S.O.V.

THE FALL CLASS OF 2015

YEARBOOK

HOLY GHOST EDITION

A Love Gift to You for a Donation of $25 or more

S.O.V. The Fall Class of 2015-Yearbook-Color
Holy Ghost Edition
Copyright © 2015 by Dr. Vicki M. Lee

ISBN-13: 978-1518772474
ISBN-10: 1518772471

Saints Of Value "World" Ministries
P.O. Box 2711 Downey CA 90242
www.SaintsOfValue.org

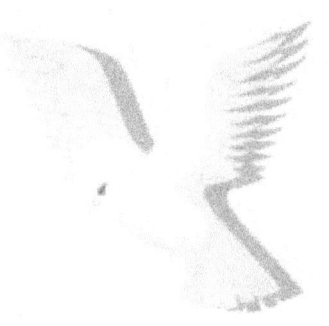

This is Your Place...
Where You Discover....
YOU ARE A
SAINT OF VALUE!

Pastors/Ministers/Leaders/Members

Disclaimer: All S.O.V. Ministers are required to renew their "Minister License" annually and submit a "Minister's Yearly Report". Please be aware that some of the ministers appearing in this yearbook may have an expired license. Information concerning the current license status of a minister is public record and any inquiries may be submitted to S.O.V. Administration

This Book Dedicated to My Mother Lovie Lee

With Our Love Respect and Gratitude

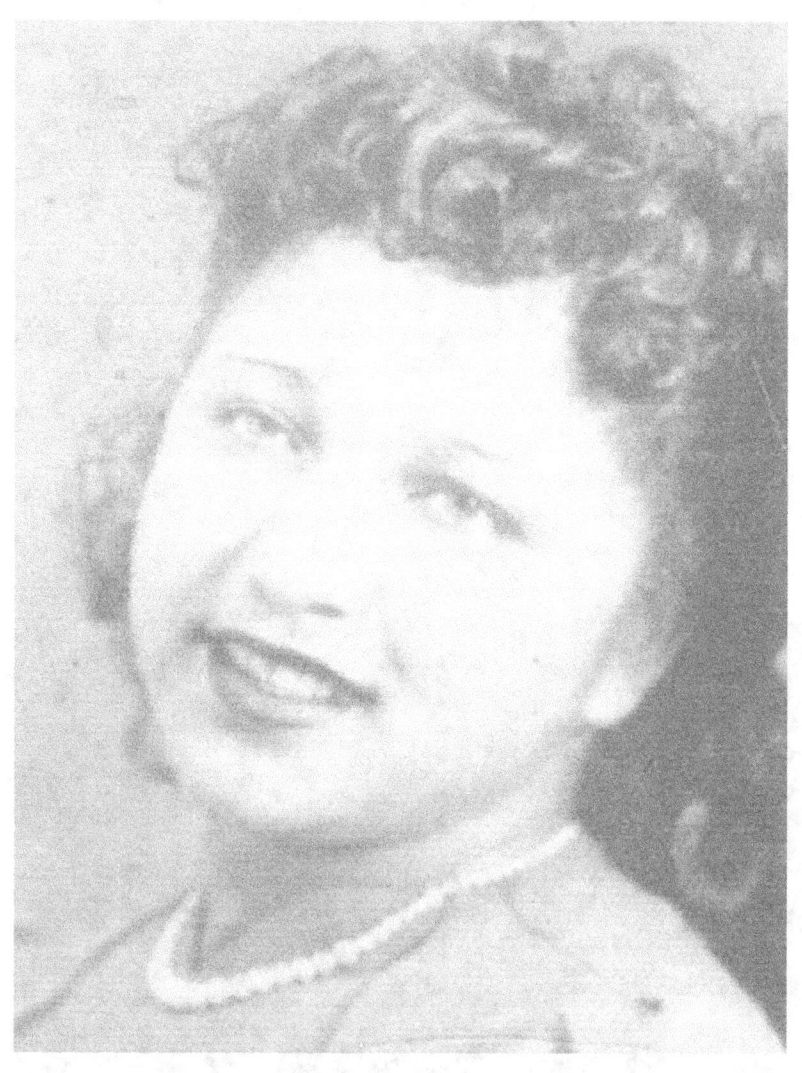

Sunrise   Sunset

August 14, 1926 - April 22, 2002

About Our Founder - Apostle Dr. Vicki Lee

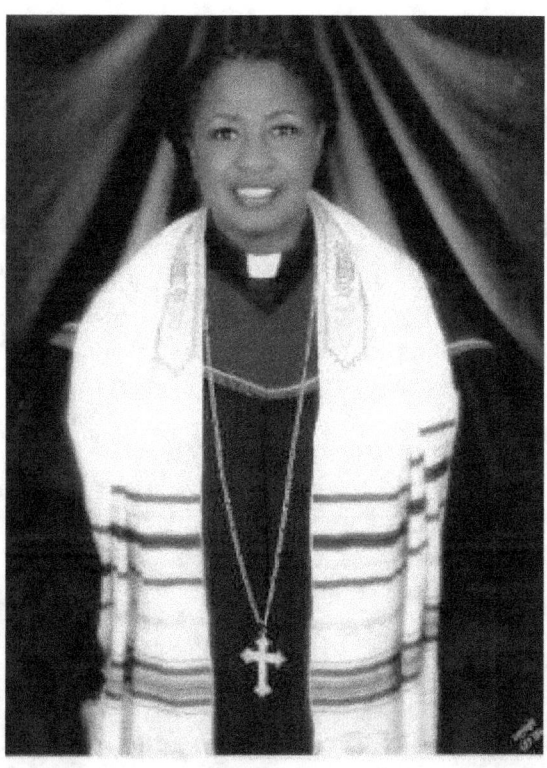

Dr. Vicki Lee is called by God to be the Founder, Director and CEO of *Saints Of Value 'World' Ministries*, a ministry designed to birth out ministers, leaders and laymen, that they may fulfill the WORD, to heal the broken hearted and set the captives free by the power of His Spirit. Dr. Lee has been supernaturally established by God to pull out the gifts and talents in the Body of Christ, calling them to order in an atmosphere of exercising them into complete and equipped ministers. Just as physical exercise is beneficial to the natural body, spiritual exercise brings us to our fullest potential in God just as He intended, before the foundation of the world.

Dr. Lee is also the director, producer and editor of *S.O.V. With Dr. Vicki Lee Television & Radio Broadcast Ministry*. Dr. Lee is a preacher, teacher, evangelist, prayer warrior, songwriter, author, and psalmist. She is devoted to serving God in any capacity so that He may be glorified. Her God-given ministry is empowered by the Holy Spirit to bring salvation, deliverance, and restoration. Dr. Lee is a woman of character, integrity, dignity and honor. She is determined, devoted, sold-out and dedicated to seeing God's righteousness prevail in the Earth.

Dr. Vicki Lee is a graduate of *Friends International Christian University*, Merced, California, where she earned a B.A. in Psychology and Biblical Counseling. Dr. Vicki Lee also received her Doctrine of Divinity from *Promise Christian University*, in August of 2006.

Giving God all the Glory!

Foundational Scriptures

In the beginning was the Word to S.O.V...

2 Timothy 2:19-21

Nevertheless the solid foundation of God stands, having this seal: "The Lord knows those who are His", and, "Let everyone who names the name of Christ depart from iniquity." 20. But in a great house there are not only vessels of gold and silver, but also of wood and clay, some for honor and some for dishonor. 21. Therefore if anyone cleanses himself from the latter, he will be a vessel for honor, sanctified and useful for the Master, prepared for every good work.

Ephesians 4:11-16

And He Himself gave some to be apostles, some prophets, some evangelists, and some pastors and teachers, 12. For the equipping of the saints for the work of ministry, for the edifying of the body of Christ, 13. Till we all come to the unity of the faith and the knowledge of the Son of God, to a perfect man, to the measure of the stature of the fullness of Christ; 14. That we should no longer be children tossed to and fro and carried about with every wind of doctrine, by the trickery of men, in the cunning craftiness by which they lie in wait to deceive, 15. But, speaking the truth in love may grow up in all things into Him who is the head Christ 16. From the whole body, joined and knit together by what every joint supplies, according to the effective working by which every part does its share, causes growth of the body for the edifying of itself in love.

S. O. V. MTC

Commencement Ordination Graduation

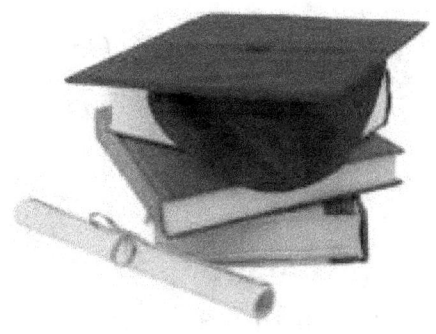

October 10, 2015
1p.m. - 3p.m.

Saints Of Value
Ministerial Training Center
P.O. Box 2711 Downey, CA 90242

562.864.4474
www.SaintsOfValue.org

Event Location: FBC
8348 2nd St. Downey CA 90241

Meet Our Candidates:
Doctorate Divinity Degree

Dr. Chaplain George McDonald
Dr. Pastor Melvin Silas
Dr. Peter Agbonlahor

Installation
Pastor Dr. Rose Sumlin - Affirmation as Apostle
Pastor G. Oliver as 1 Year Staff Pastor

2 Years Full Pastor Credential
Pastor Venus L. Burton
Pastor Peggy Gentry

1 Year Full Pastor Credential
Pastor Maalo Fetelika

1 Year Intern Pastor Credential
Pastor Jennet Guerrrero, **Pastor Prisca Wilfred**
Pastor Michael Curry
Pastor Schylar Oneal, **Pastor Minnie Dixion** *& Pastor Cecelia "Sally" Molina*

20 hour Addition Training Certificates
Evang. Katrinia B. Seymour, Evang. Kelly Rayford & Min. Earnestine Colbert

Intern Credential
Minister Loretta Andrews

Diploma
Emma Coleman, **Lahonda Johnson**
Margo Williams, *Silvia Sealey*
Mary Bakaimani, **Ana Zapata**
Jose Macias, *Loretta Andrews &* **William Lee**

Certify Instructor License Certificates
Lesha McCall-Lewis

Special Recognition Certificates
Christine De La Santos

The Processional Intro Pastor Gloria Levine

MC: Dr. Richard Bryant

Opening Prayer: Dr. Richard Bryant

Praise & Worship:

Pastor Henry Newton & Holy Ghost Choir

Welcome By: Dr. Earline Long Weaver,

(Accountability Team Member)

What is S. O. V. MTC?

By Spanish Dean: Pastor Maria Perez

Song: Brother Darren Jeter

Awards of Recognition-Installations

By Dr. Vicki Lee &

Pastor Jessica Downton, Downey -Dean

Announcements: Dr. Nawania Lyles

Amazing Grace Seed Time – Elder Minger

Word of Exhortation (10 min)

Dr. Mary Sims M.D.

The Sax by: Bro Pablo Guerrero

Introduction of Speaker-Dr. Lee

Dance: Evangelist Kelly Rayford-(Las Vegas, NV. Dean)

Speaker: Dr. Ron Roberson **(20 min)**

Bio Reader - Dr. Nawania Lyles

2 min WORD from the Honored Doctors

Presentation of Doctorate Degrees by

Dr. Ron Robeson & Doctorate Team

Charge: Dr. Darlene Alexander

Laying on of Hands- of the Elders

Certificate Presentations-Readers

Dr. Melvora Fulton & Dr. Mary Sims

Closing Remark **& Prayer:** Apostle Dr. Vicki Lee Founder / President

MEET THE "FALL" DOCTORS 2015

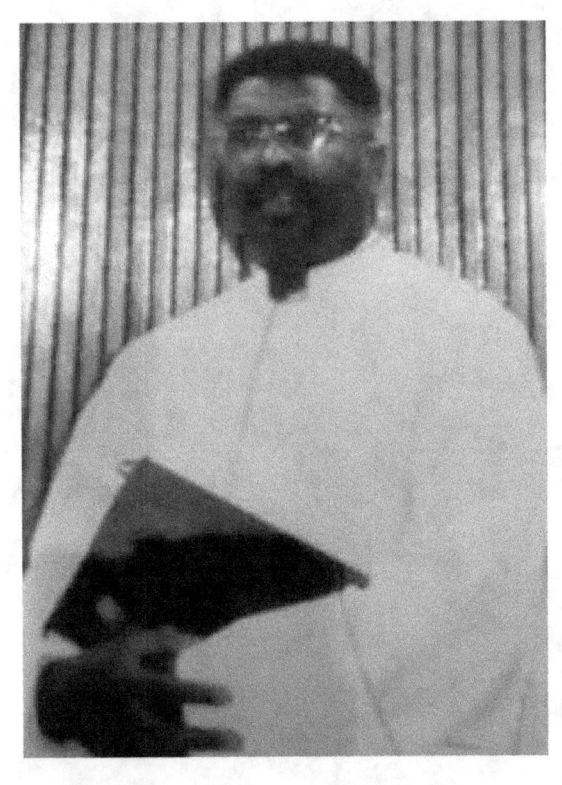

Dr. George J. McDonald:

Chaplain George J. McDonald has been in Prison Ministry for more than thirty-five years. He has been the Volunteer Senior Chaplain at both the Los Angeles Men's Central Jail in Los Angeles and The Institution of Men, Department of Correction for the past 25 years. Prior to those assignments, he was the Volunteer Senior Chaplain at Los Padrinos Juvenile Hall in Downey, California for more than 9 years. He was the Outreach Evangelism Coordinator Volunteer for 16 years at the California Institution for Men, Department of Corrections. He also ministered at Los Angeles Probation Department Juvenile Halls and Camps, Nevada State Department of Corrections, San Quentin, Wayside Honor Ranch, Los Angeles Men's Central Jail, and various other institutions. At these institutions, he has coordinated protestant religious services for prison chapel services, Cell to Cell ministry, inmate one on one counseling, Conflict resolution, Inmate mediation and advocacy. He has conducted weekly Bible studies, group mentoring, coordinated youth focus activities, Promoted positive youth development, volunteer recruitment and planned concerts and volunteer activities for Holiday functions and coordinated donations for youth. He is a member of the Western Baptist State Convention and Director of Prison Ministries. He received Ministerial License and Ministerial Ordination by Bishop E.E. Cleveland Bishop of Second Jurisdiction Churches of God in Christ. He is a member of Praises of Zion Baptist Church, Pastor Joe B. Hardiwick and is currently working with Family of Prayer and Praise Church of God In Christ in Los Angeles, where Dr. Donald Ferguson is Senior Pastor. He has been married to Tonya for 29 years and have 7 children; Lamar, Shamko, Kier, George III, Jasmine, Nathan, and Kandis.

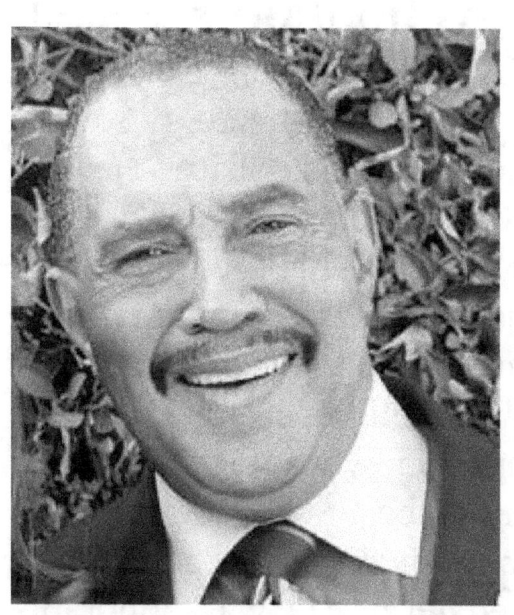

Dr. Melvin Silas better known as (Pastor Mel) spent a great deal of his life on the run from God, which caused him to spend many years within prison going in and out of jail for many different crimes. On one cold snowy night, in the state of Ohio while sitting in a cell. Pastor Mel accepted the call of God. For the next several years while still in prison he commenced studying the Word of God to know more about the God that had saved him while sitting in that cell. Pastor Mel wrote a letter to Kenneth Hagin Sr. Pastor of Rhema Bible College, and asked for help. The man of God (Pastor Hagin Sr.) sent Pastor Silas a bible correspondence course. This course changed his life. He learned what it meant to live by faith!! Thank God for Pastor Kenneth Hagin Sr. and all the brothers and sisters at Rhema that invested in his life. Upon being released from prison Pastor Mel attended Crenshaw Christian Center School of Ministry under Dr. Fredrick KC Price. Where he learned the excellence of ministry, along with the required disciple needed for a man of God to serve God and the people of God. After which Pastor Mel went on to attend ZOE Christian Leadership School under Bishop Frank Stewart for another two years and graduated. Pastor Mel is now a dynamic and anointed Teacher and Preacher of the Word sharing the Gospel with electrifying presentation his life experiences through the Word of God to help others, communicating with unmistakable clarity which challenges the believer to walk in faith and live in fullness as God desires. His God given messages presents uncompromising truths with a unique and matchless style that reaches far into the hearts of listeners of young and old, of all ethnic origins. Pastor Silas is the senior Pastor of the The Great "I AM" Faith Center in the city of Los Angeles, California.

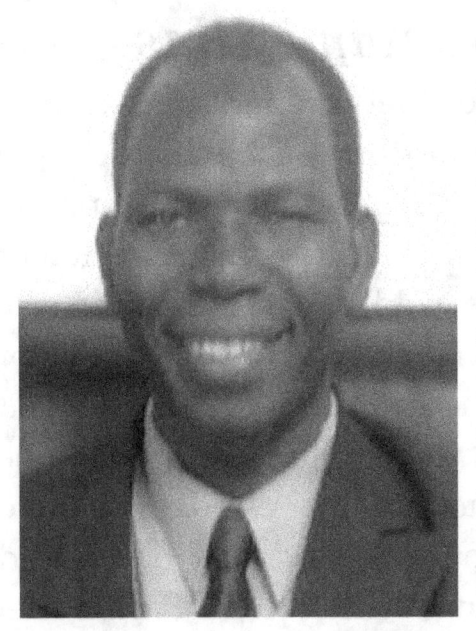

Dr. Peter Agbonlahor, currently ministers on OCN Broadcasting Network in Los Angeles and also mentors several ministries in the USA and Africa. He was born in Benin City where he grew up as a Muslim. In 1964 he gave his life to the Lord and Savior Jesus the Christ. He was enlisted into the Nigerian Air Force in the year 1970 and served in the intelligence for six years. He was popularly known as an Evangelist and a Pastor and since the call of God was so heavy upon him, he requested a discharge after his required term. He was honorably discharged to go and serve his Lord. Dr Peter N. Agbonlahor is married to the Beautiful Pastor Ifeanyi F. Agbonlahor. He attended All Nation For Christ Bible Institute in Benin City, Dr. Morris Cerullo's school in San Diego, Faith School of Theology, Beulah Heights University, and Atlanta University. He has established Churches and held Crusades and Conferences all over the world. In 1984 he started a radio ministry on WTJH and WXLL in Atlanta metro area. In the same year, his school campus bible study group grew into a church call Prince of Peace which was located on memorial Dr. He has pioneered churches in Atlanta GA, Griffin GA, Irving TX, and Altamonte Springs FL, Pastor Peter takes delight in motivating, counseling and praying for people of all Nationalities. His passion is to be more like Christ, to know him and the power of his resurrection and to be made conformable onto his death. Through the special grace of God, cancer, tumor, demonic swelling, blind has been healed and in addition to this, God used his to raise four dead people back alive. It is not by human ability, but by the Holy Spirit of God. Dr Peter is a member of Saints Of Value under the great leadership of Dr. Apostle Vickie Lee of whom he really appreciates and thanks God for Sending her. I have been taught many things at SOV.

THE
FALL
CLASS
OF
2015

2 Year Full Pastoral Credential

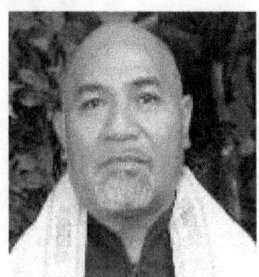

Youth Pastor Venus Burton of Downey, CA
Ministry of Helps Dec. 11, 2004
S.O.V. Diploma October 12, 2013*Intern Ordination October 12, 2013
Intern Youth Pastor Installation October 11, 2014
*** 2 Year Full Youth Pastor Installation October 10, 2015

Pastor Peggy Ramos of Downey, CA
S.O.V. Diploma October 12, 2013 * Intern Ordination October 12, 2013
Accounting Department 2014 *Instructors License January 11, 2014
Intern Pastor Installation October 11, 2014
*** 2 Year Full Pastor Installation October 10, 2015

1 Year Full Pastoral Credential

Pastor Maalo Fetelika of Downey, CA
* Diploma *Intern Pastor Ordination October 11, 2014
***1 Year Full Pastor Credential October 10, 2015

1 Year Intern Pastor Credential

Minister Michael Curry of Los Angeles, CA
Minister Certificate July 12, 2014 * Diploma & Intern Ordination Oct. 11, 2014
1 year Intern Pastor Credential October 10, 2015

Minister Jennet Guerrero of Los Angeles, CA
* Diploma *Intern Ordination October 11, 2014
1 year Intern Pastor Credential October 10, 2015

Minister Prisca Wilfred of Los Angeles, CA
* Diploma *Intern Ordination October 11, 2014
1 year Intern Pastor Credential October 10, 2015

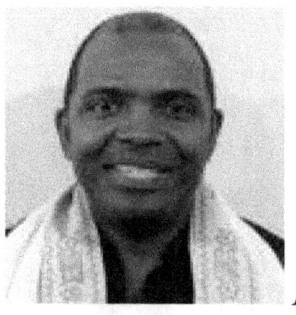

Minister Schyler Oneal of Los Angeles, CA
* Diploma *Intern Ordination October 11, 2014
1 year Intern Pastor Credential October 10, 2015

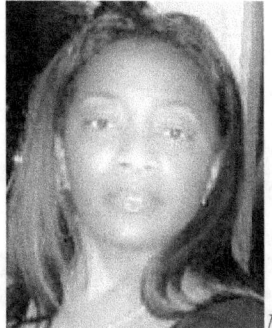

Minister Minnie Ola Moore - Dixon of Las Vegas, Nevada
* Diploma *Intern Ordination October 11, 2014
1 year Intern Pastor Credential October 10, 2015

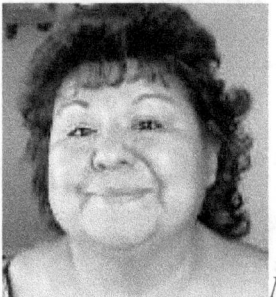

Minister Celia "Sally" Molina of Las Vegas, Nevada
* Diploma *Intern Ordination October 11, 2014
1 year Intern Pastor Credential October 10, 2015

Installations

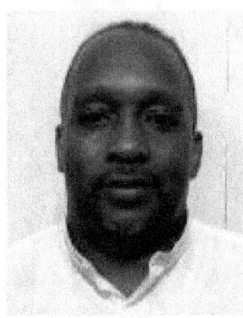

Pastor Gale Olivia Jr. of Santa Ana, CA.
S.O.V. Diploma October 12, 2013 * Intern Pastor Ordination October 12, 2013
Intern Staff Pastor Installation October 11, 2014
Full Staff Pastor Installation October 10, 2015

Prophetess Dr. Rose Sumlin of Las Vegas, Nevada
S.O.V. Diploma Oct 13, 2012 *Staff Pastoral Installation Oct 13, 2012
1 year Salute of Excellent Service October 12, 2013 Prophetess Installation October 11, 2014***Apostle Installation October 10, 2015

20 *hour Addition Training Certificates*

Evangelist Kellarice Hughes-Rayford of Las Vegas, Nevada
S.O.V. Diploma October 2, 2010 Intern Minister Ordination October 2, 2010
Full Credential Evangelist Installation Oct. 8, 2011
20 hour Addition Training Certificates October 10, 2015

Evangelist Katrina Seymour of Norwalk, CA
Intern Ordained June 5, 2005 Full Ordination July 8, 2006
20 hour Addition Training Certificates October 10, 2015

Evangelist Earnestine L. Colbert of Norwalk, CA
S.O.V. Diploma April 2010   Intern Minister Ordination April 3, 2010
Full Credential Installation July 9, 2011
20 hour Addition Training Certificates October 10, 2015

Certify Instructor License Certificates

Lesha D. B. McCall-Lewis of Downey, CA
*Ministry of Helps July 11, 2015 ***S.O.V. Diploma** July 11, 2015
Certify Instructor License Certificates: October 10, 2015

Intern & Diploma

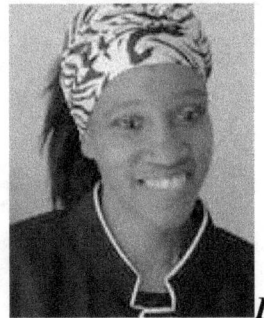

Intern Minister Loretta Andrews, of Southwest Los Angeles, CA
Diploma & Intern Ordination October 10, 2015

Diploma

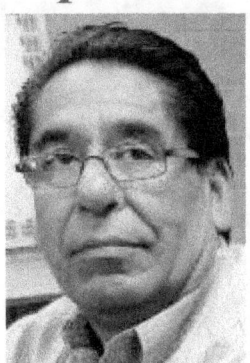

Jose Macias, of Downey CA
Diploma October 10, 2015

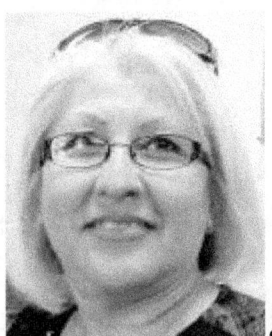

Silvia Sealey, of Downey CA
Diploma October 10, 2015

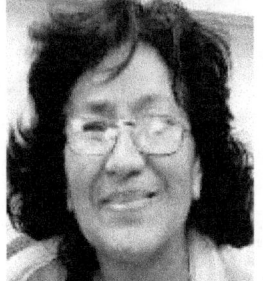

Ana Zapata, of Downey CA
Diploma October 10, 2015

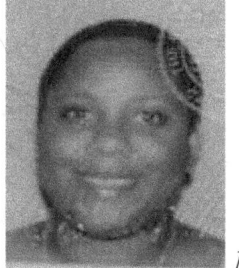 *Margo Williams*, of Southwest Los Angeles, CA
Diploma October 10, 2015

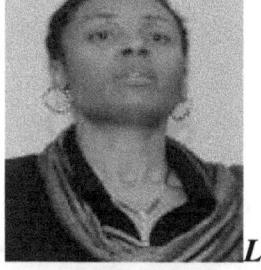 *Lahonda Johnson*, of Southwest Los Angeles, CA
Diploma October 10, 2015

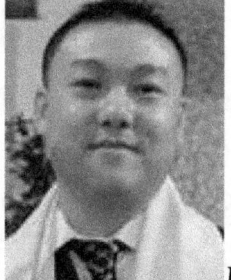 *William Lee*, of Southwest Los Angeles, CA
Diploma October 10, 2015

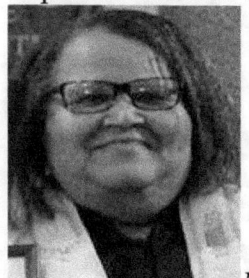 *Mary Bakaimani,* of Southwest Los Angeles, CA
Diploma October 10, 2015

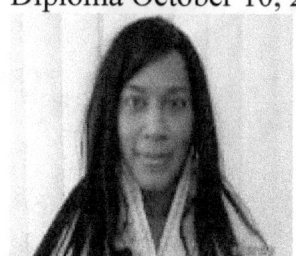 *Emma Coleman*, Houston Texas
Diploma October 10, 2015

Special Recognition Certificates

Christine De La Santos, of Downey CA
Special Recognition Certificate October 10, 2015

Southwest Los Angeles
MTC Fall Class of 2015

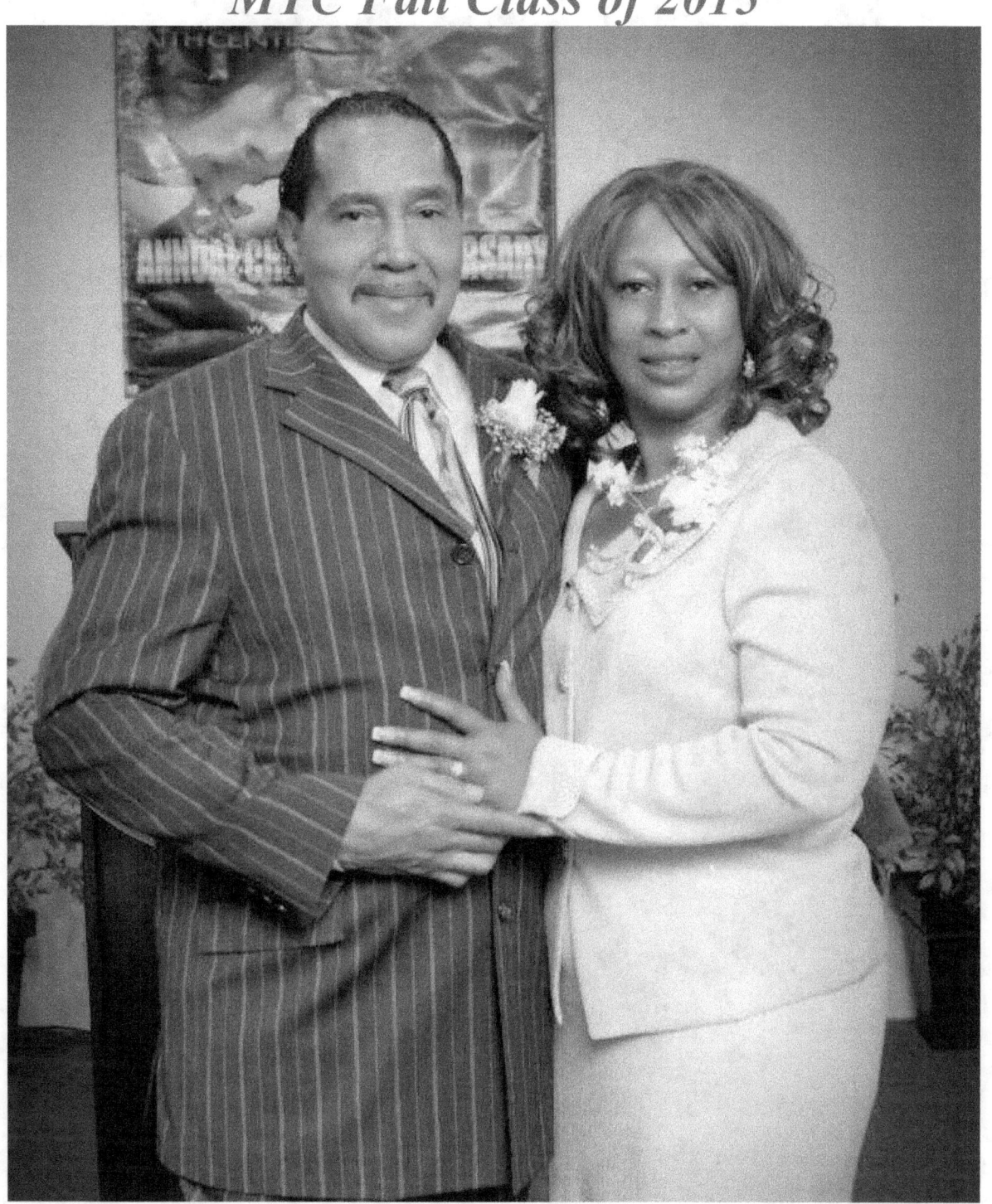

Dr. Melvin Silas - Dean & Assitant Lady Beverly Silas

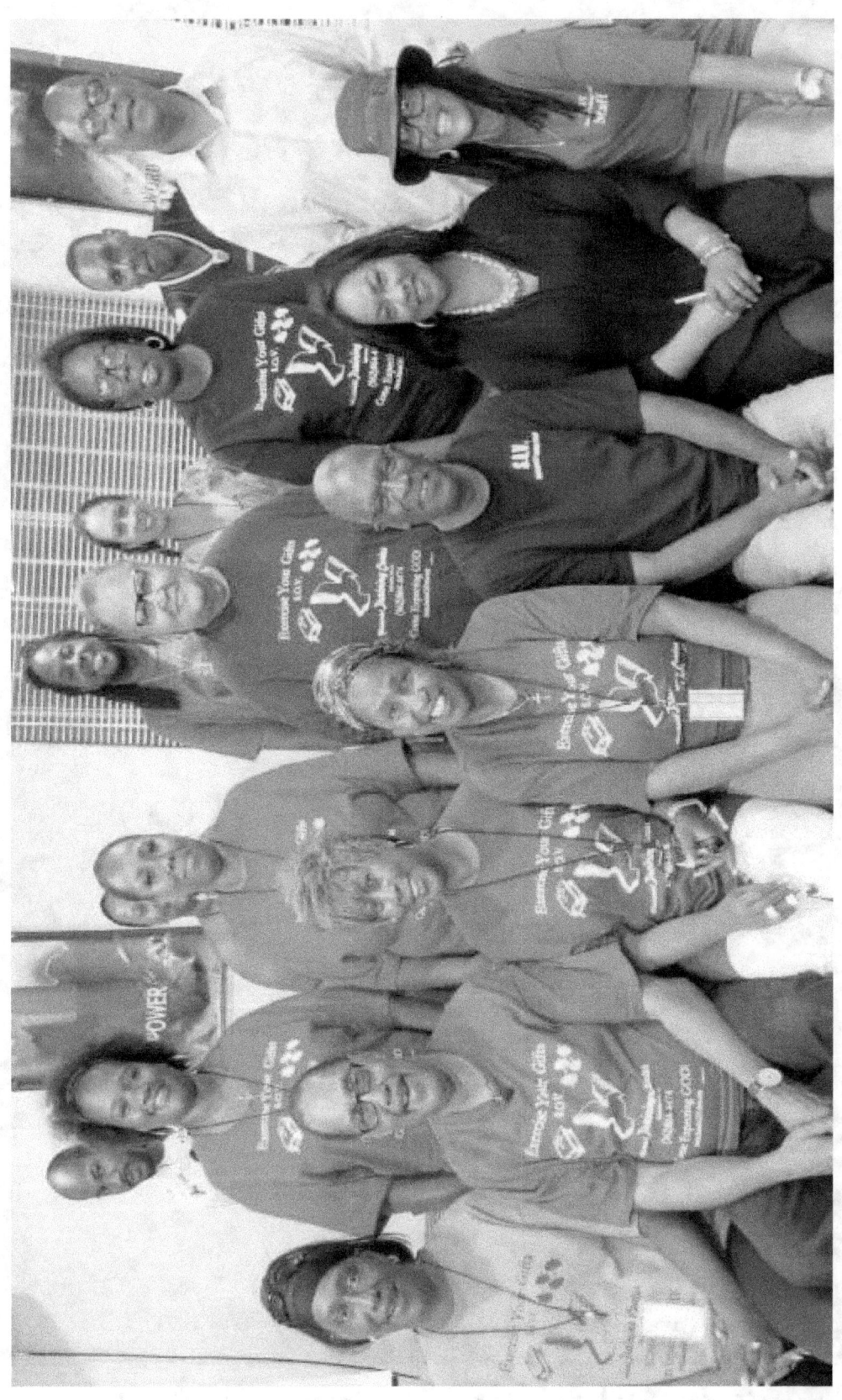

Southwest Los Angeles MTC
Fall Class of 2015

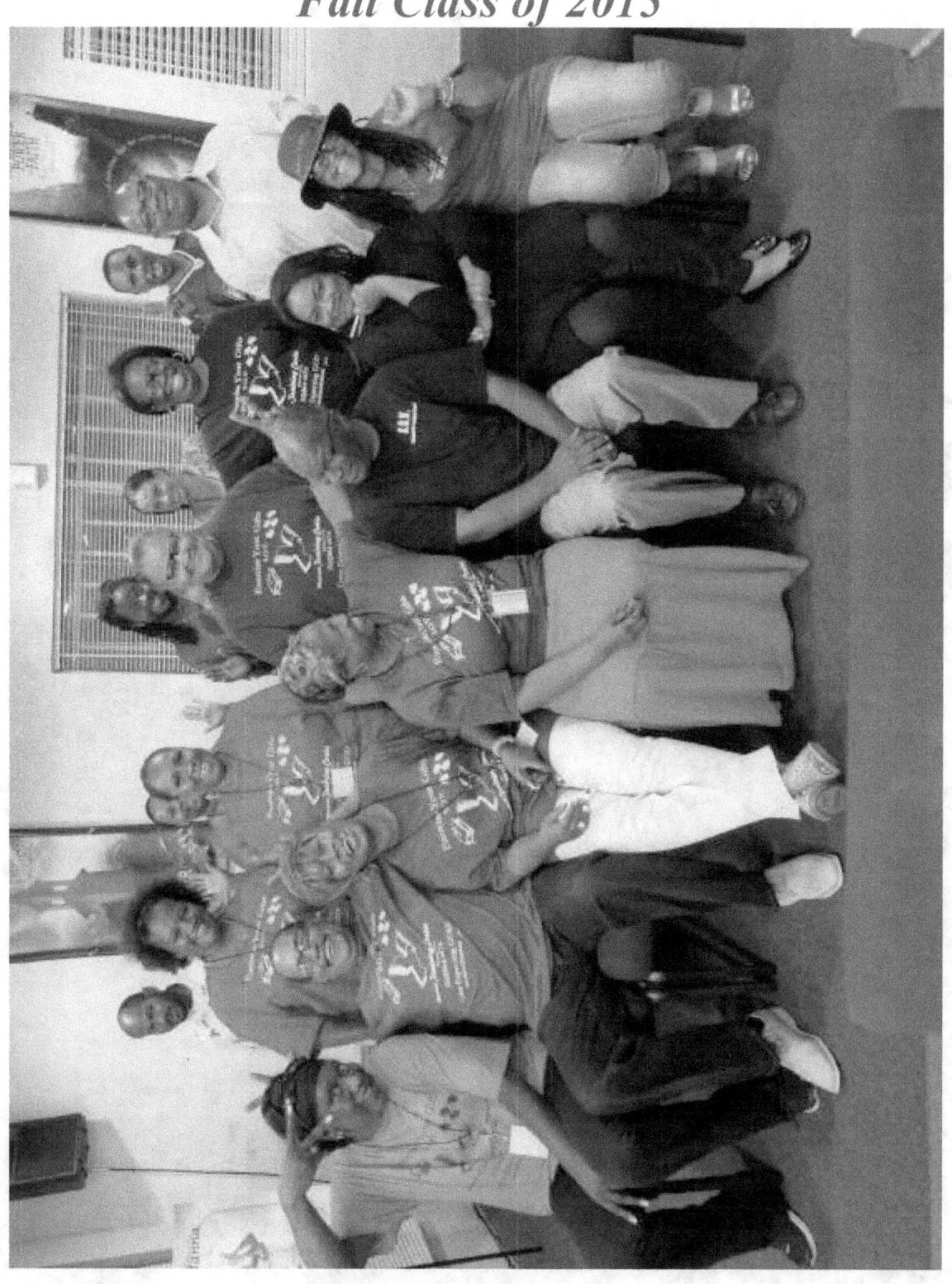

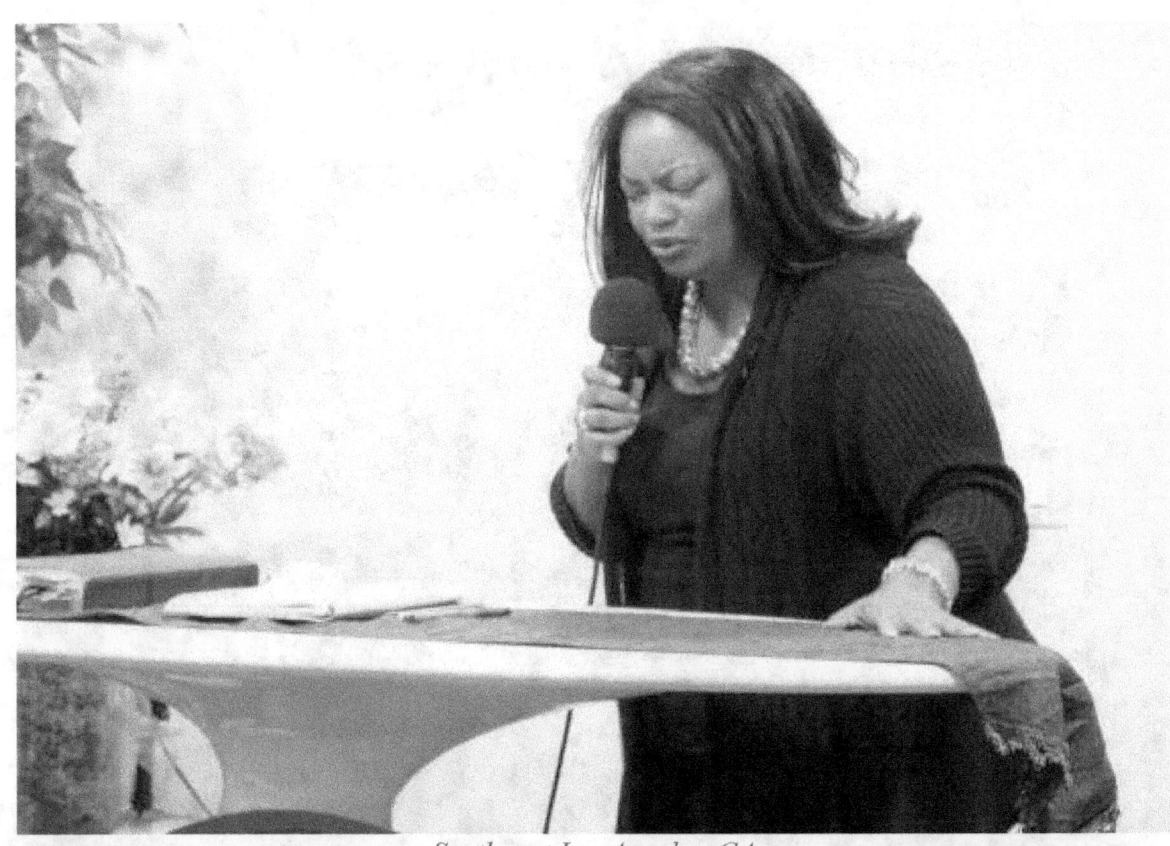

Southwest Los Angeles, CA

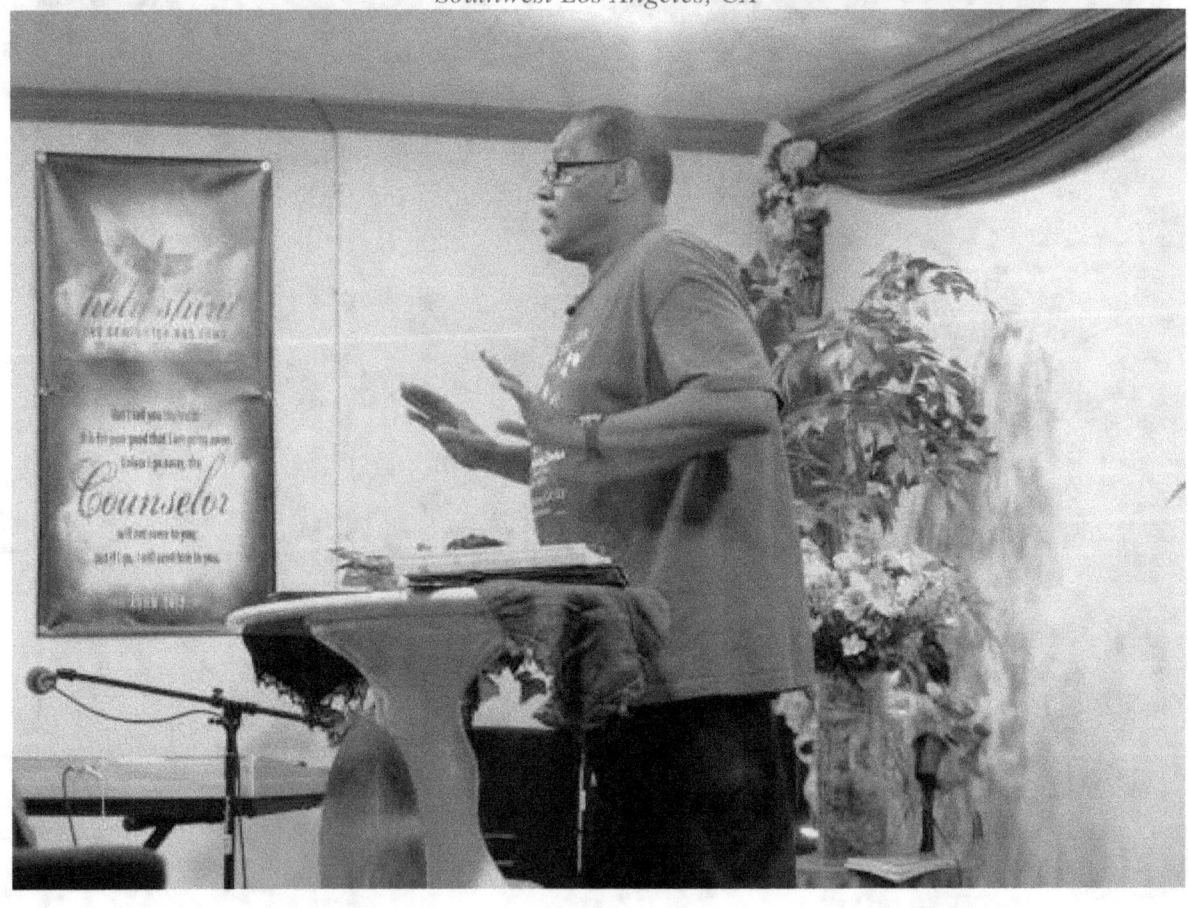

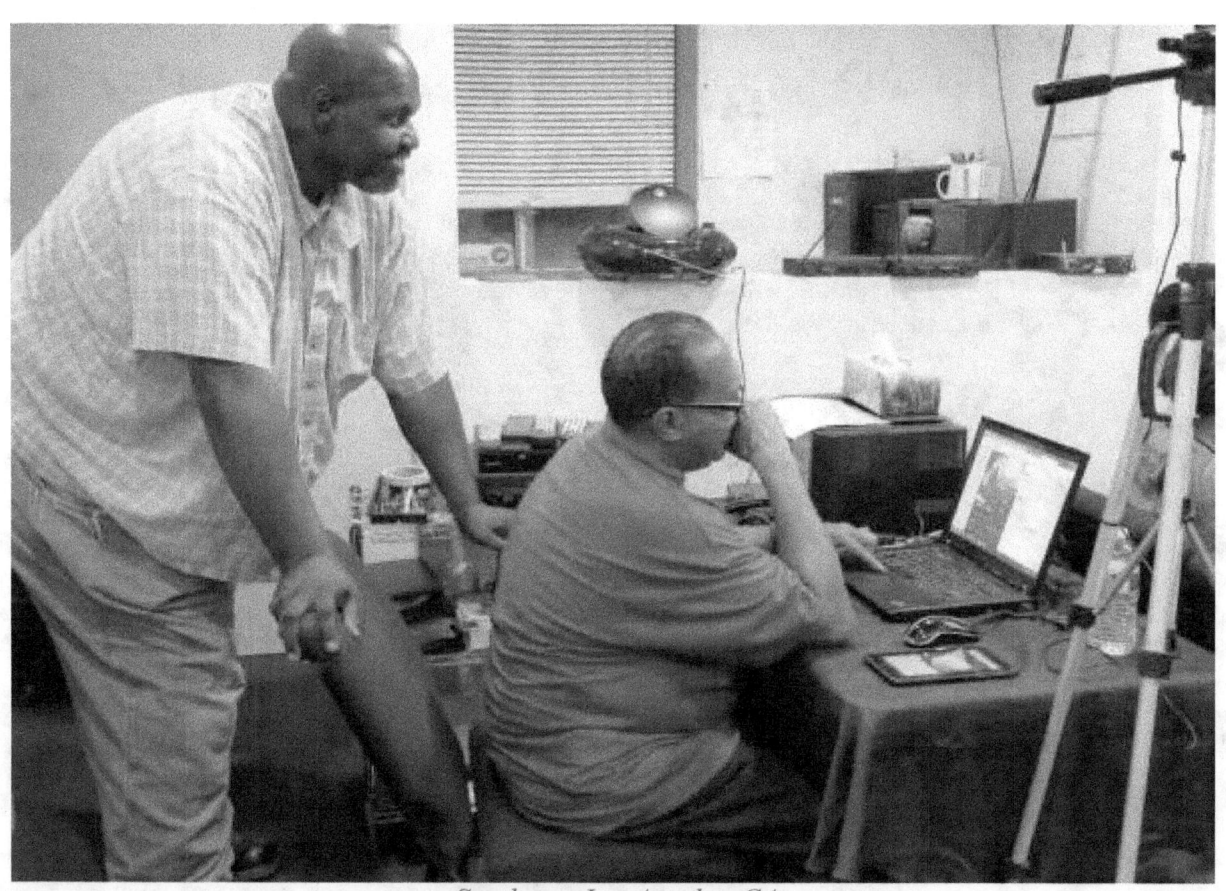

Southwest Los Angeles, CA

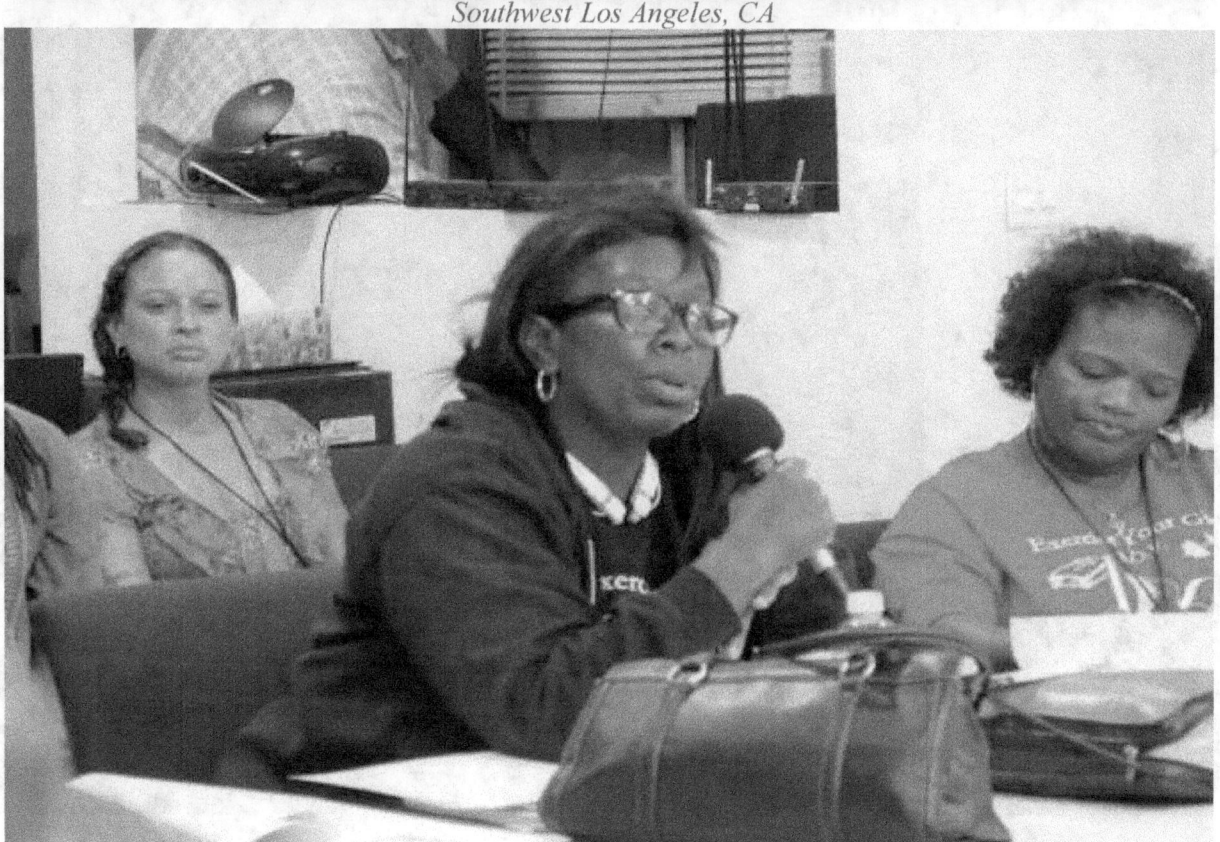

35

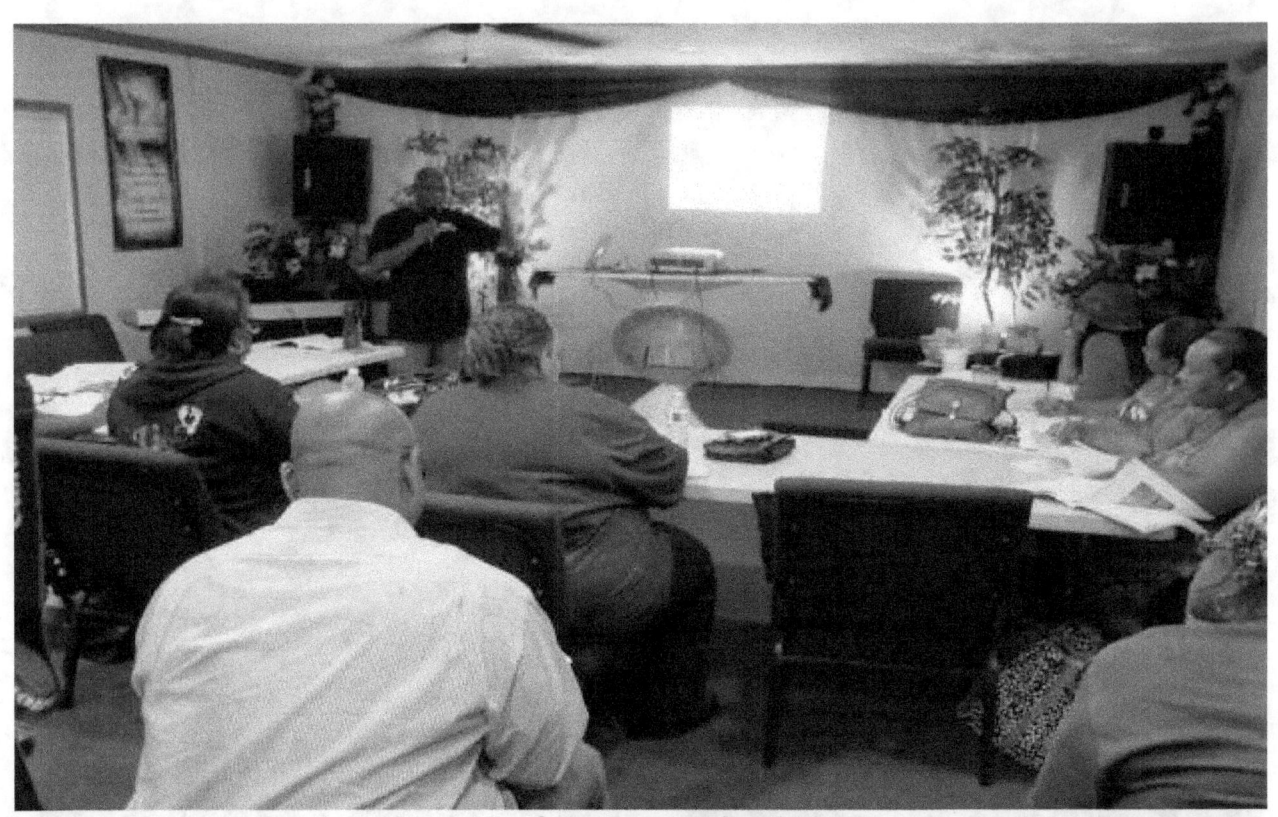

Southwest Los Angeles, CA

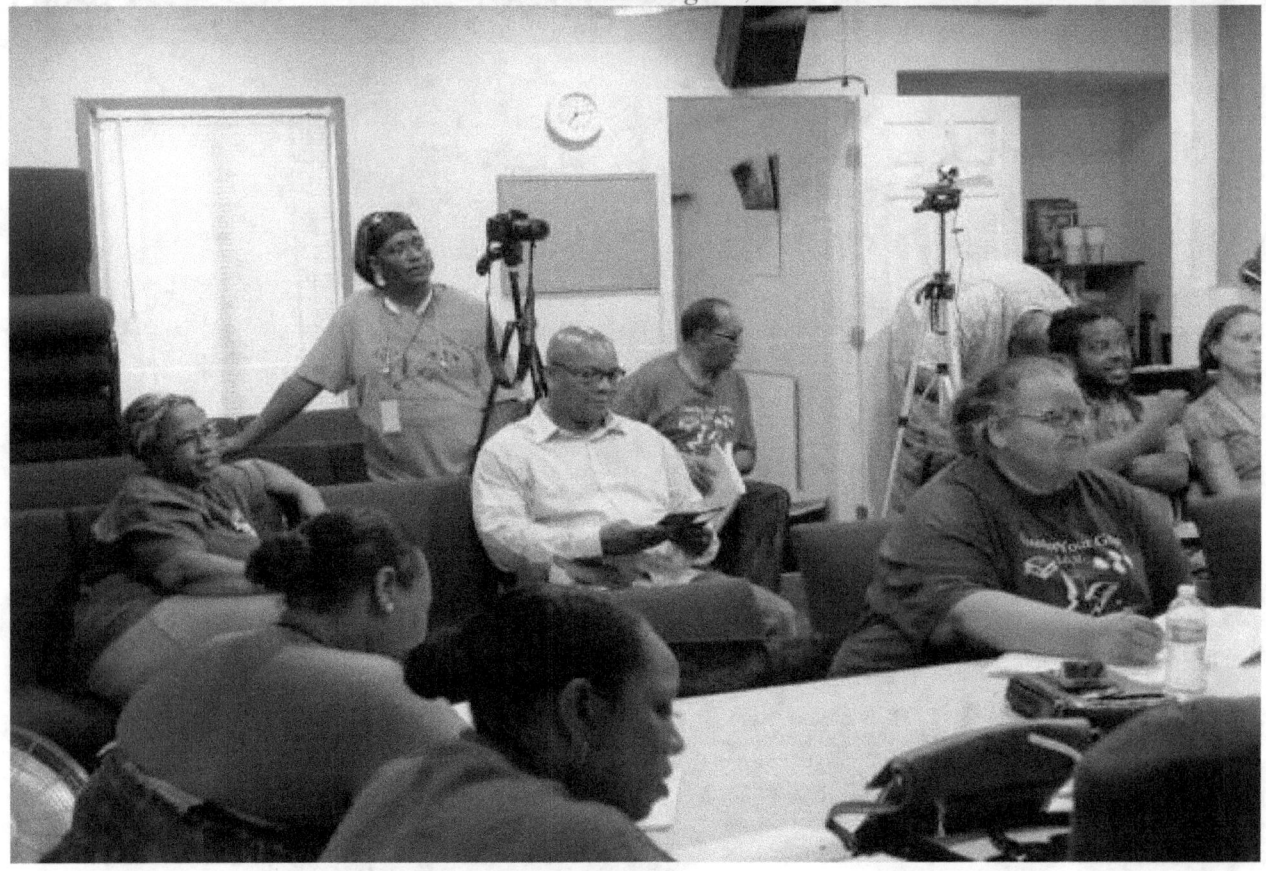

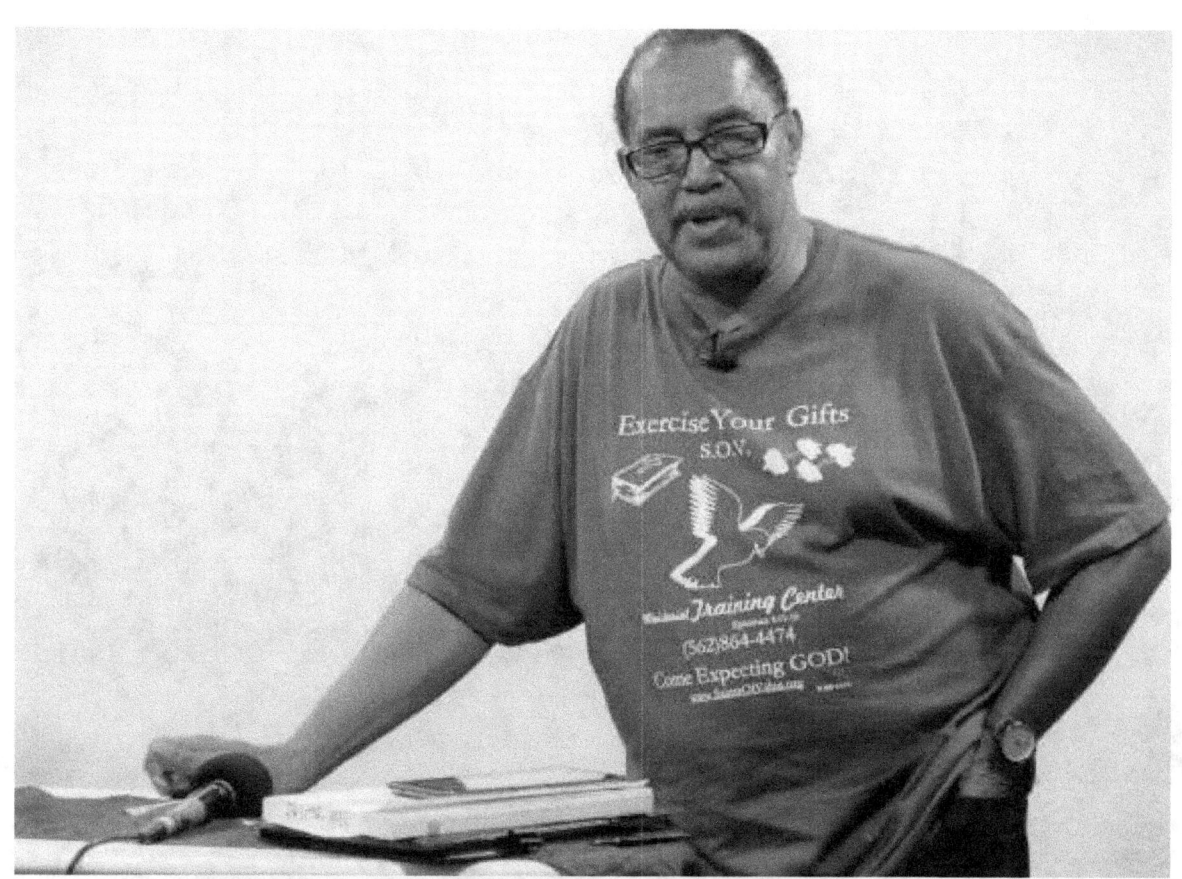

Southwest Los Angeles, CA

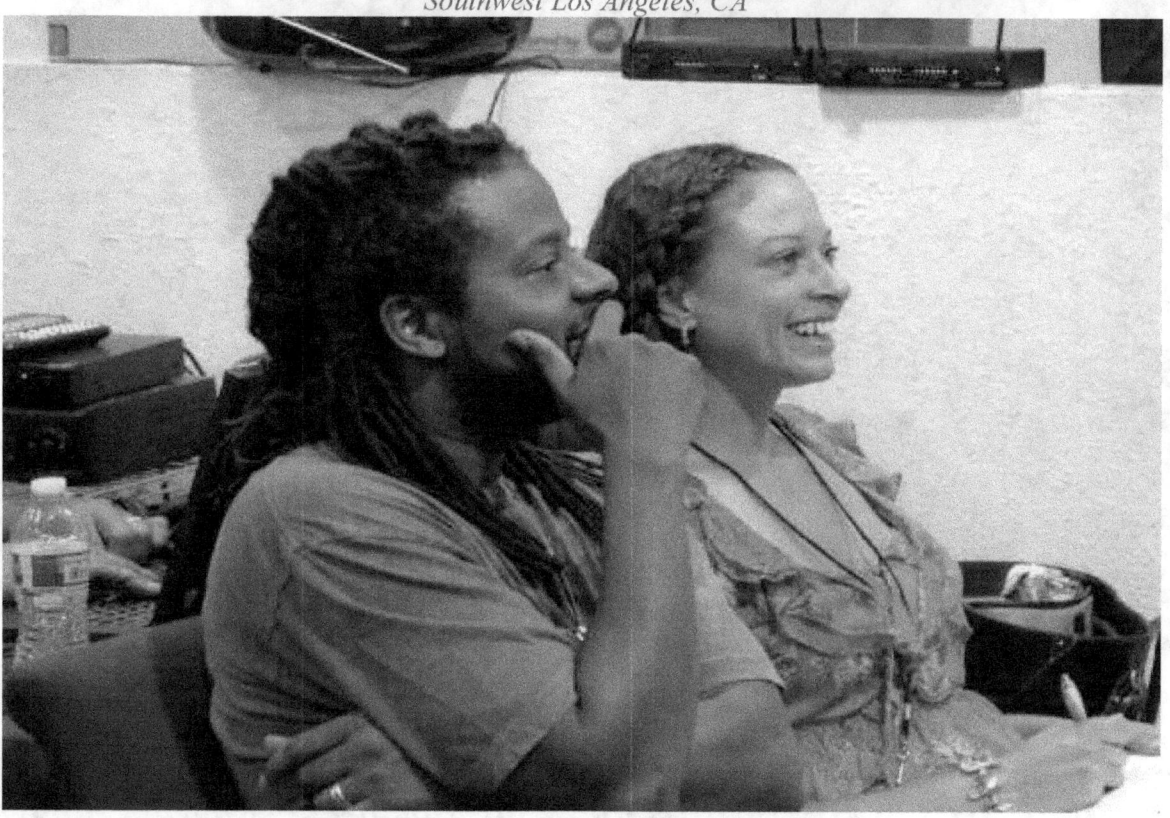

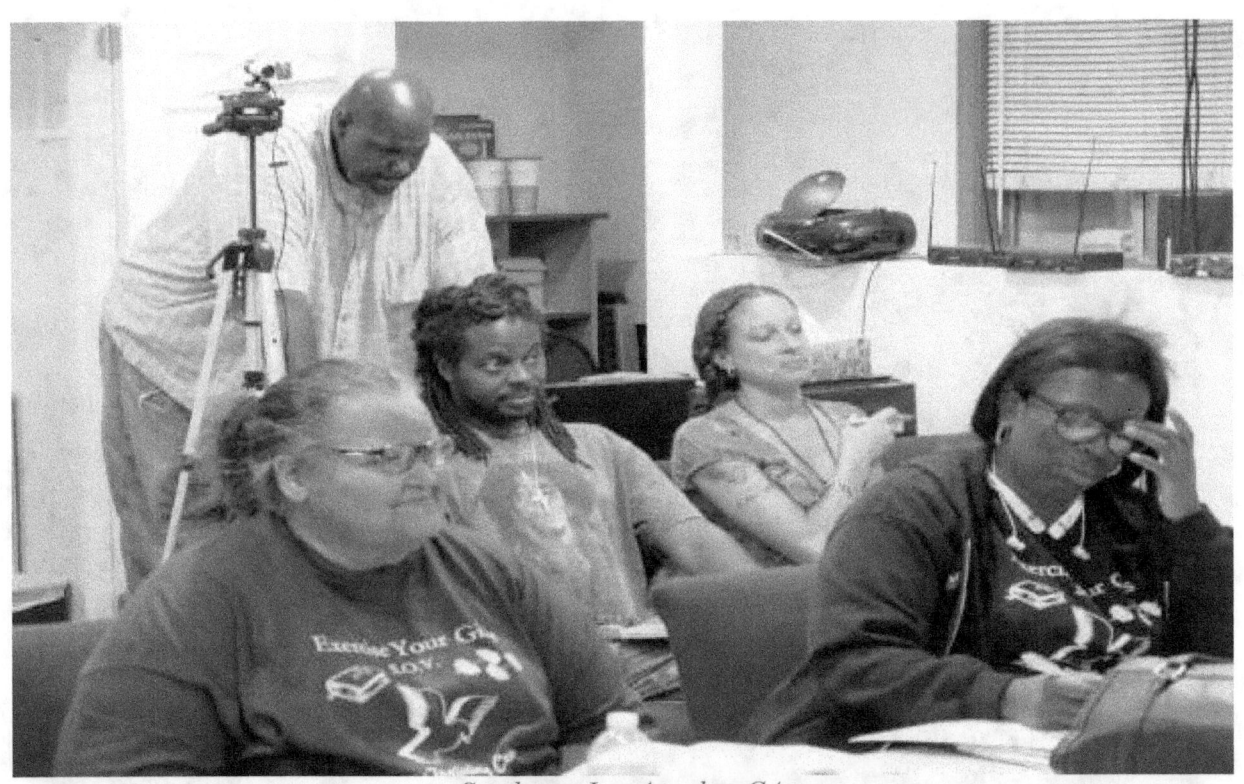

Southwest Los Angeles, CA

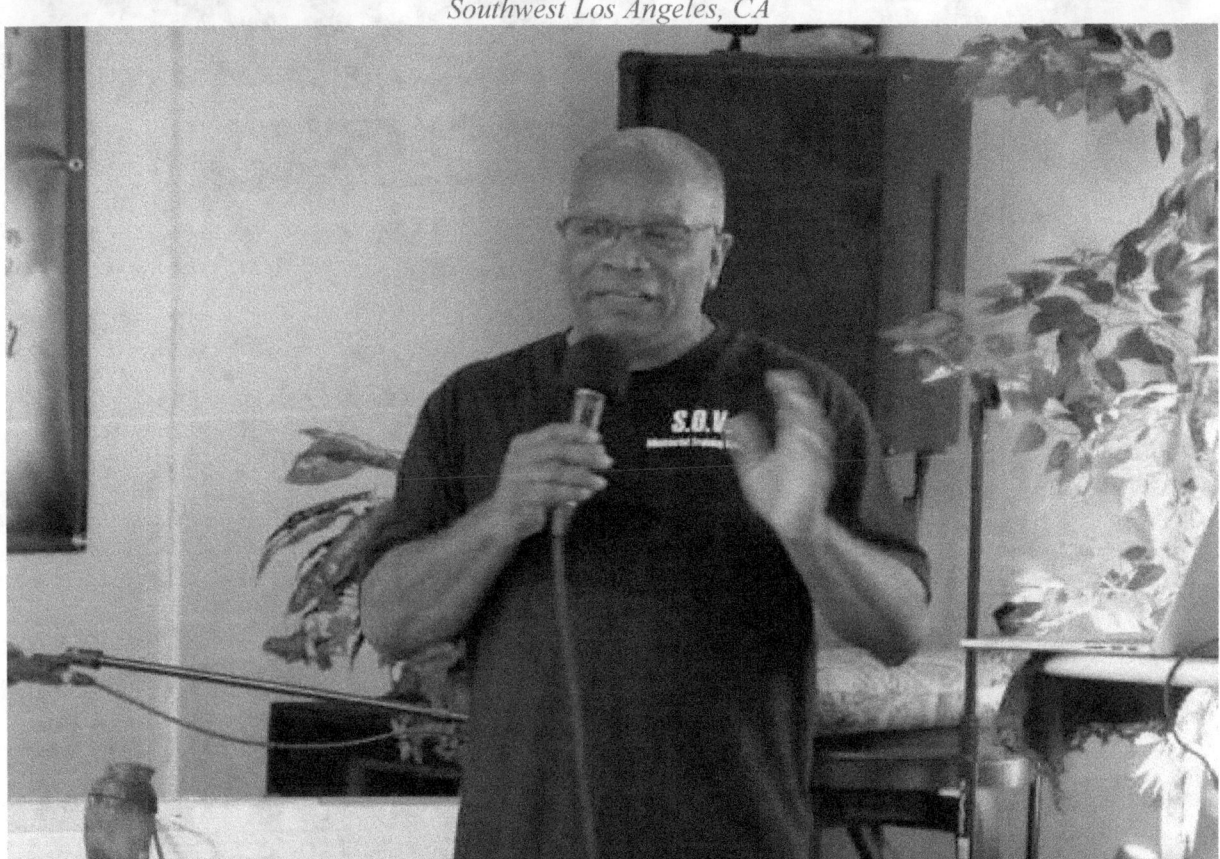

***Dr. Ron Roberson** – Director of the Doctorate Program (above)*

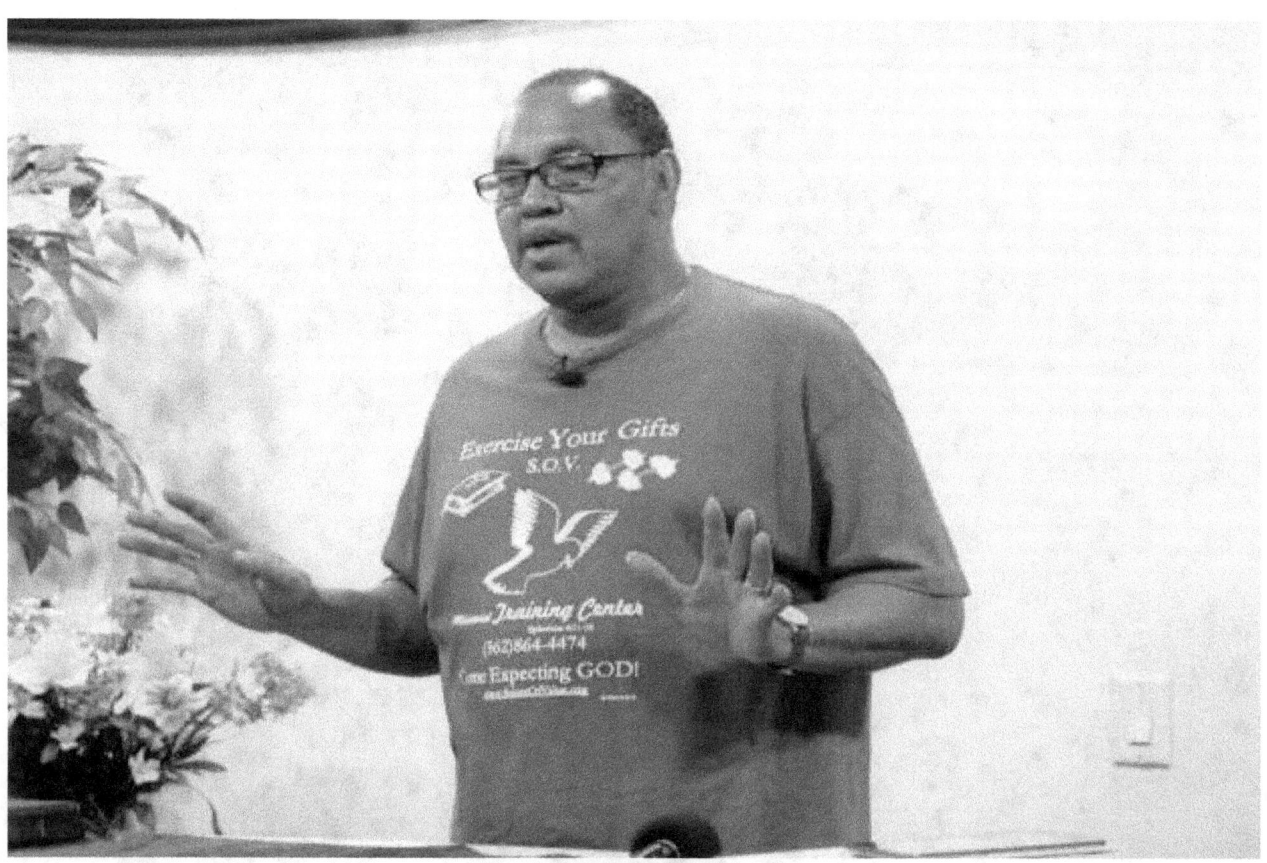

Southwest Los Angeles, CA

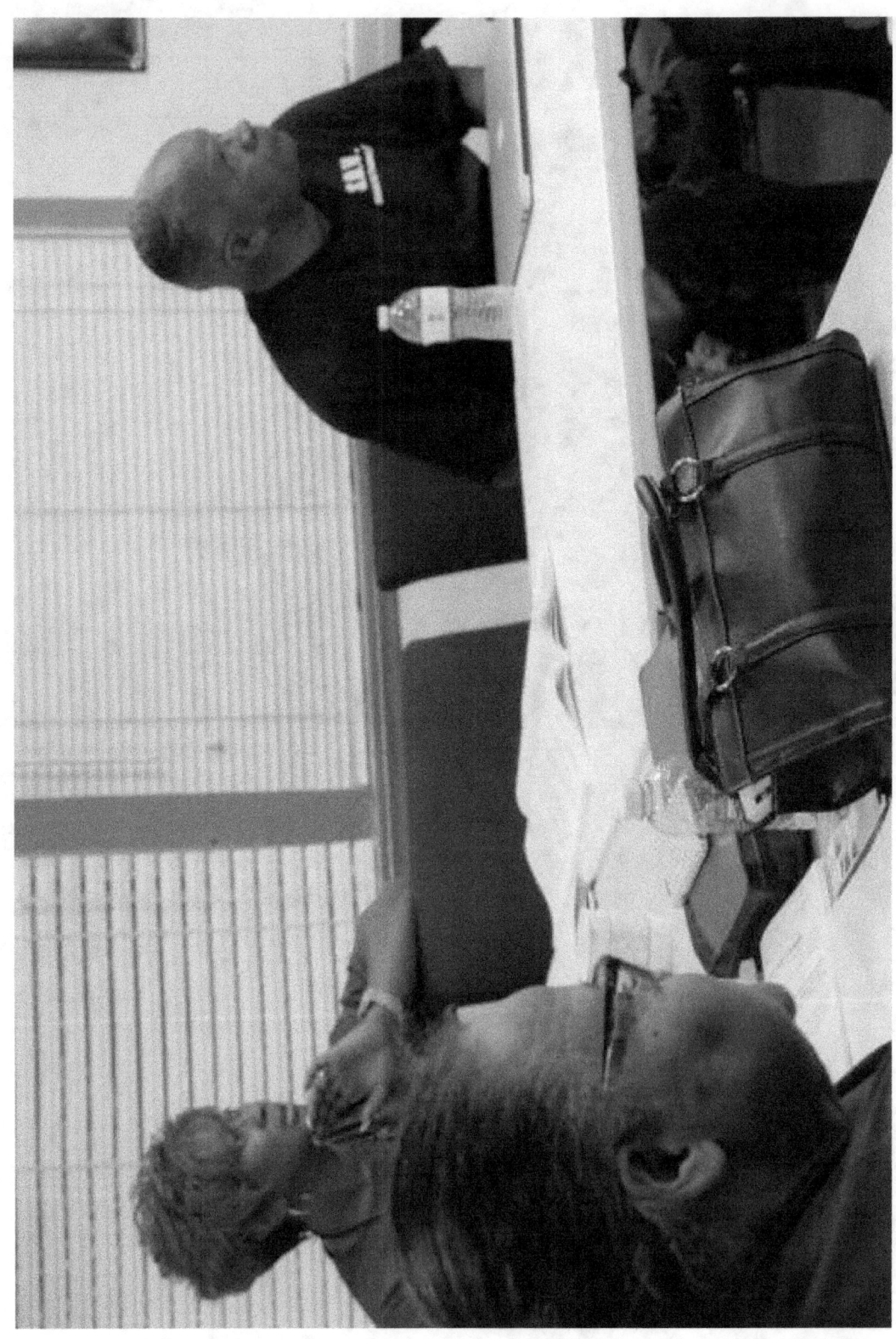

North Las Vegas, Nevada

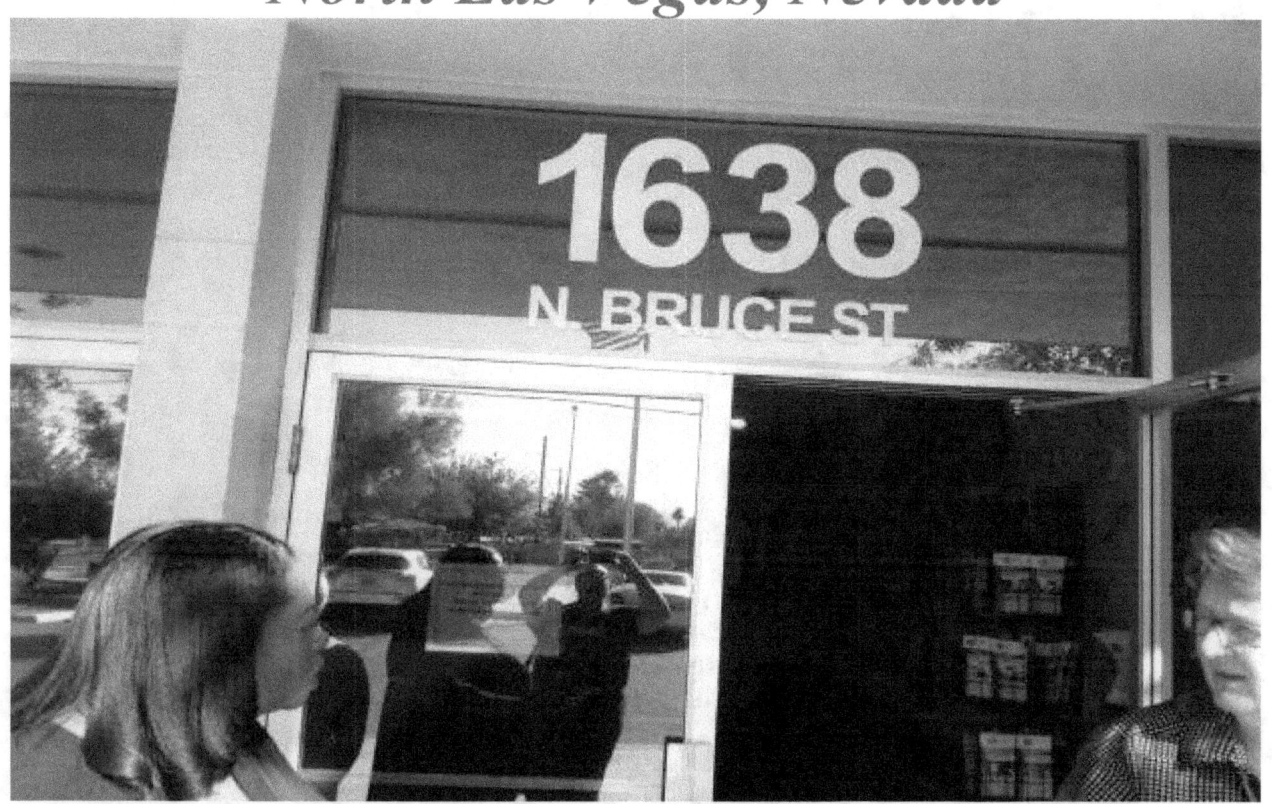

S.O.V. MTC Fall Class of 2015

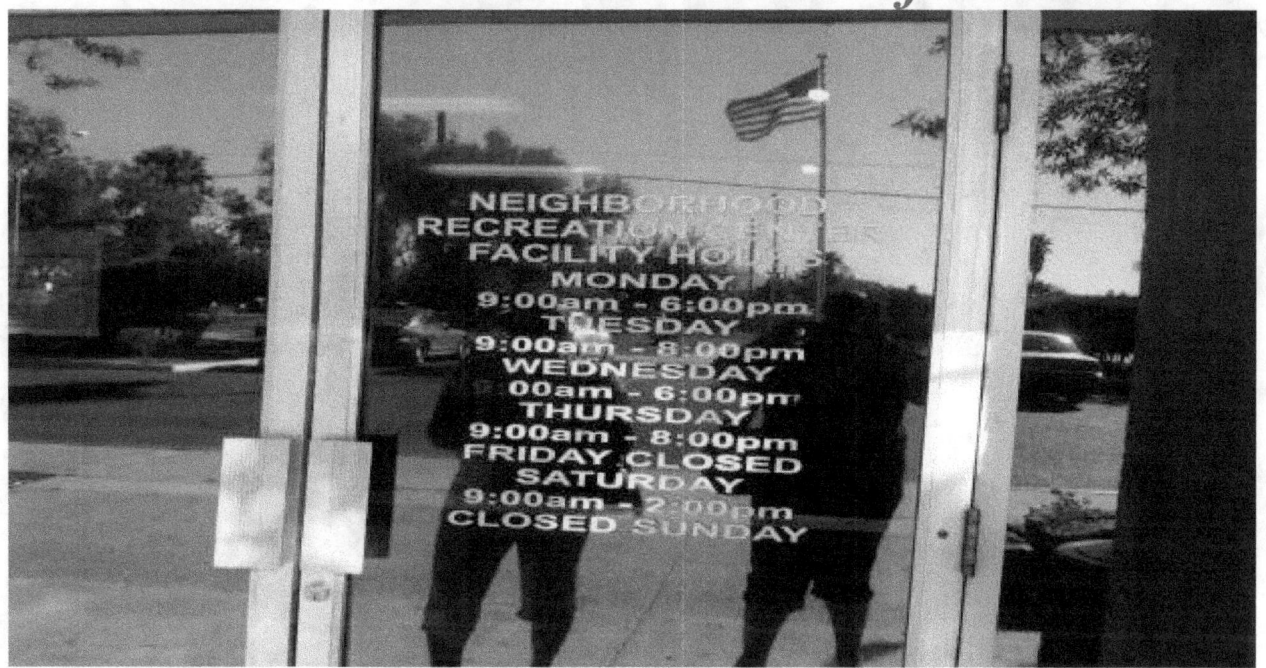

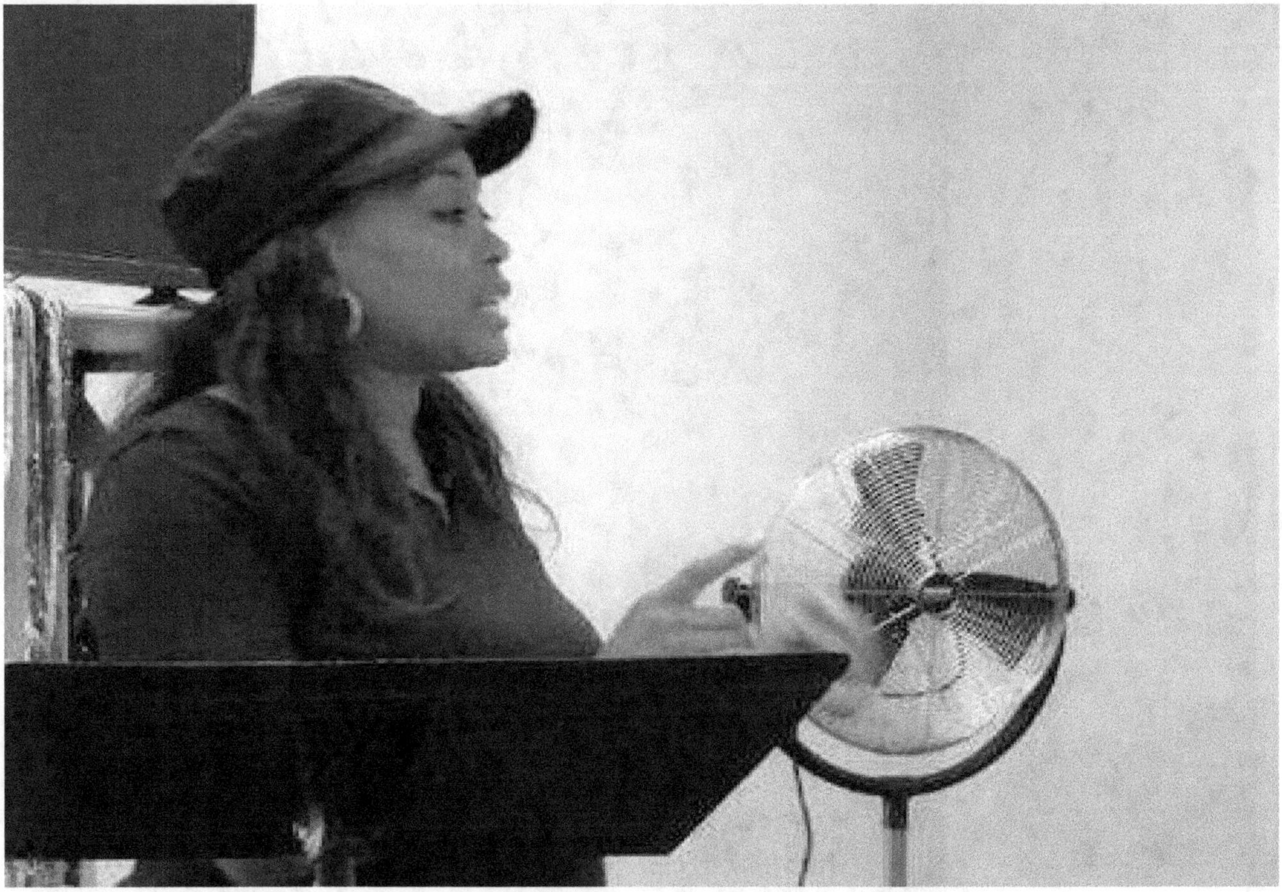

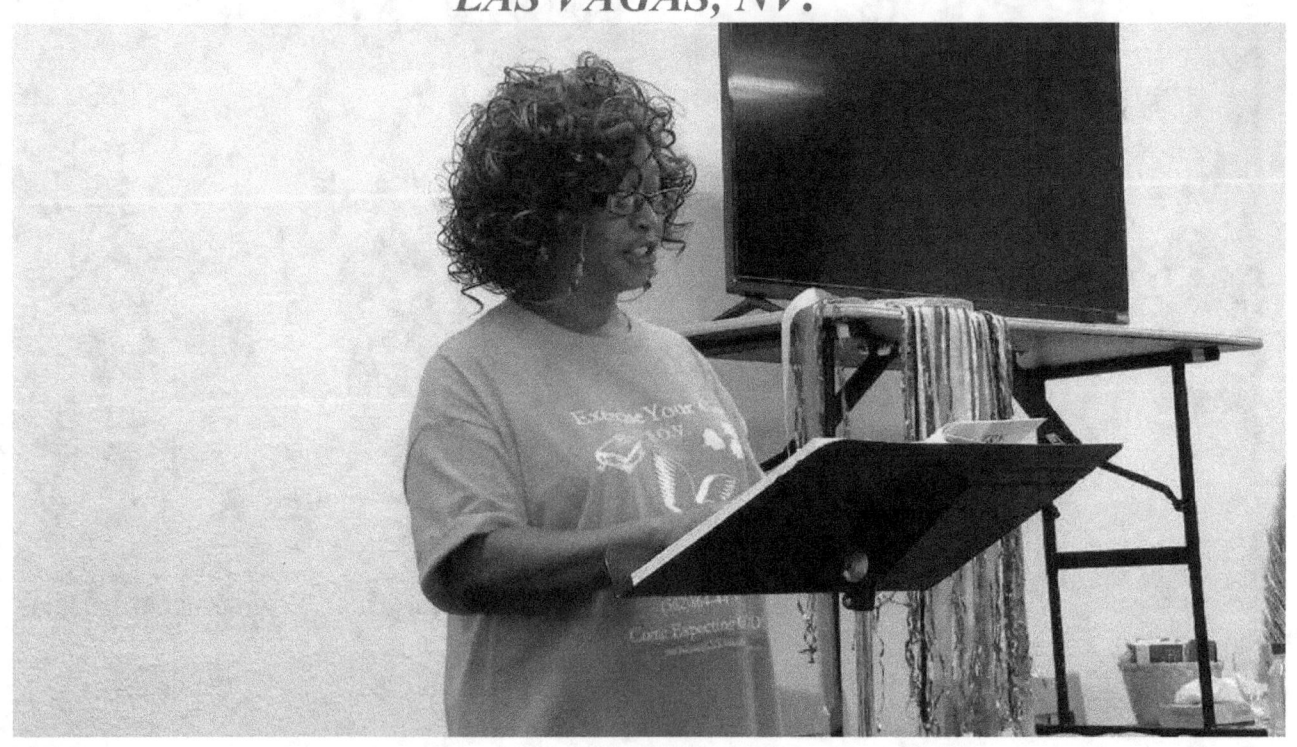

Evangelist Kelly Rayford -MTC Dean-(above)
LAS VAGAS, NV.

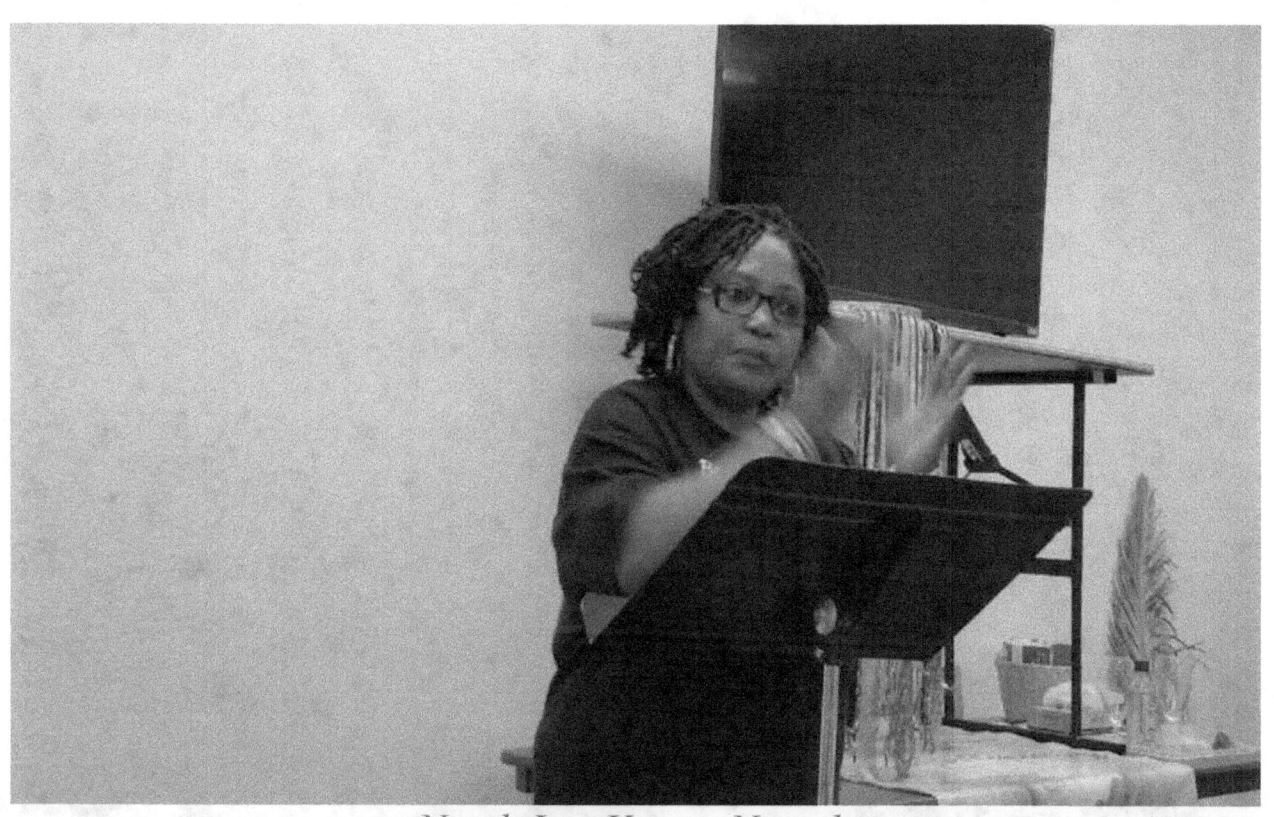

North Las Vegas, Nevada

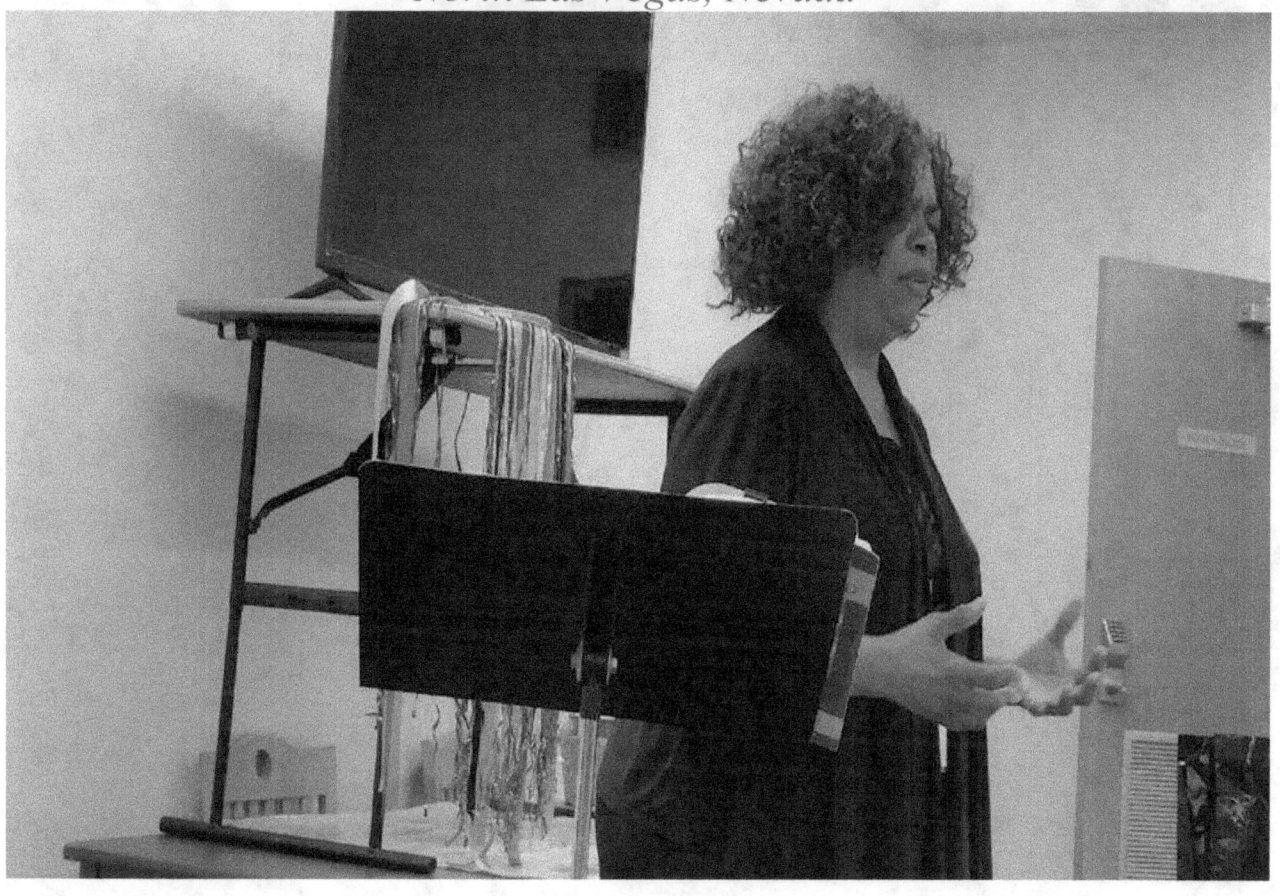

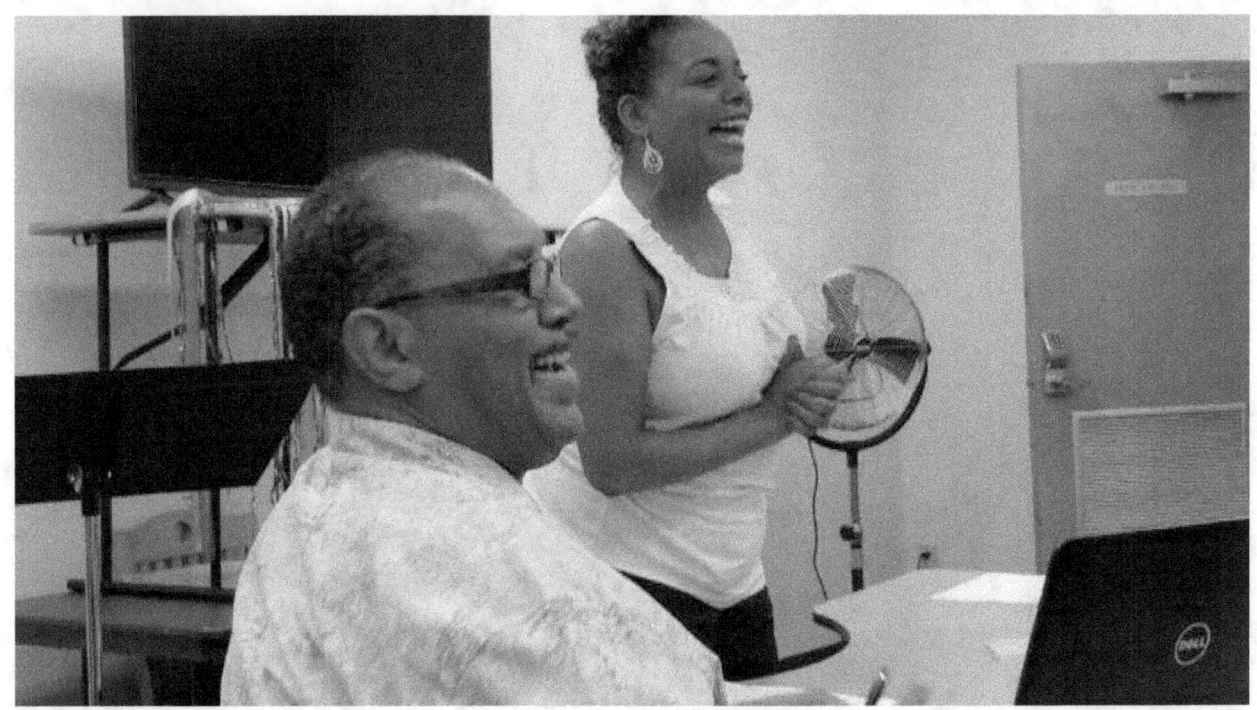

North Las Vegas, Nevada

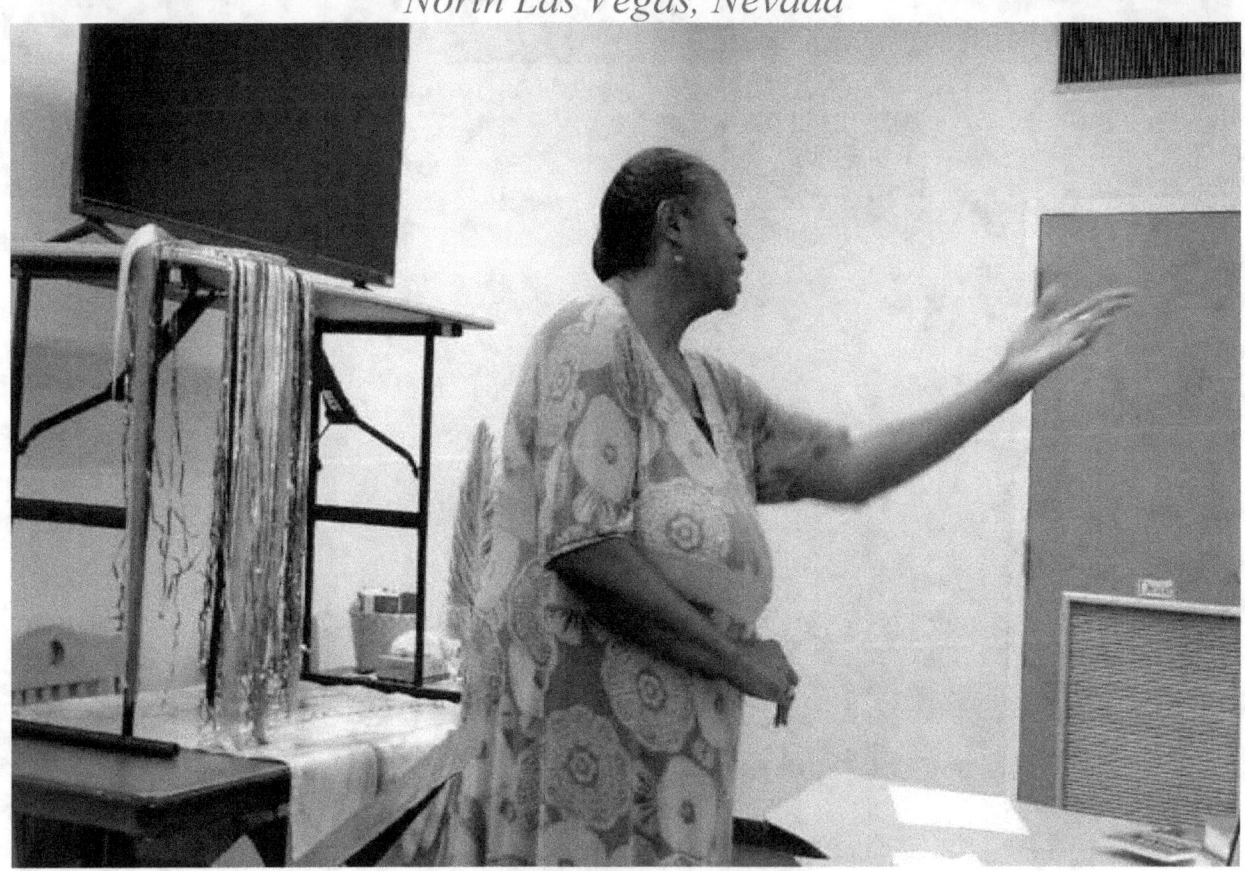

Apostle Rose Sumlin

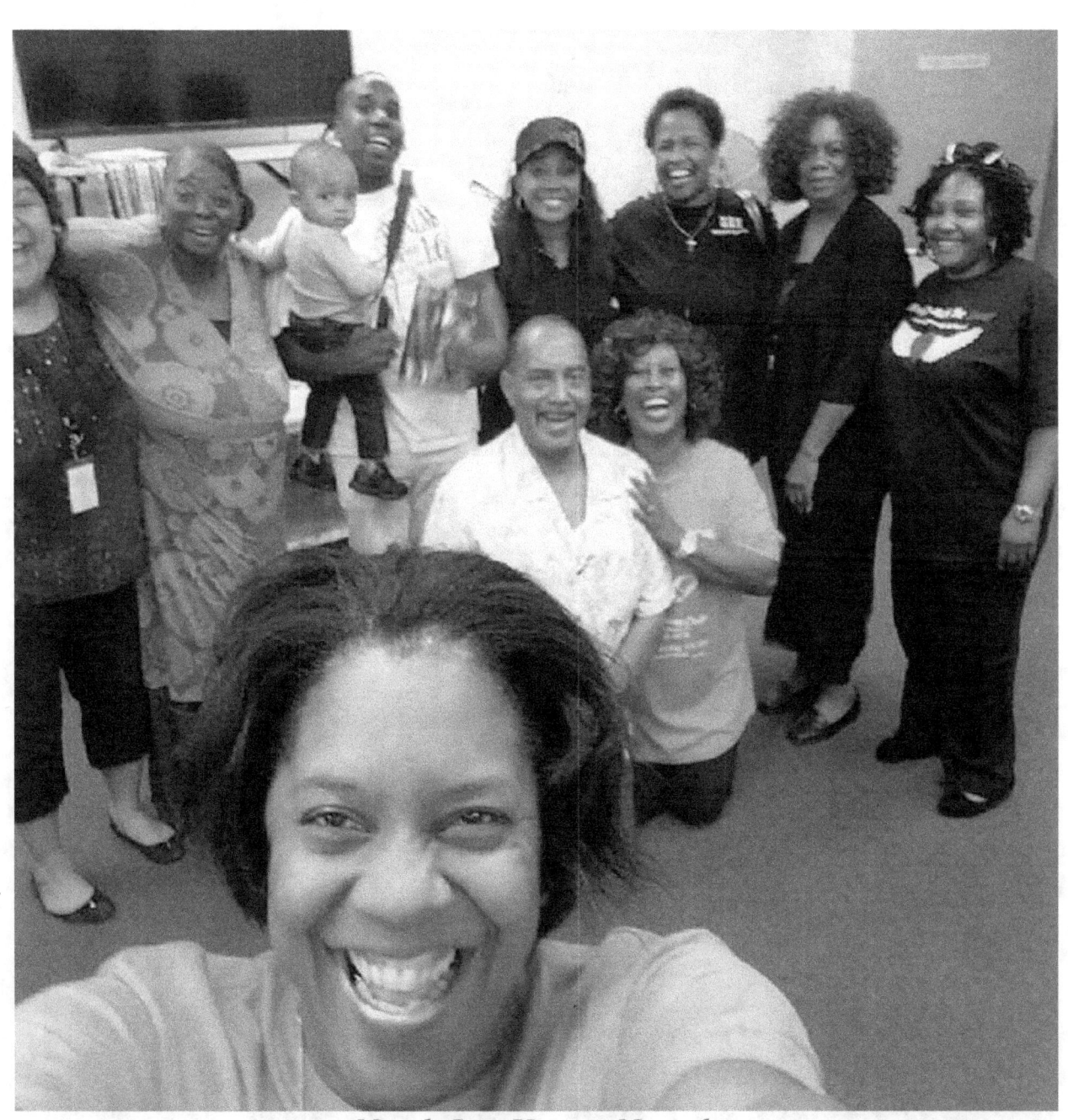

North Las Vegas, Nevada

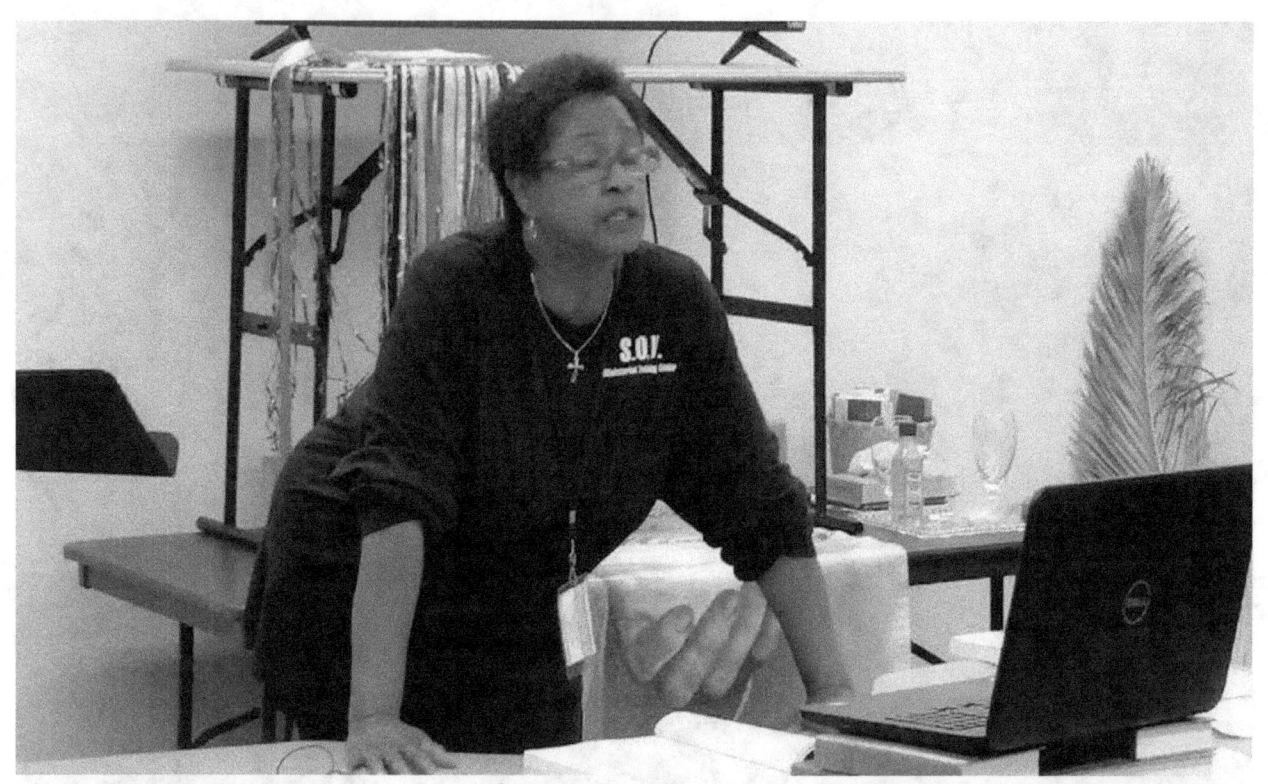

North Las Vegas, Nevada

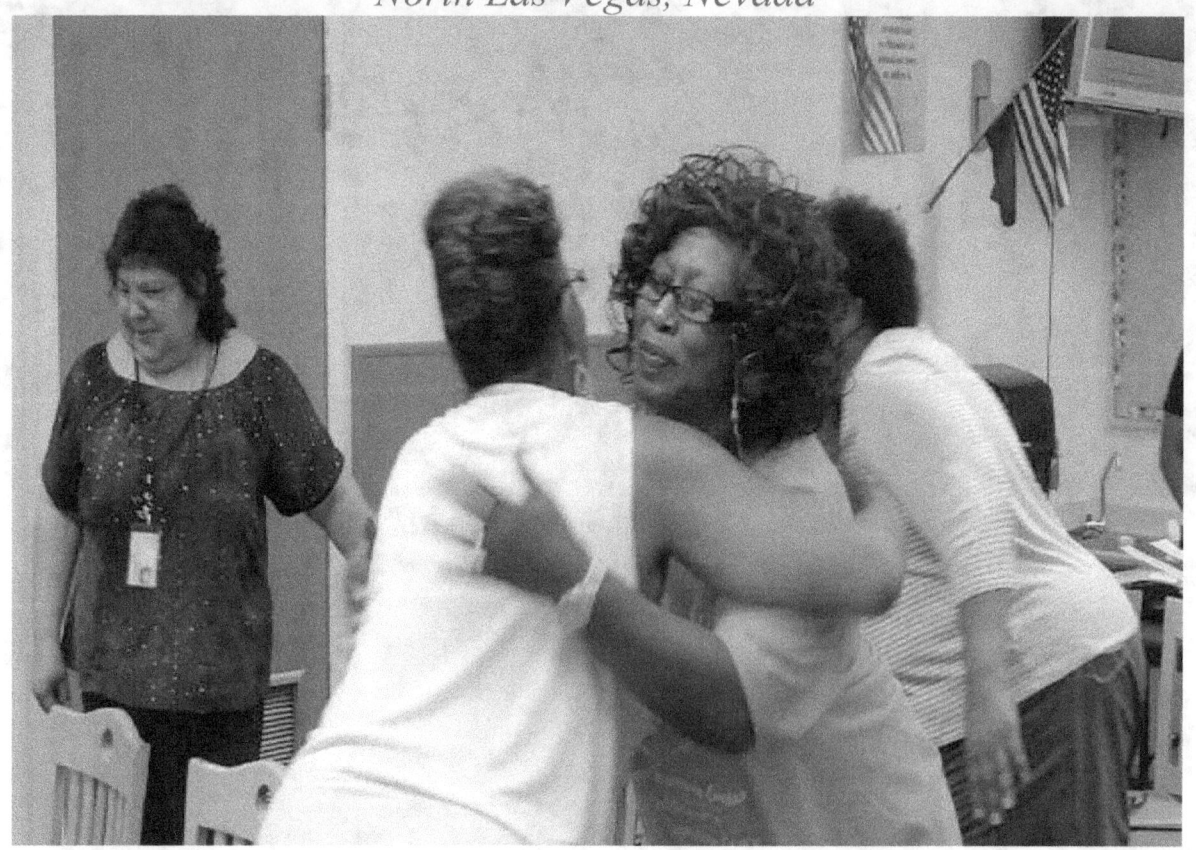

North Las Vegas NV- S.O.V. MTC Fall Class of 2015

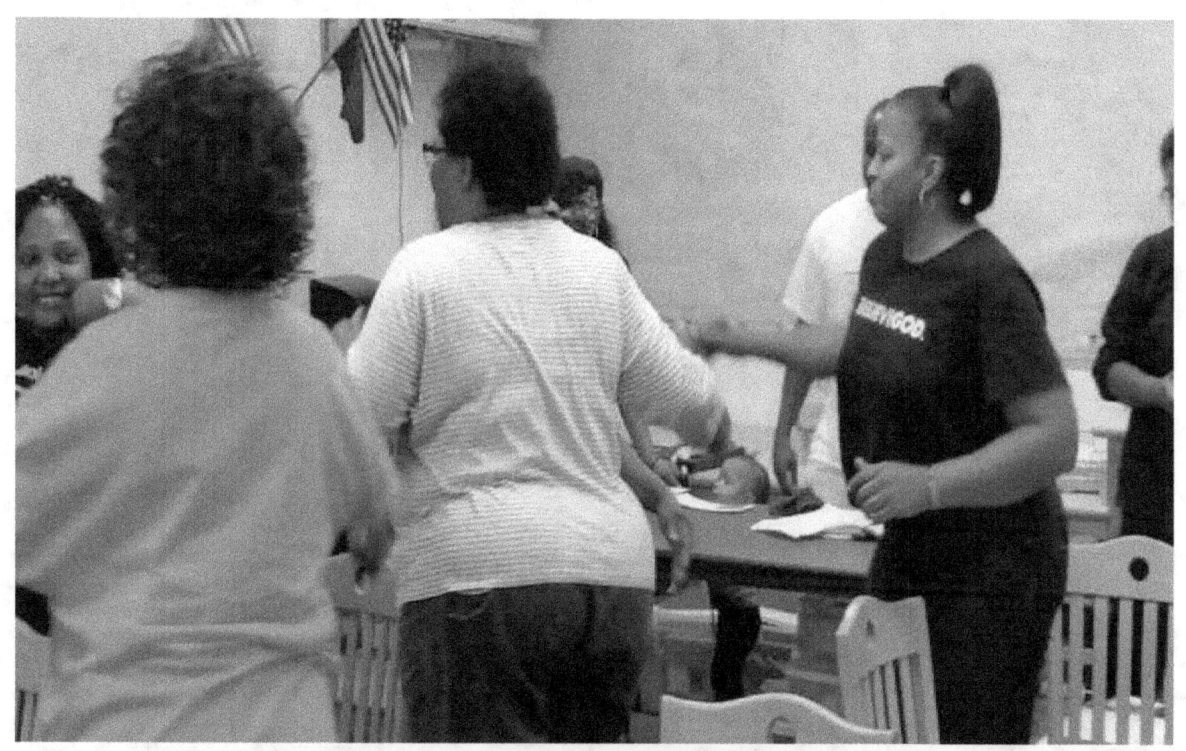

North Las Vegas, Nevada

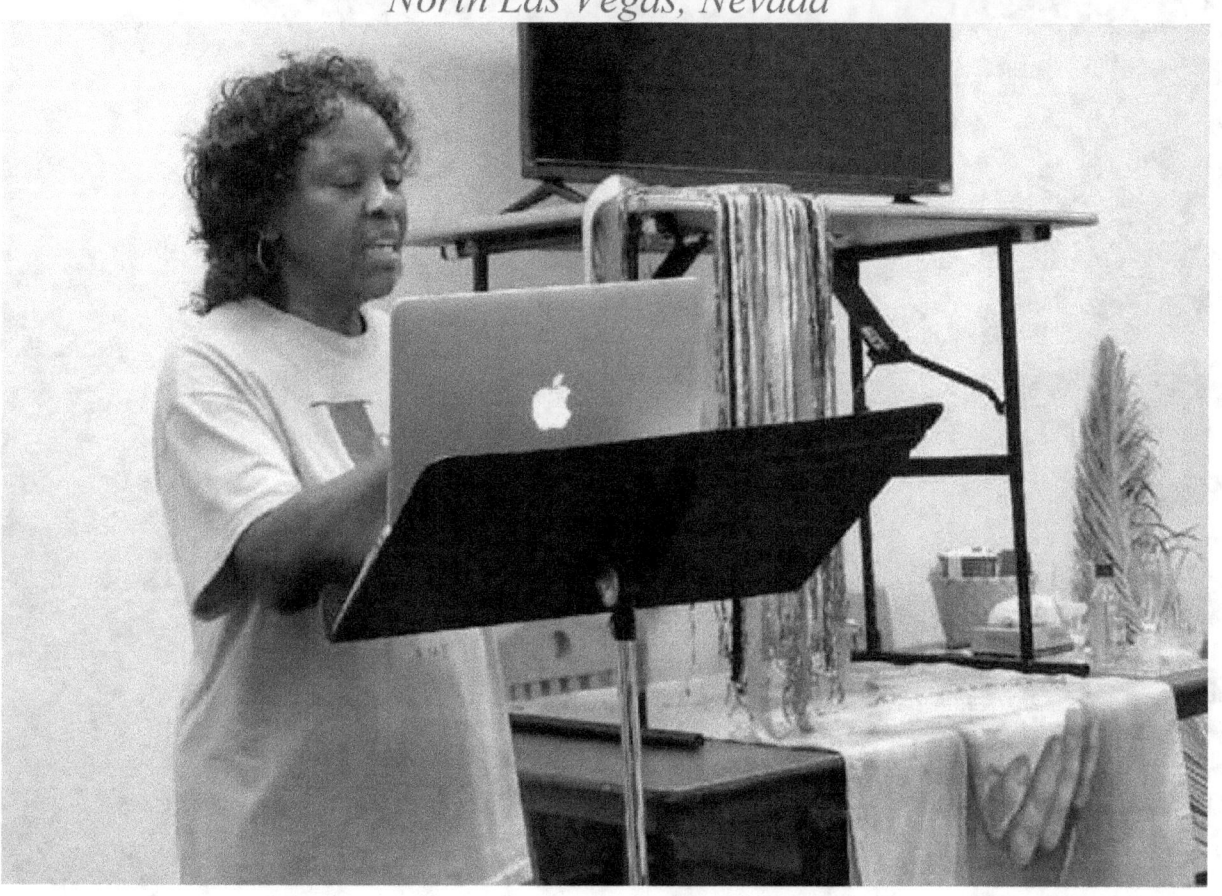

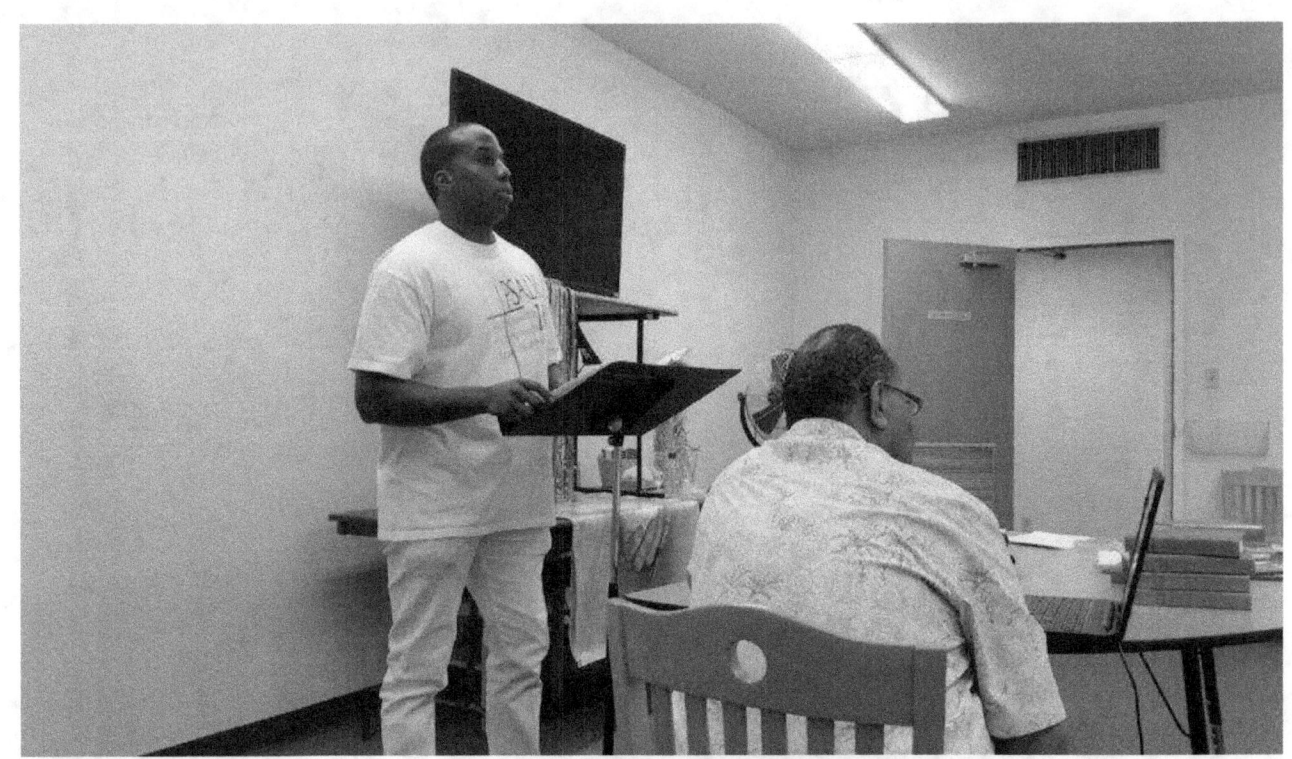

North Las Vegas, Nevada

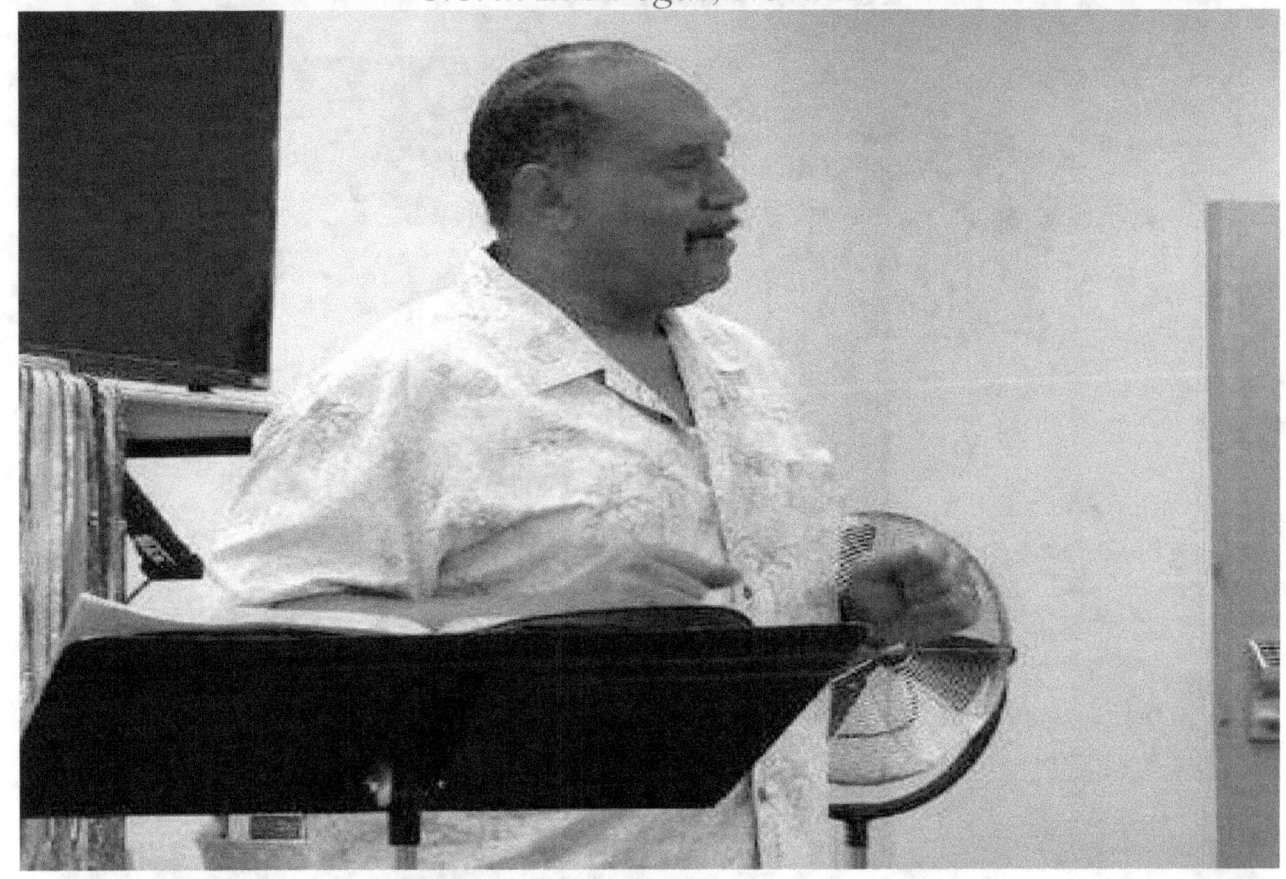

North Las Vegas NV- S.O.V. MTC Fall Class of 2015

Meet the Downey CA
S.O.V. MTC
Fall Class of 2015

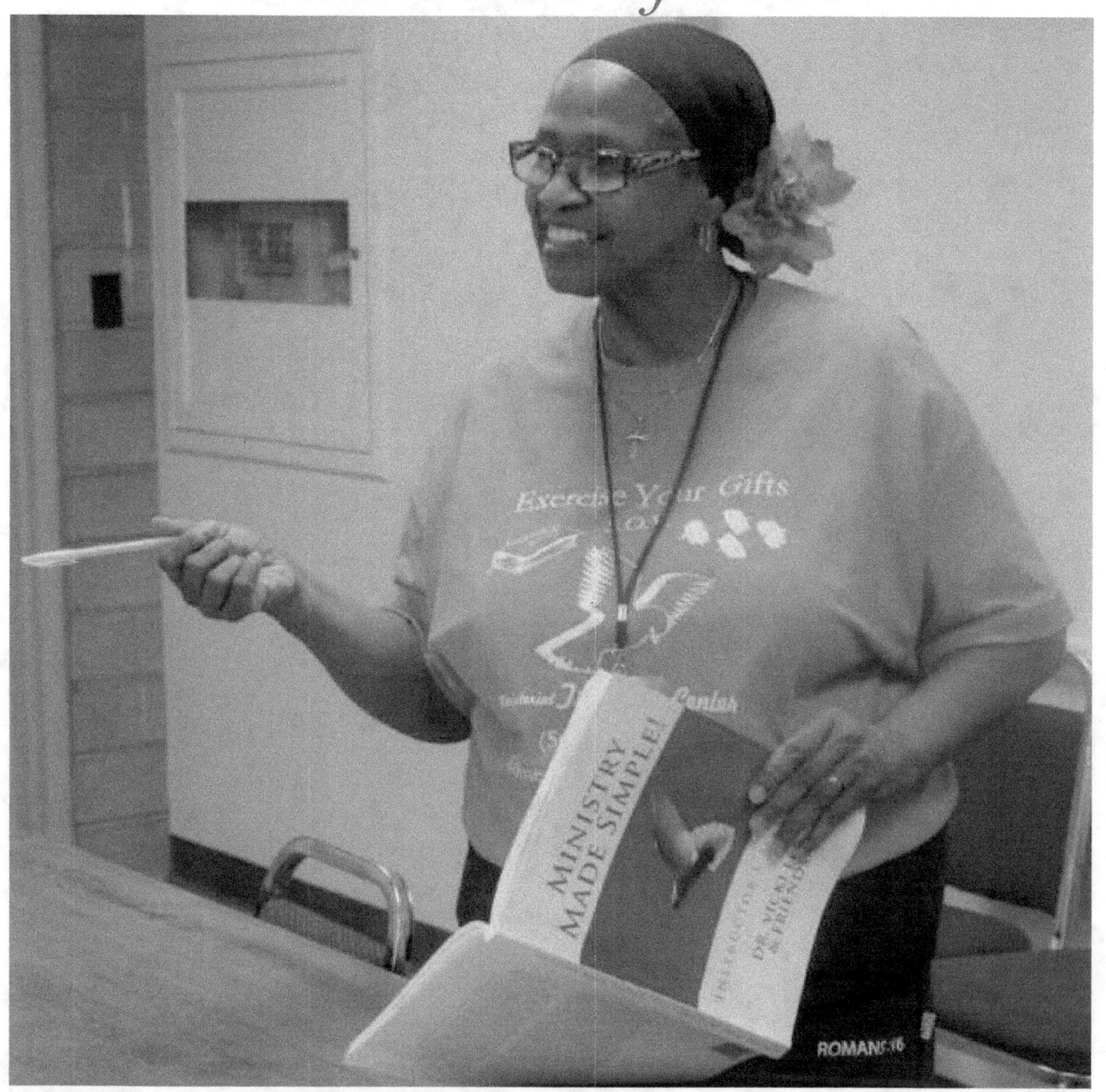

Apostle Dr. Vicki Lee –Founder / CEO

Pastor Jessica Downton, Dean of Students

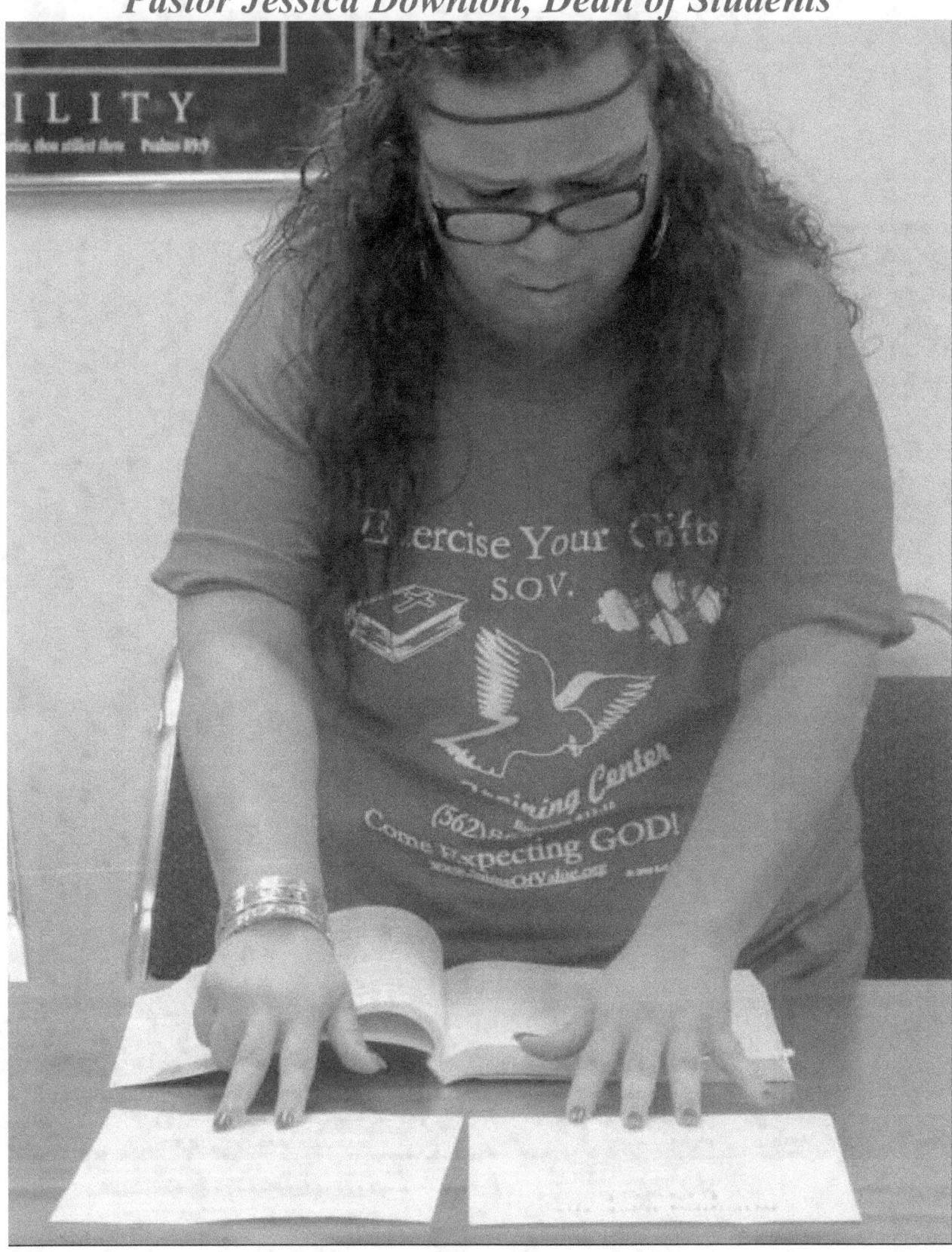

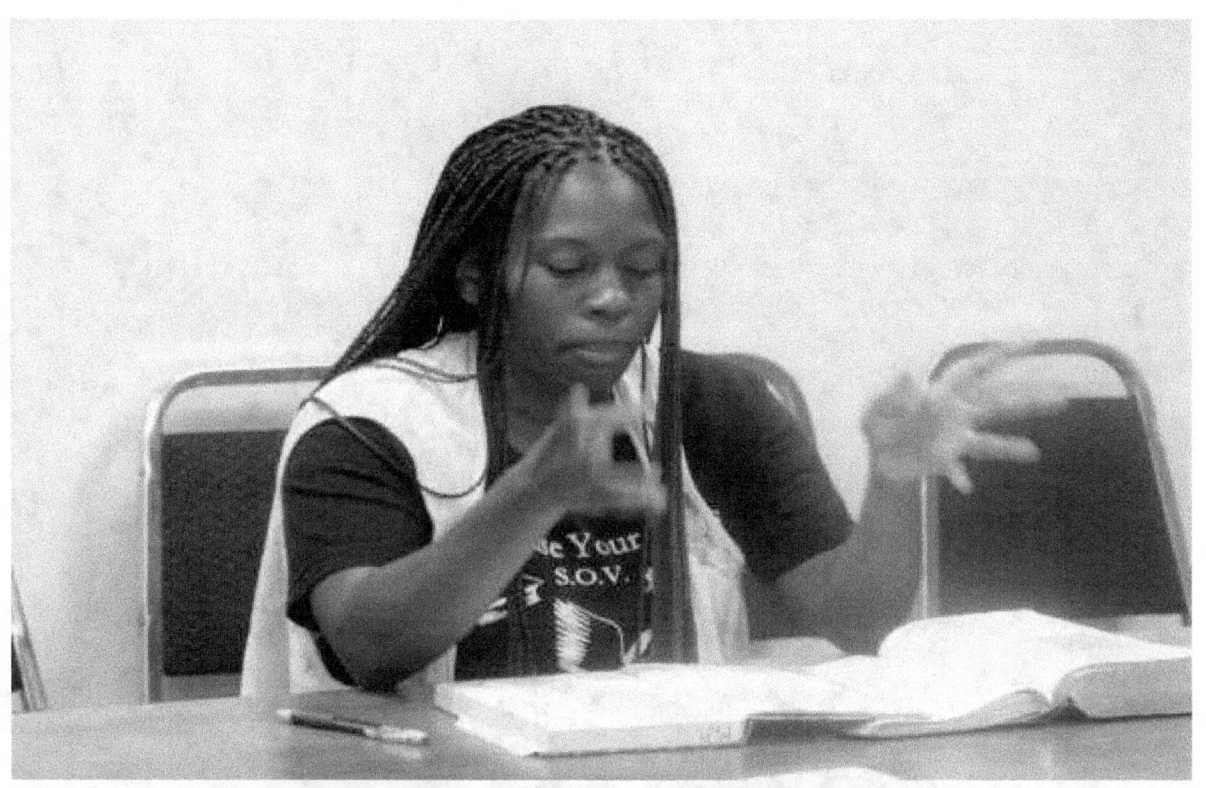

Prophetess Beatrice Brazil

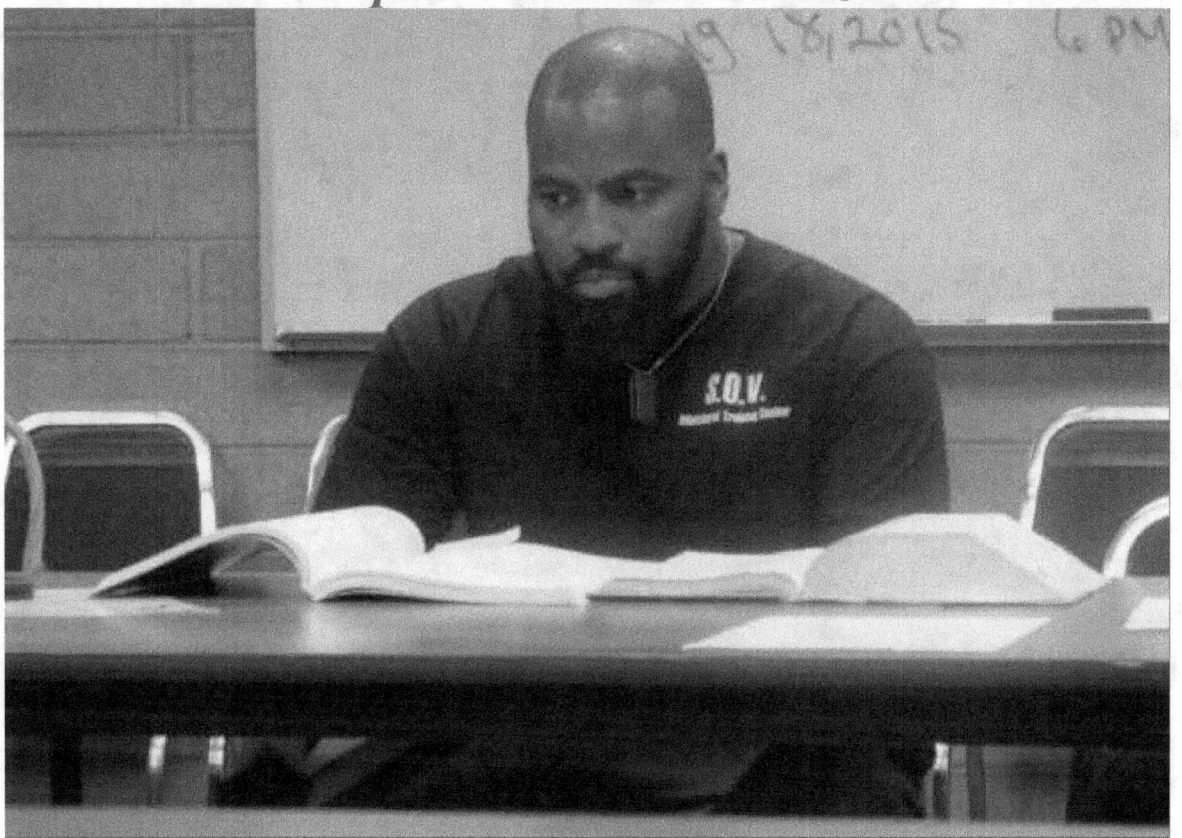

Apostle / Prophet Jason Green

Downey CA - S.O.V. MTC
Fall Class of 2015

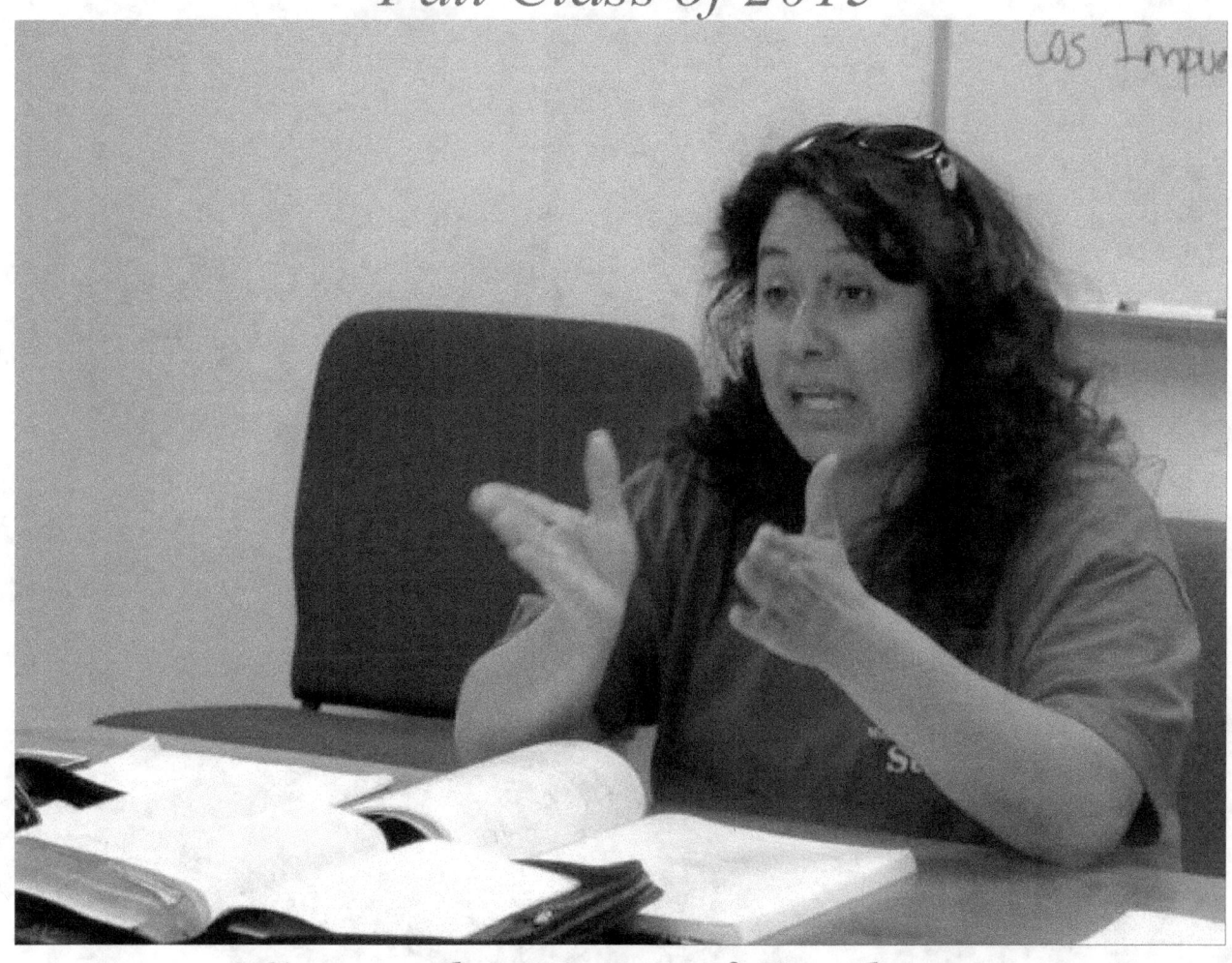

Spanish Dean of Students
Pastor Maria Perez

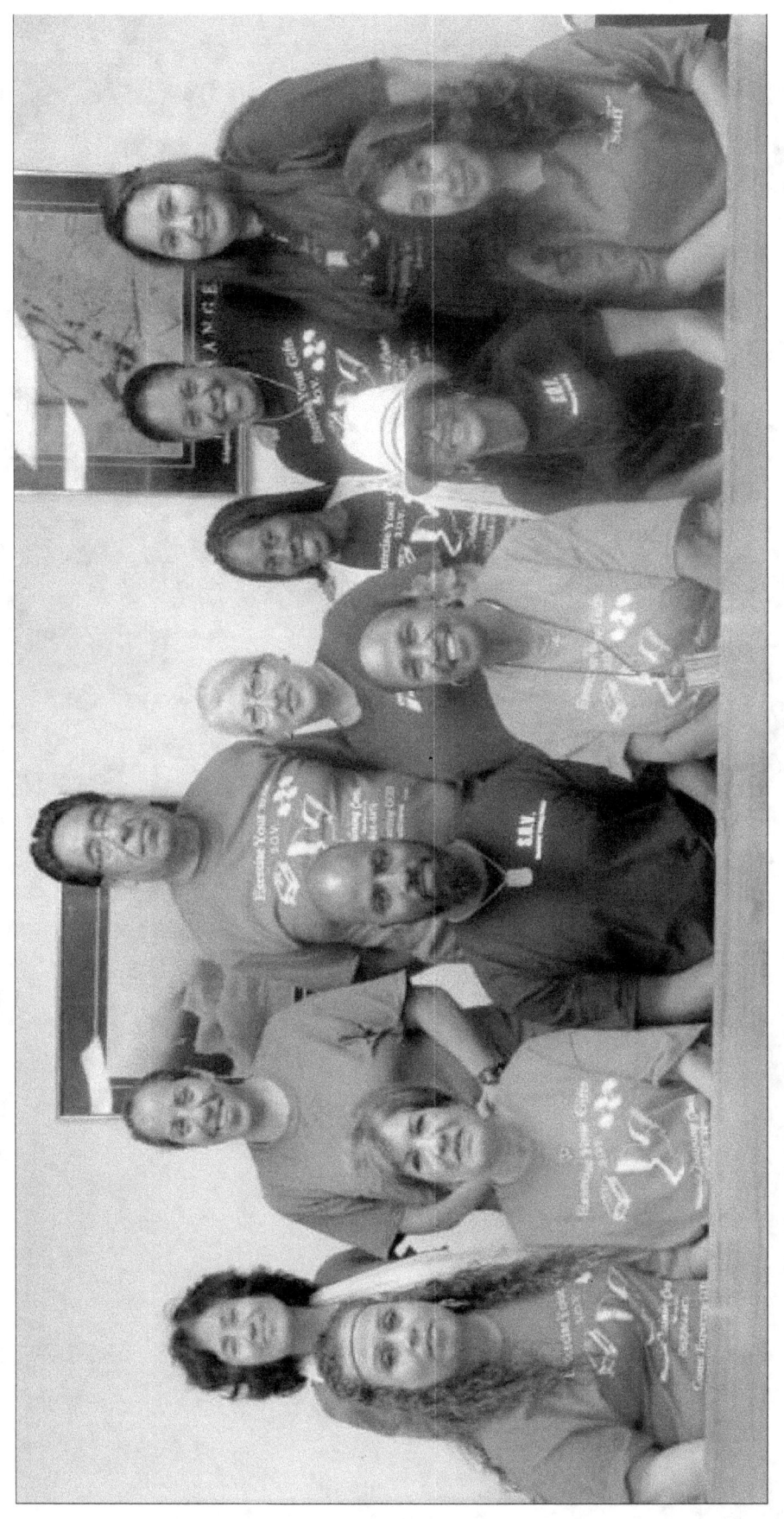

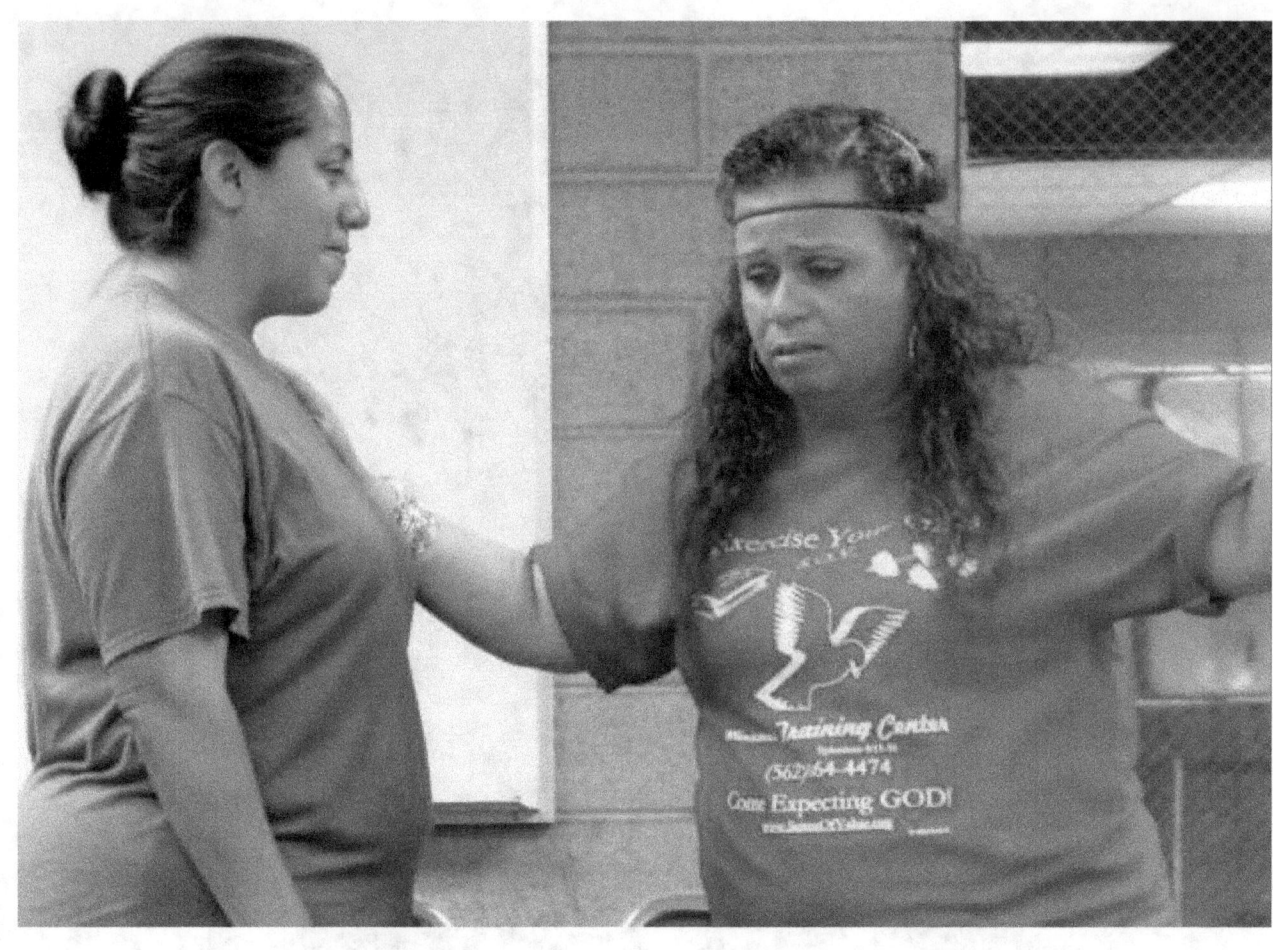

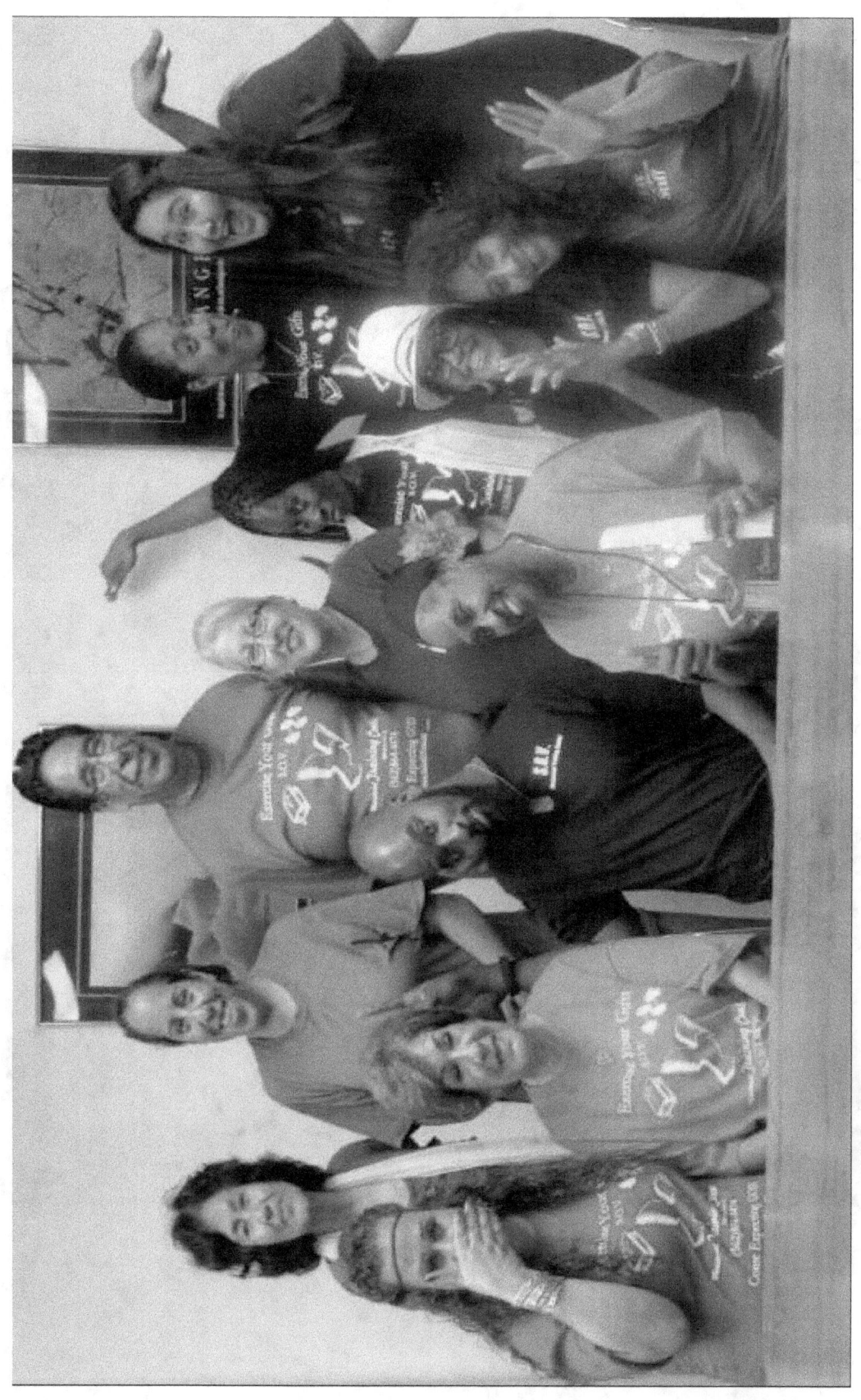

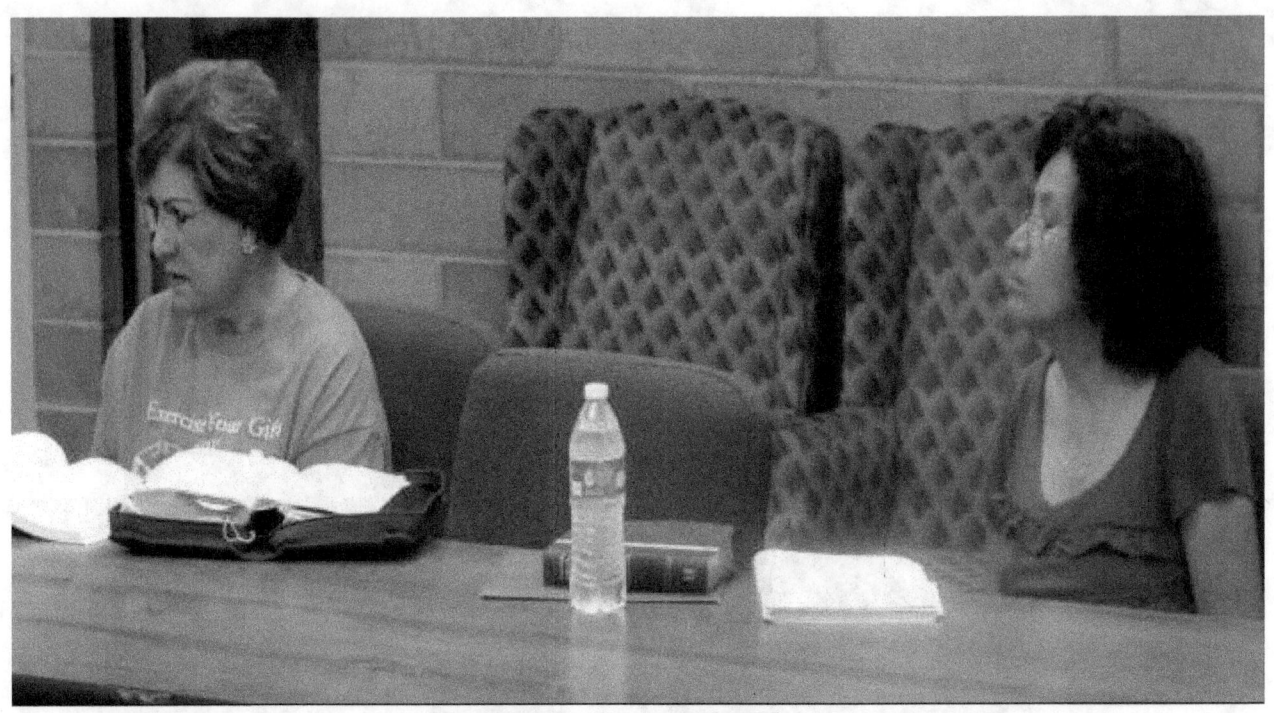

Downney Spanish Class

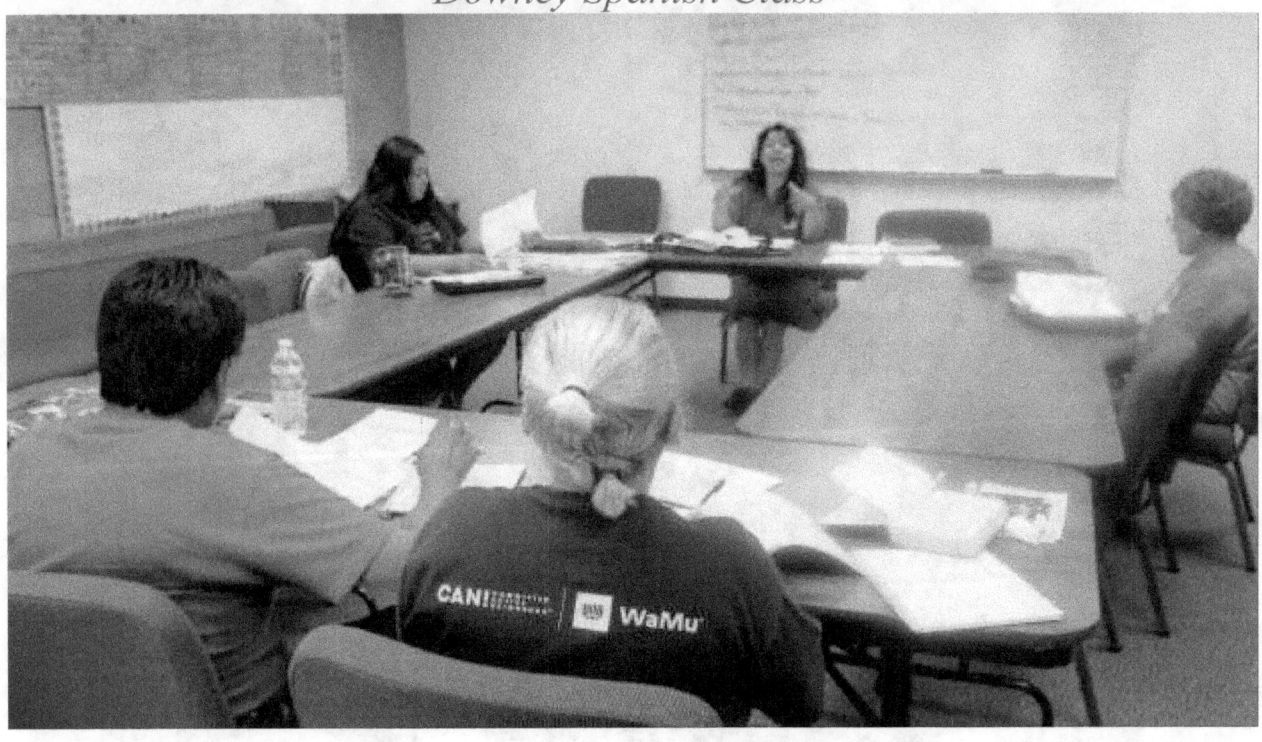

Asst. Spanish Dean Youth Pastor Natalie Pérez

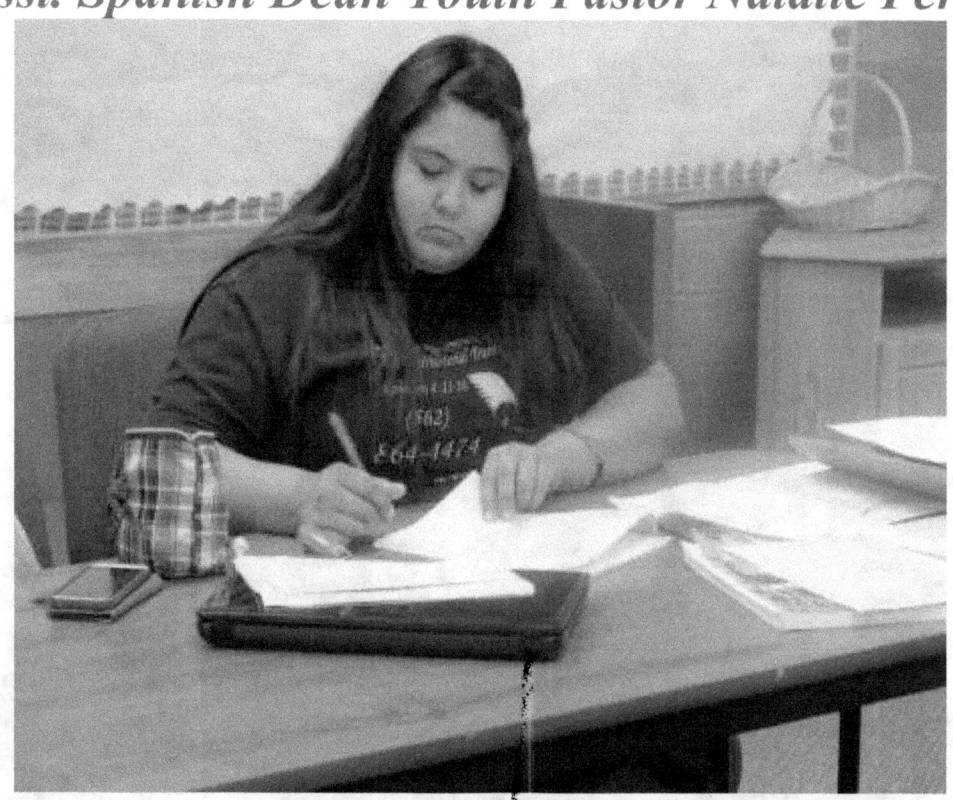

Downey, California

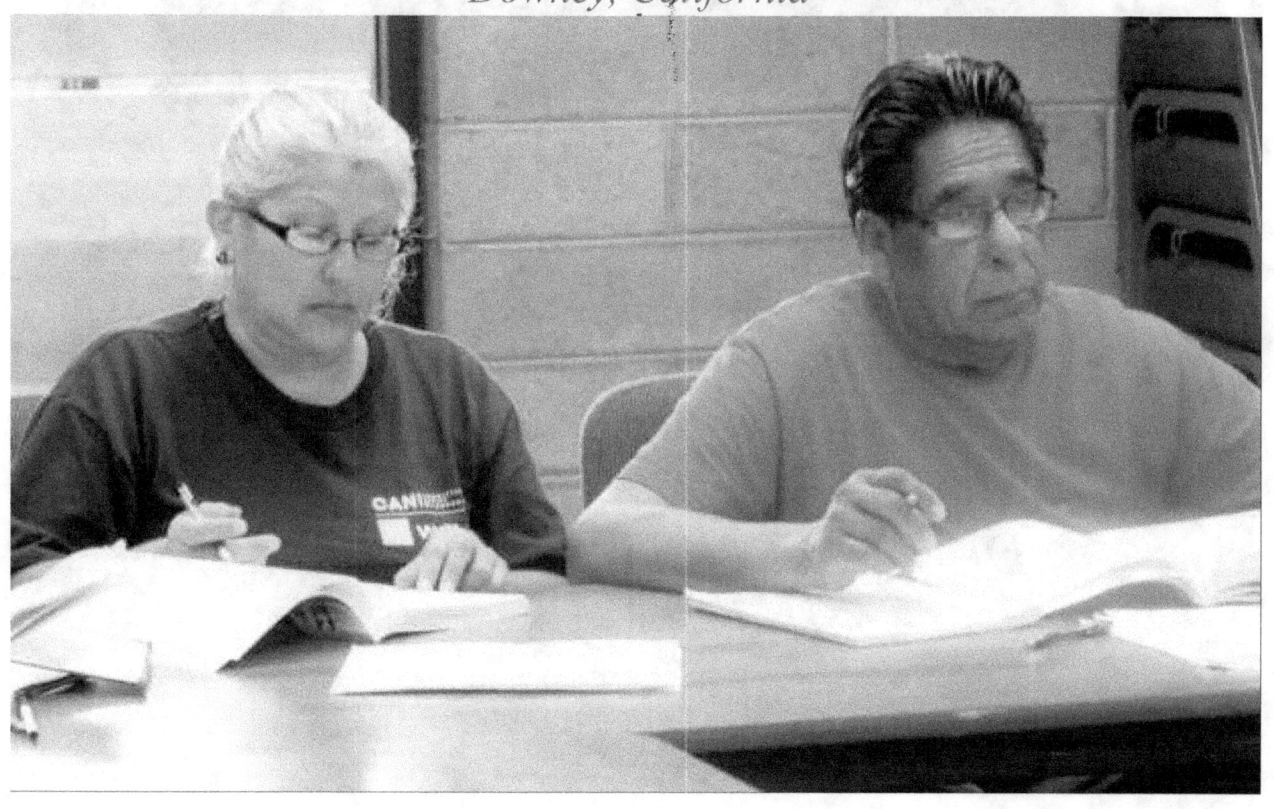

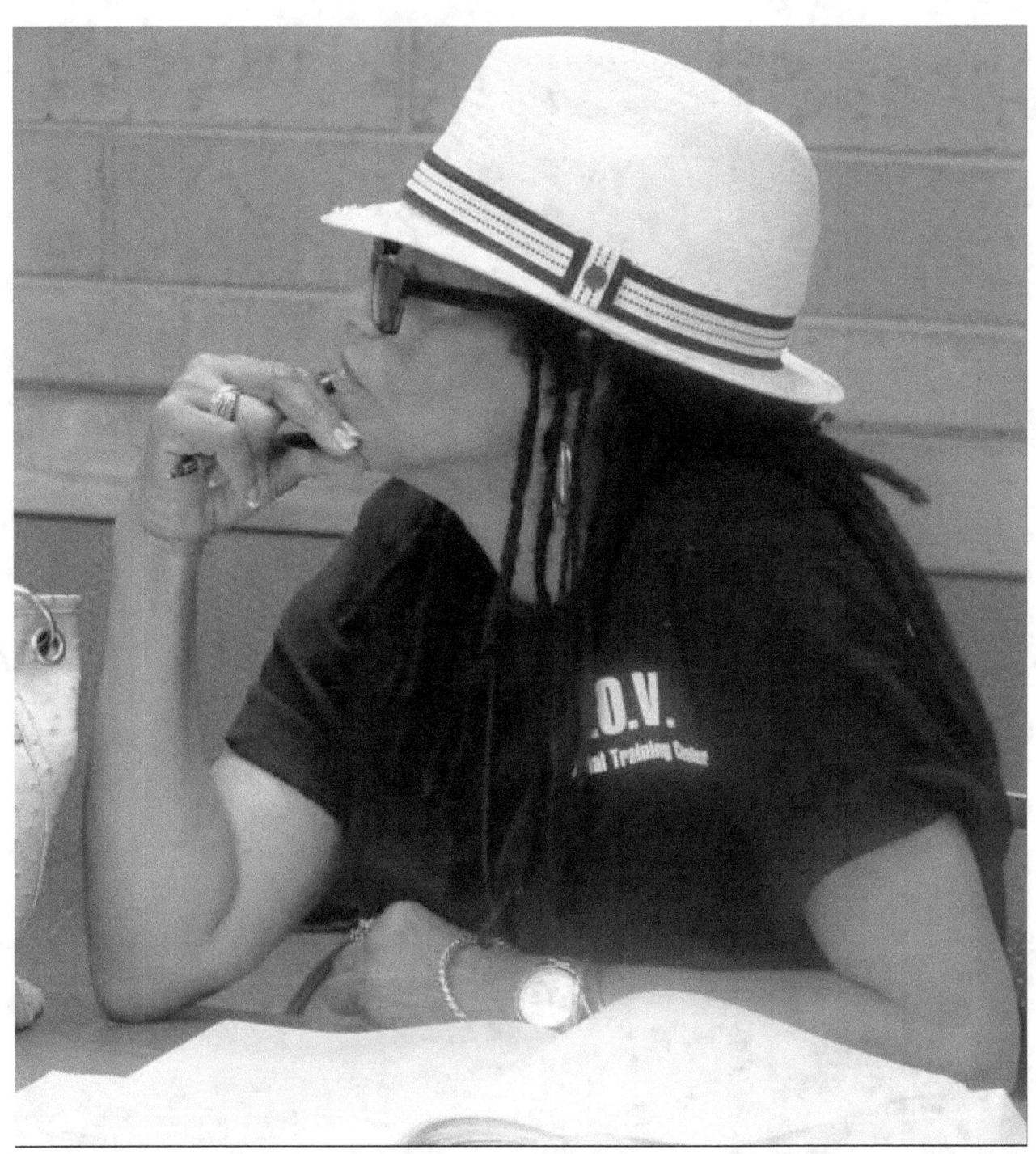

Dr. Pastor Pinky Cunningham
Head Intercessor

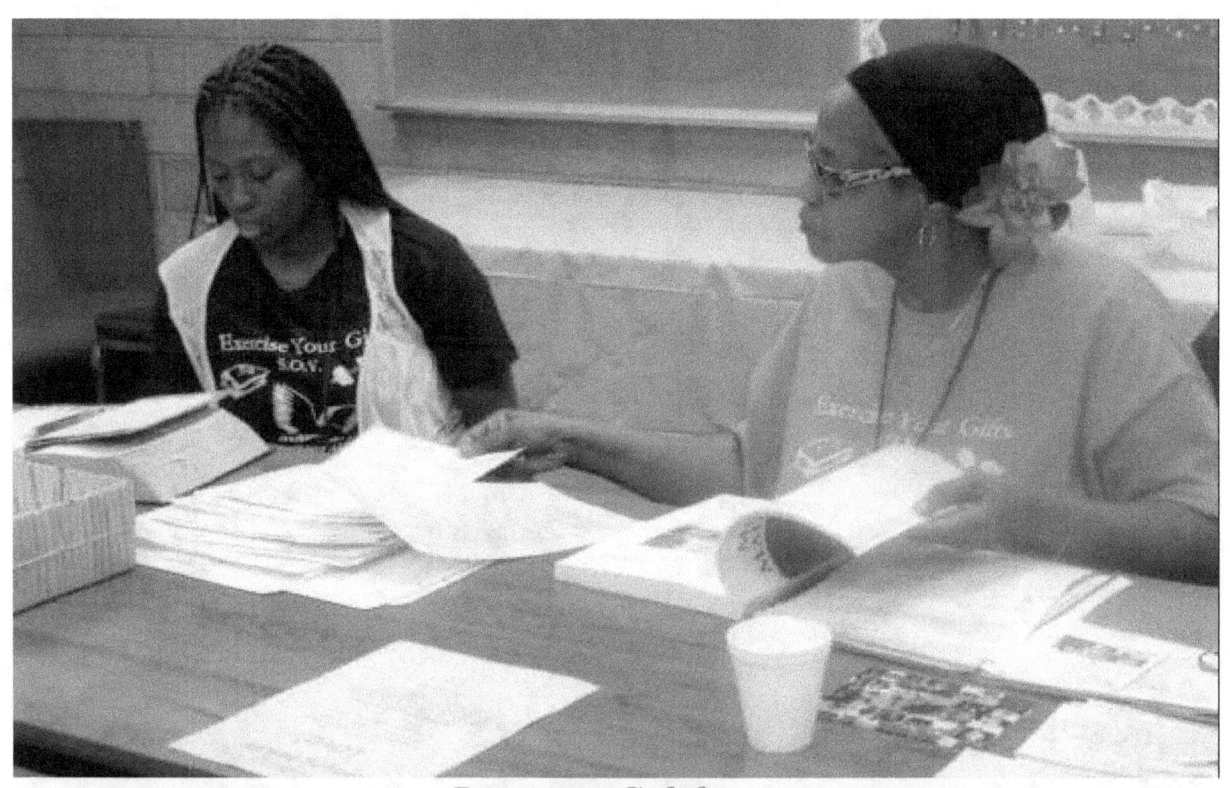

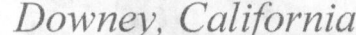
Downey, California

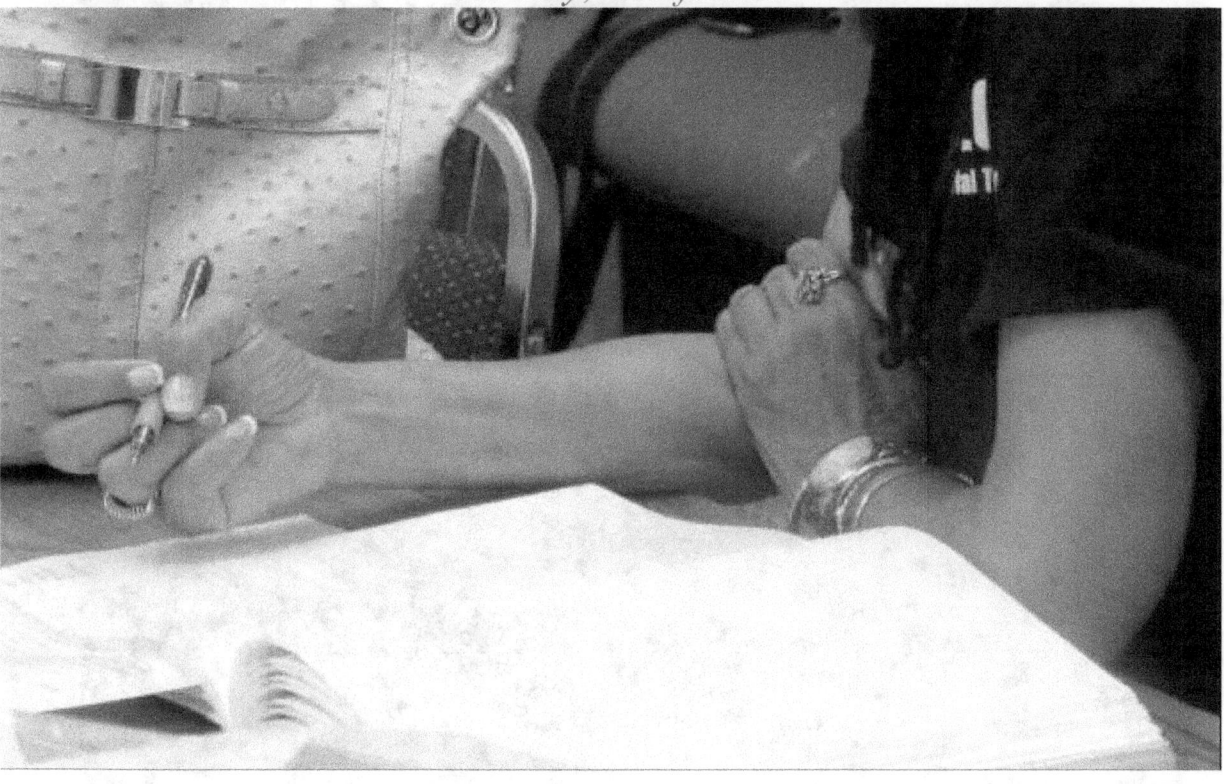

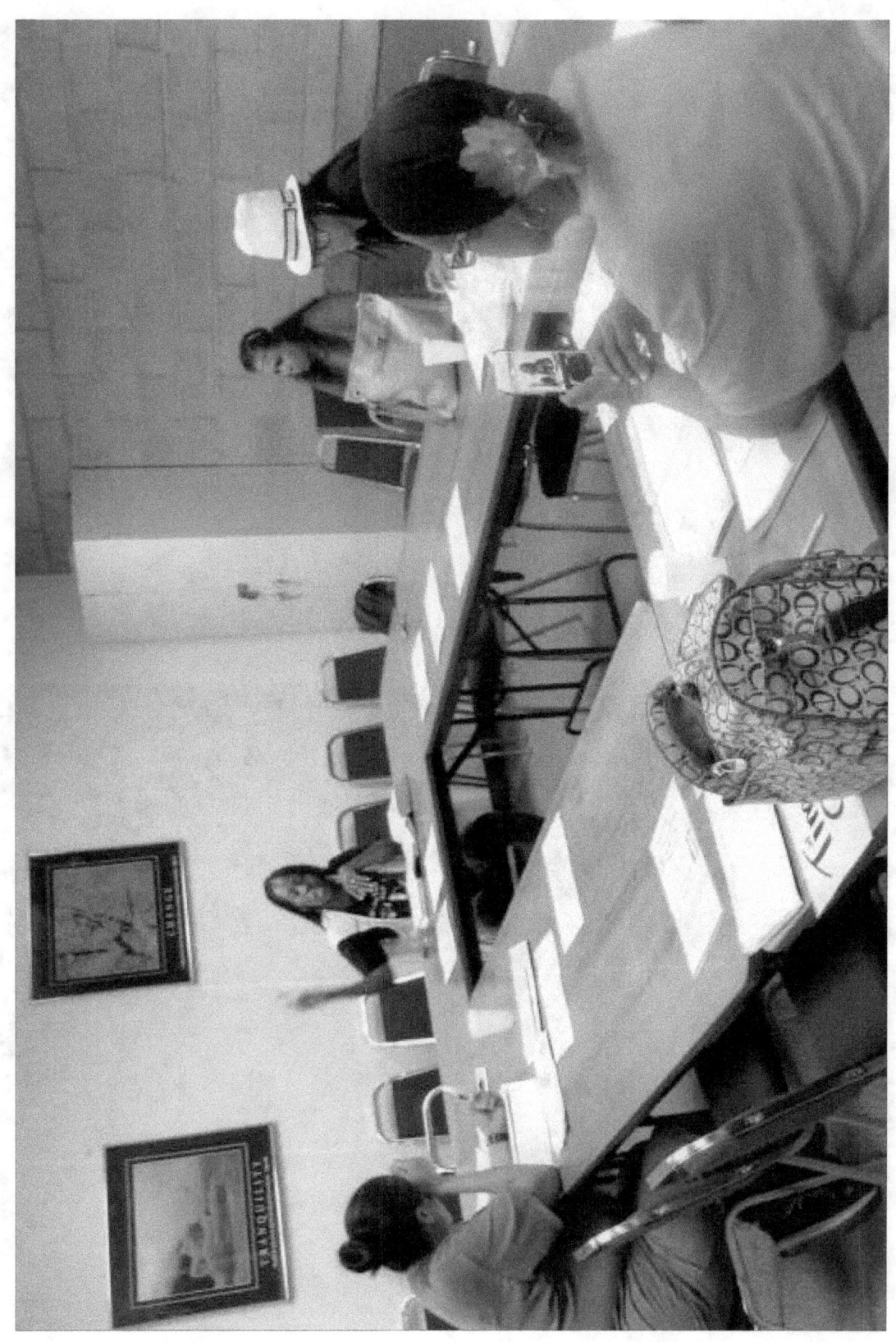

Meet The Houston, Texas
S.O.V. MTC Fall Class of 2015

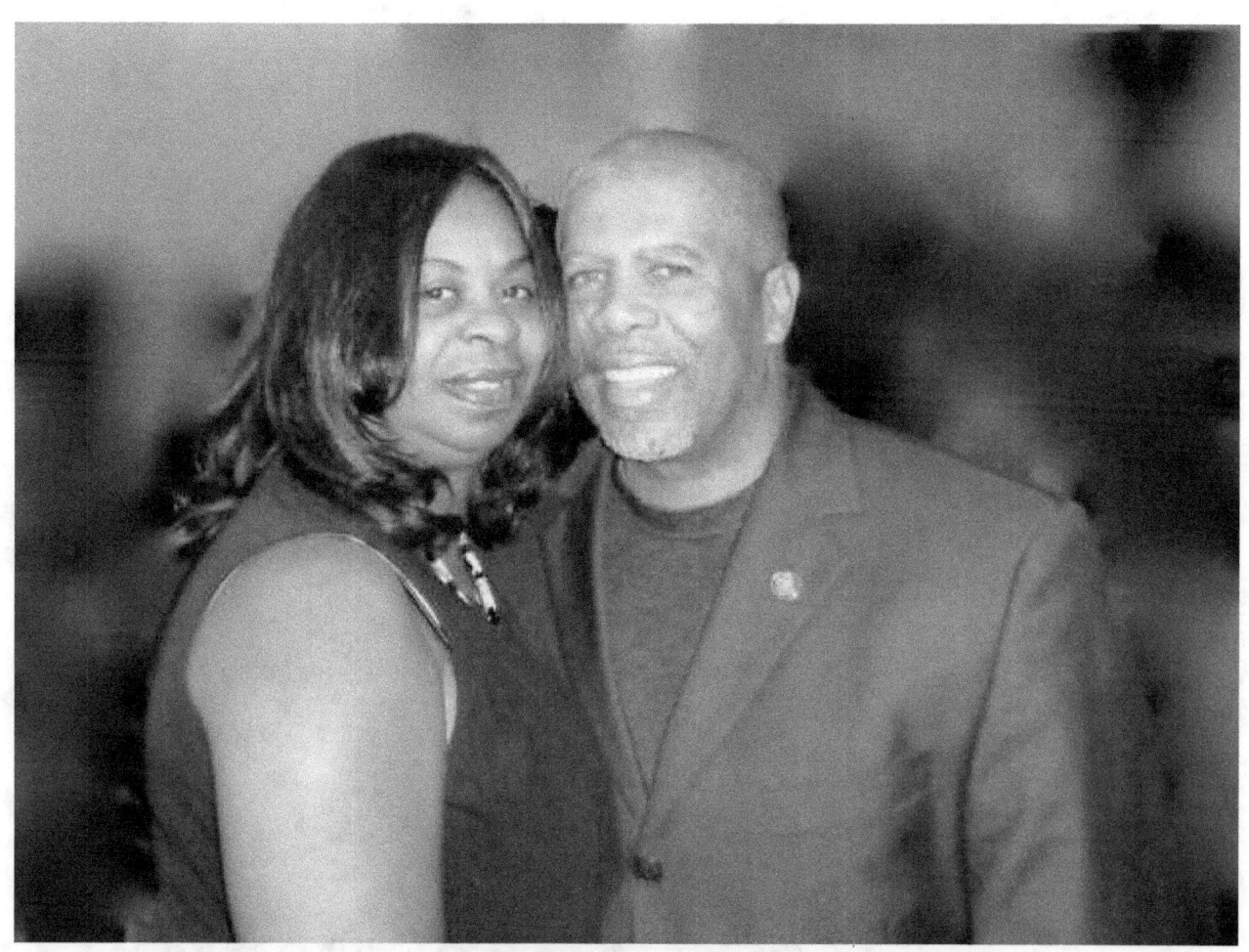

Dr. Kenneth Thomas Dean of Students
& Pastor Toni Thomas Asst. Dean

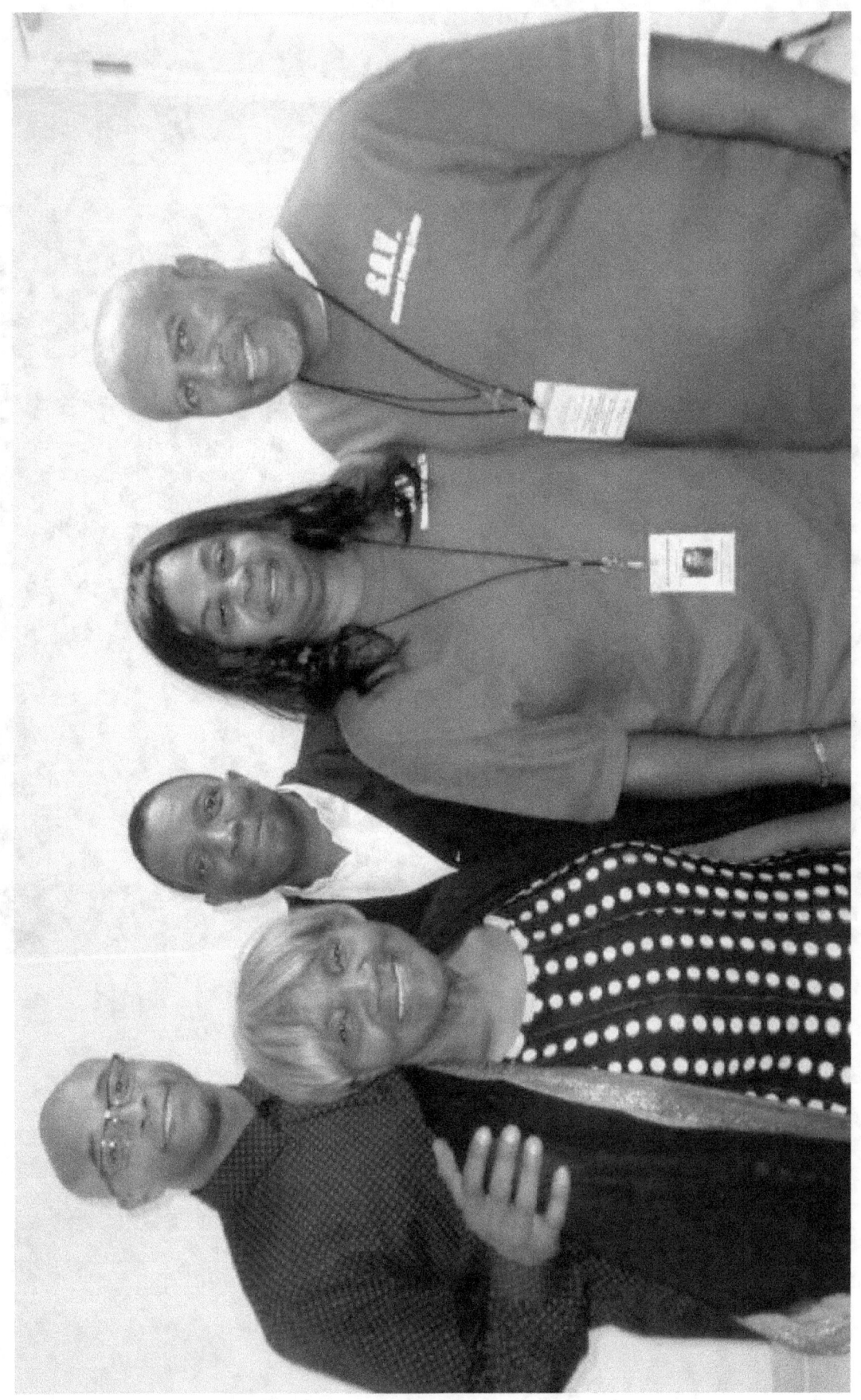

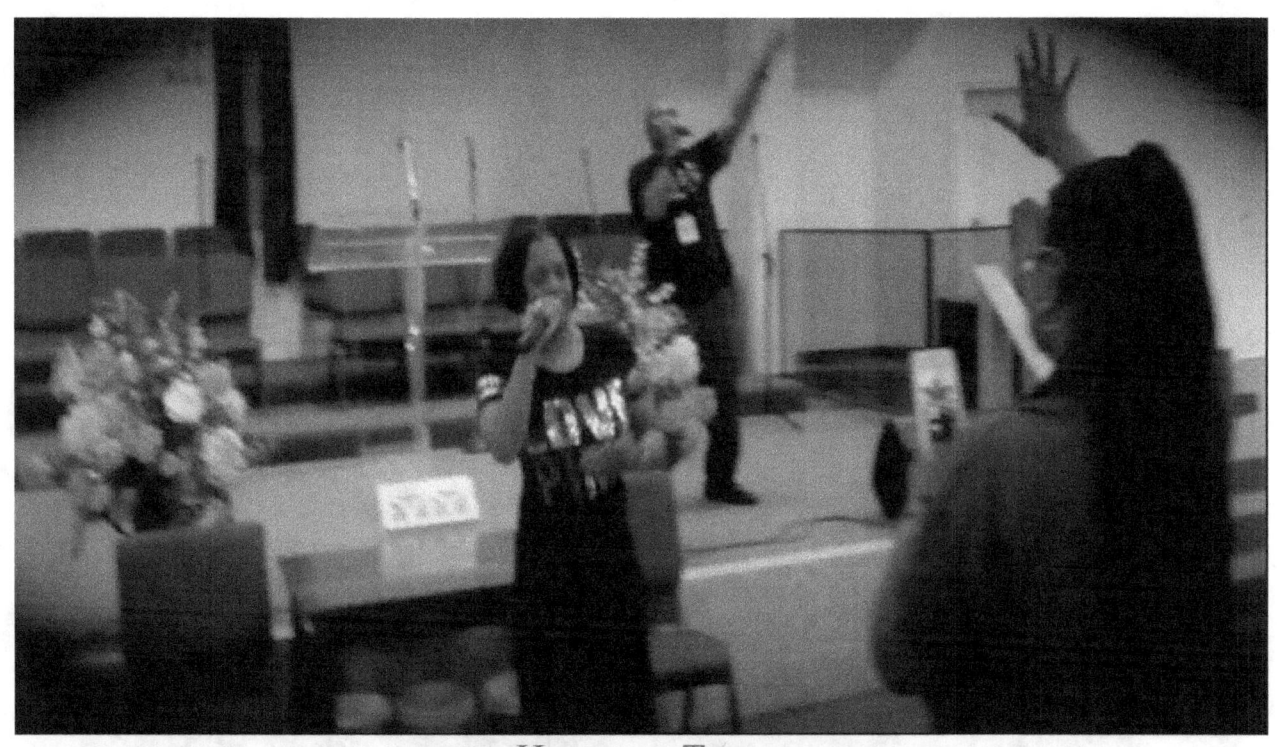

Houston, Texas

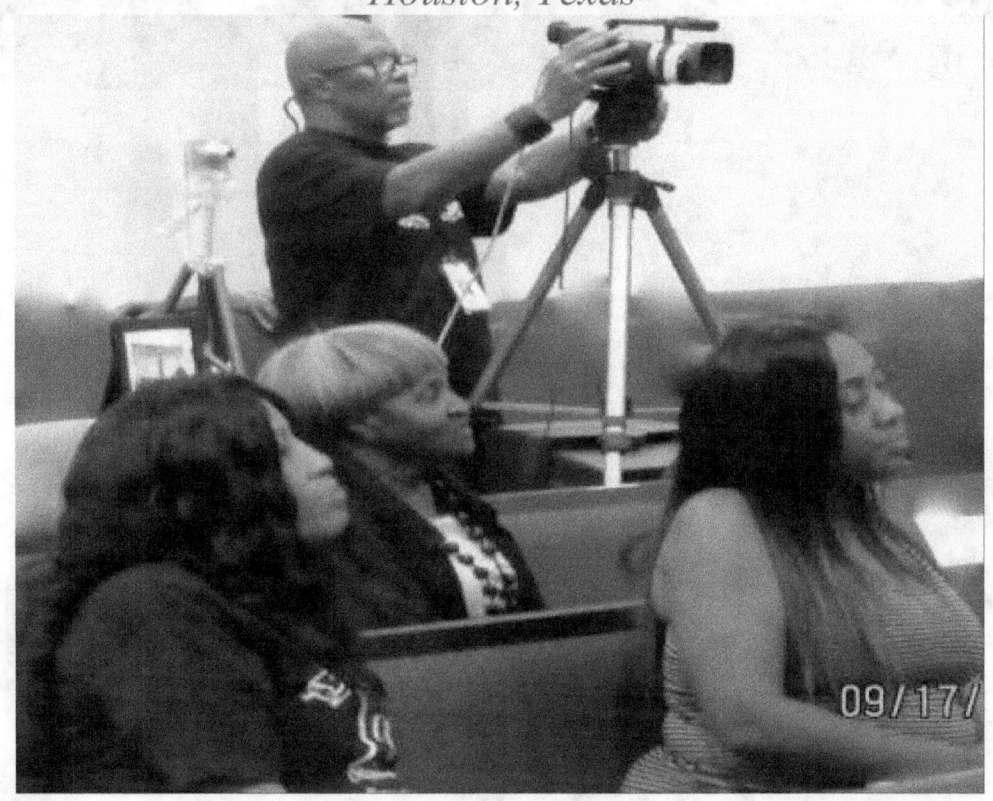

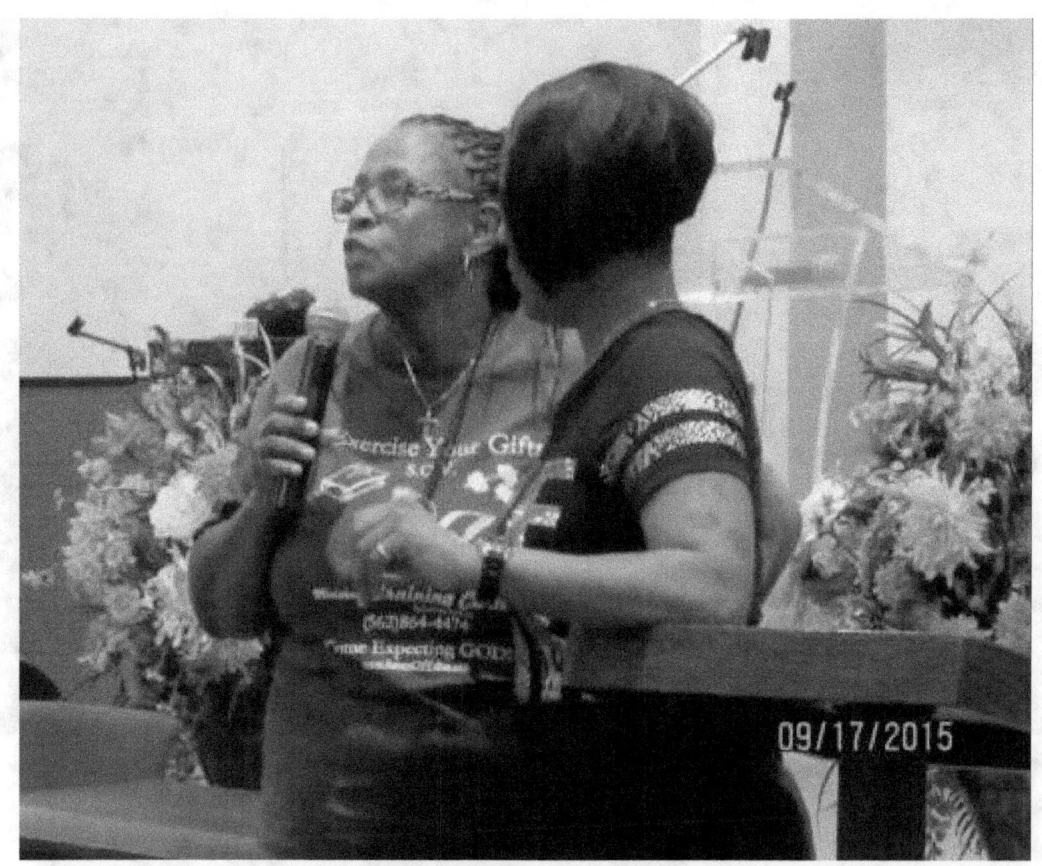

Houston, Texas

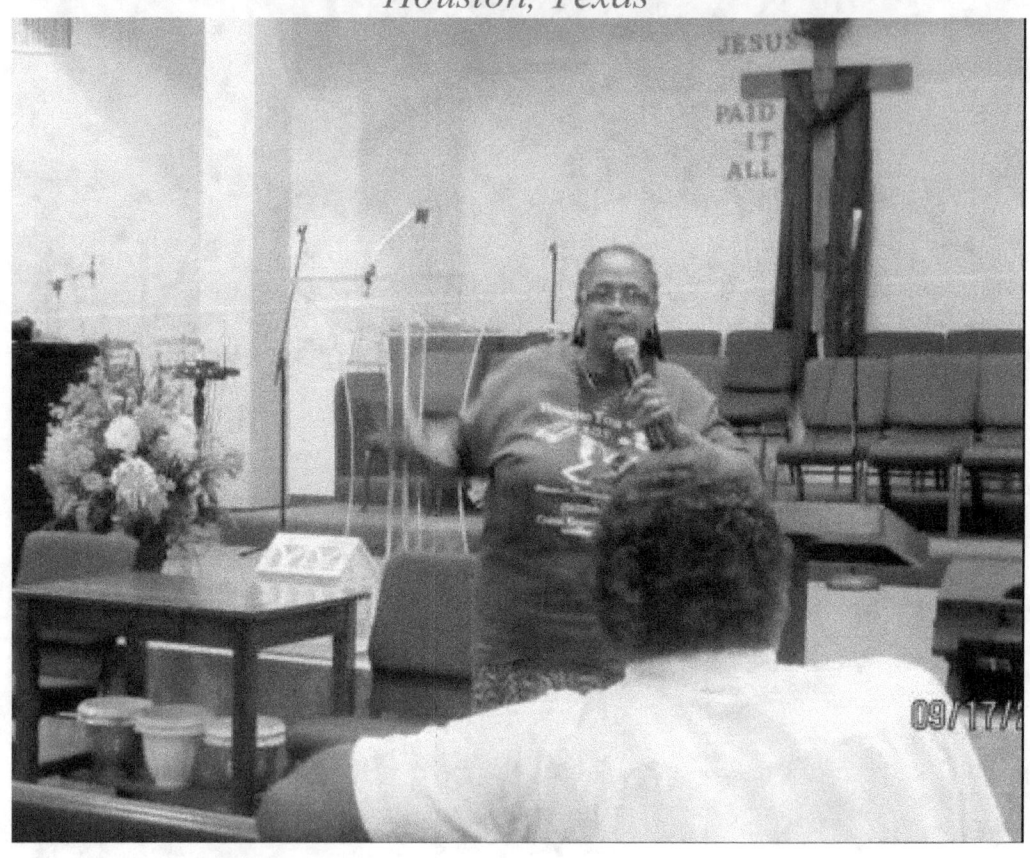

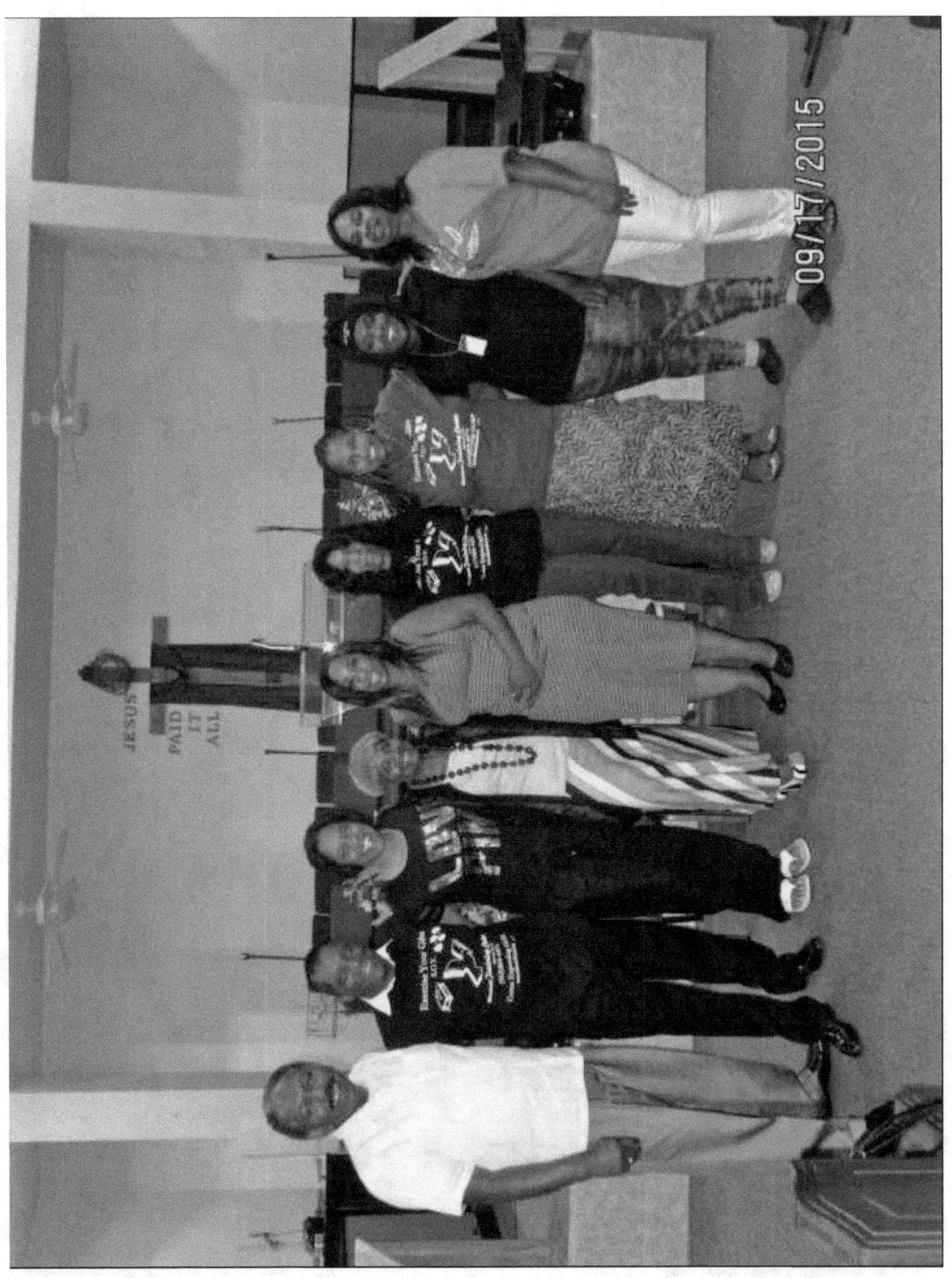

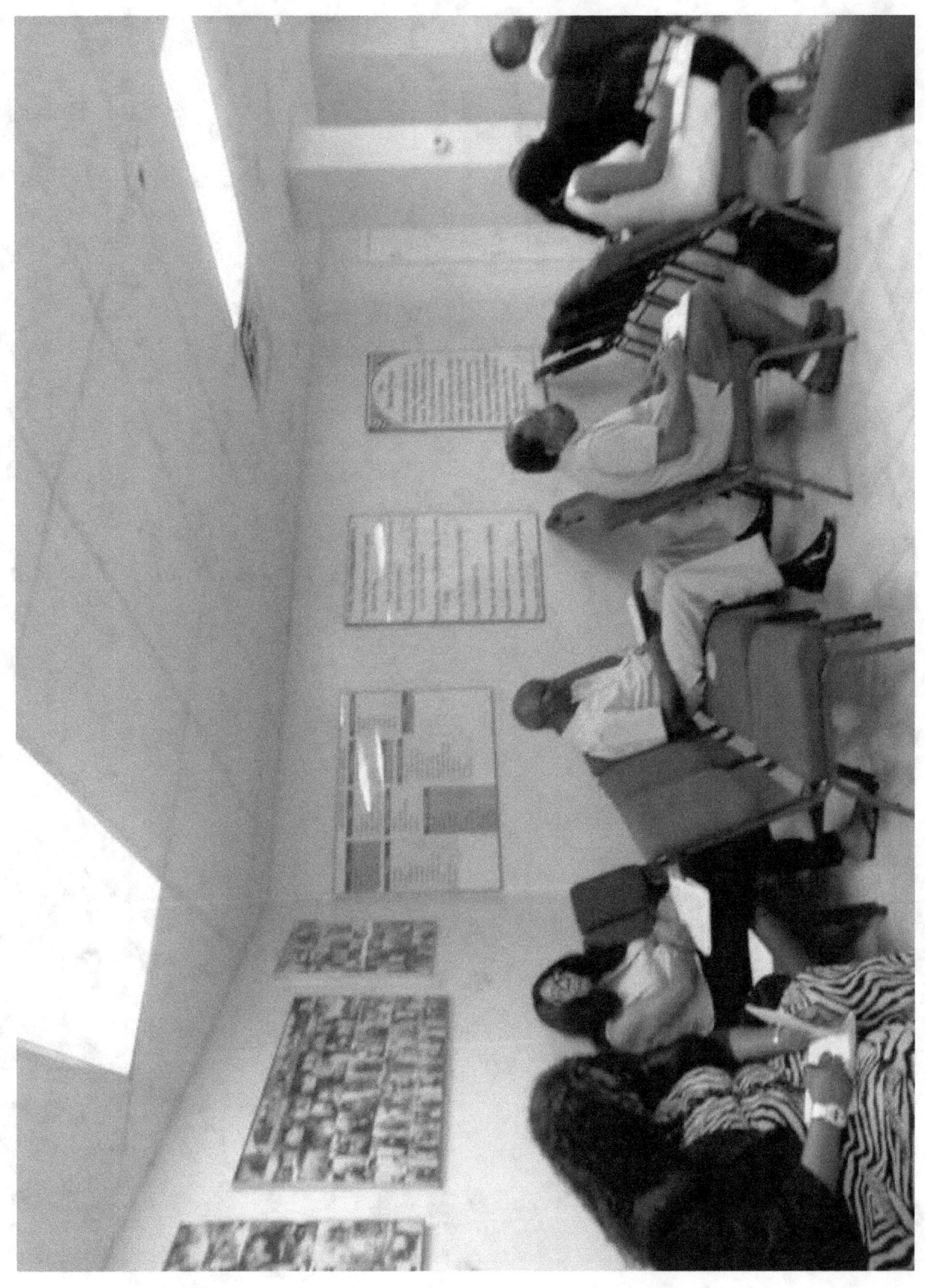

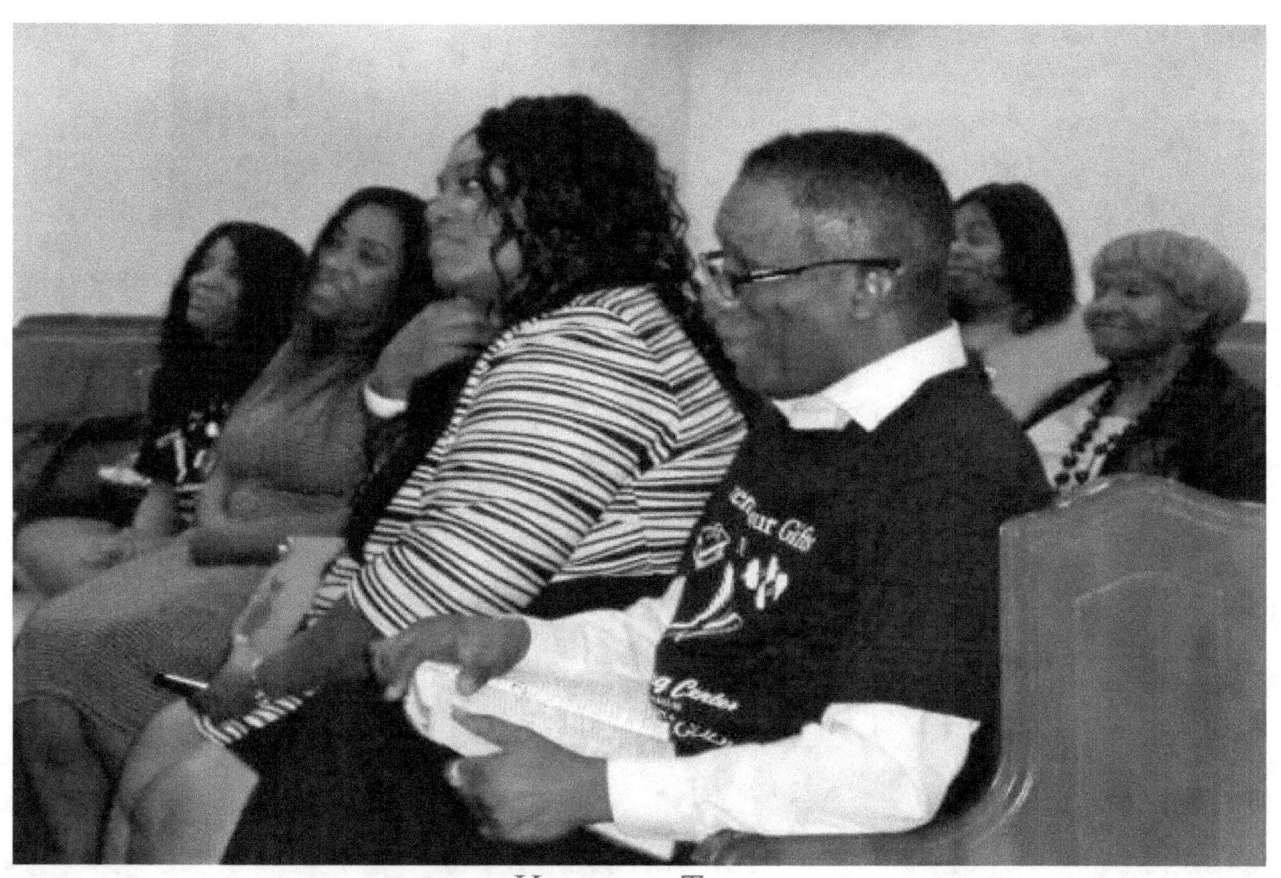

Houston, Texas

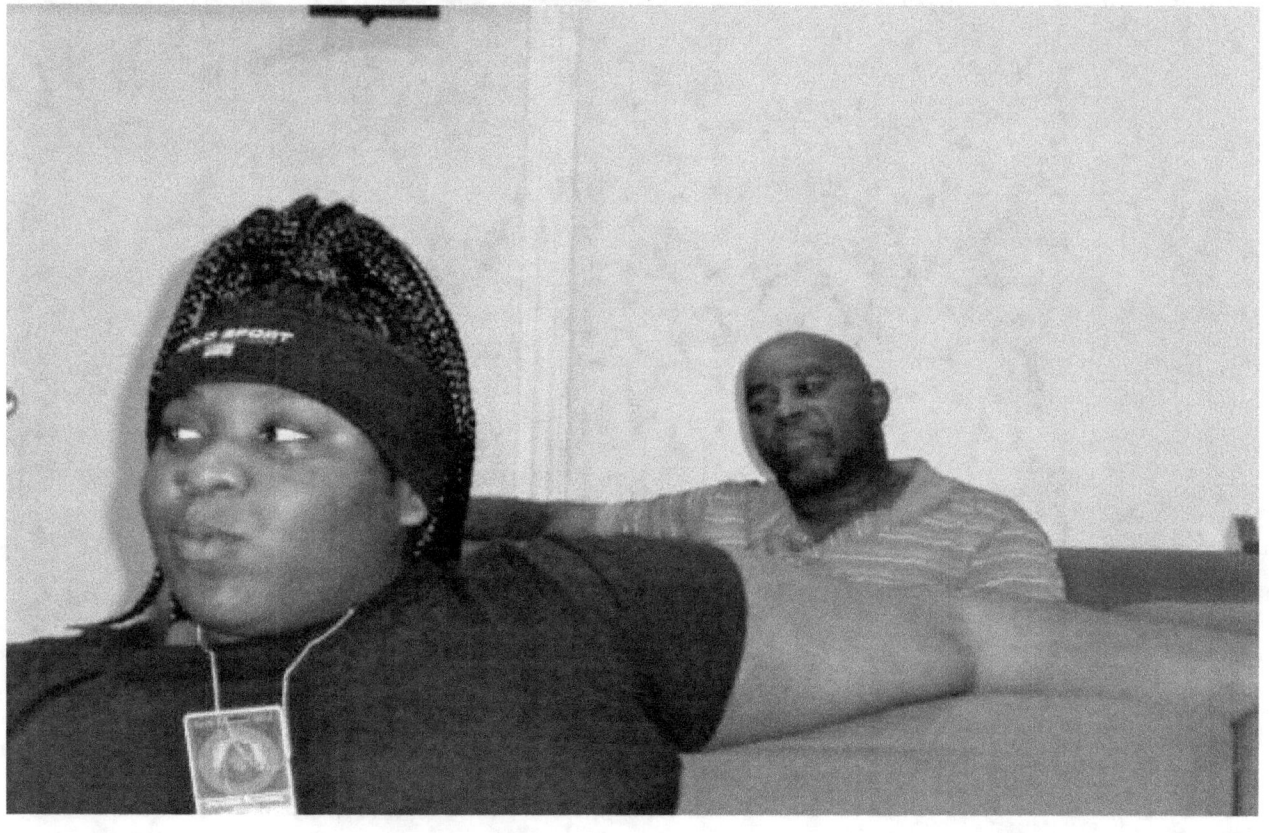

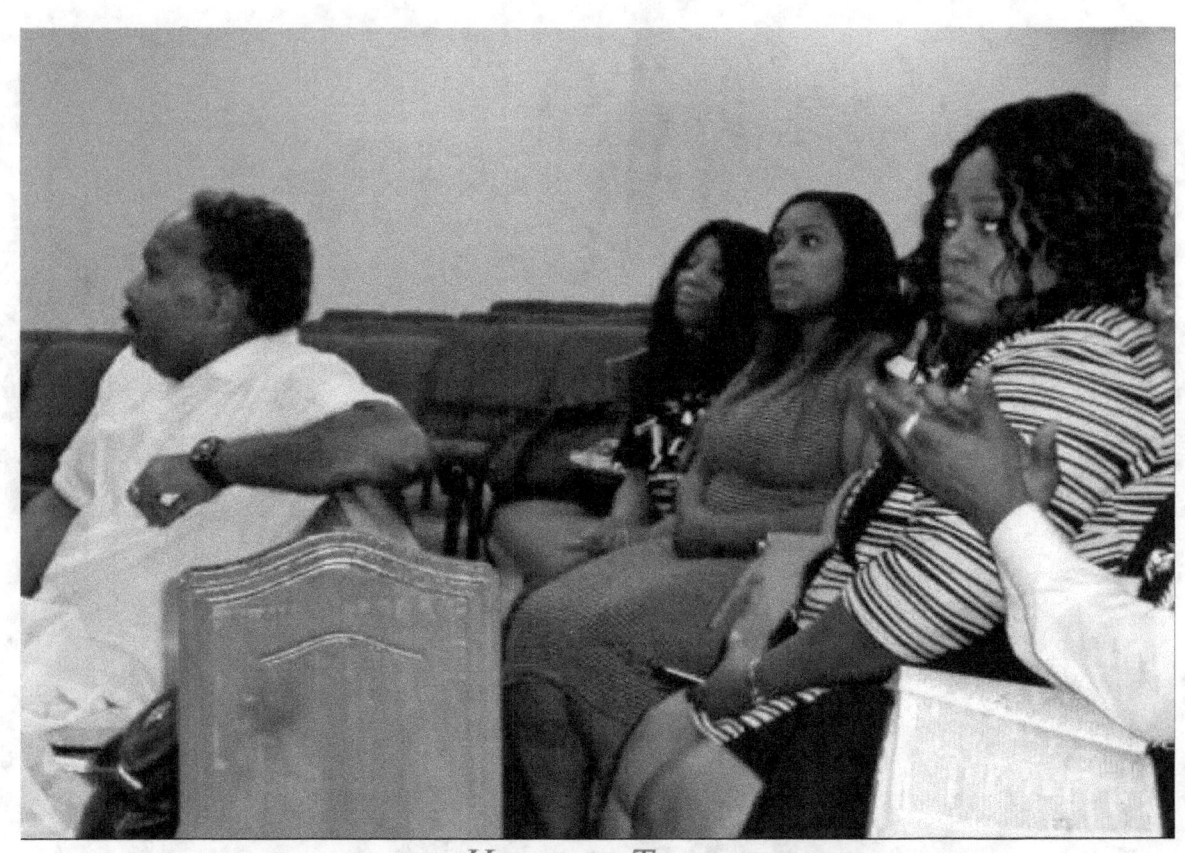

Houston, Texas

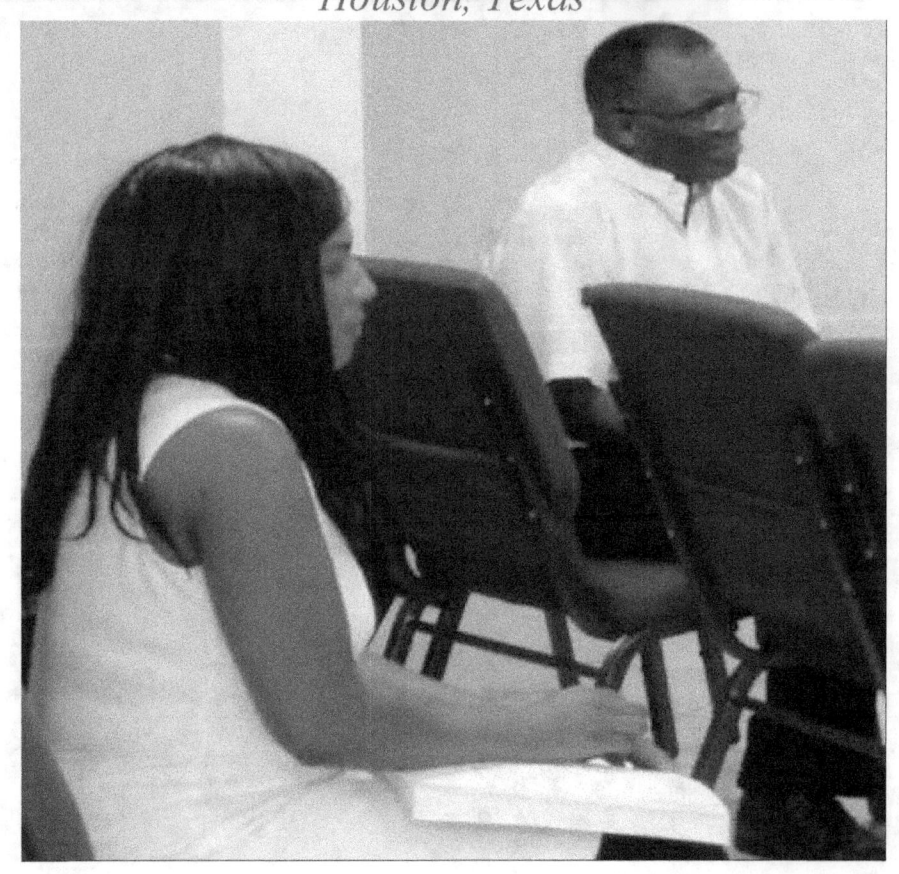

THE ORDINATION DAY
10-10-2015

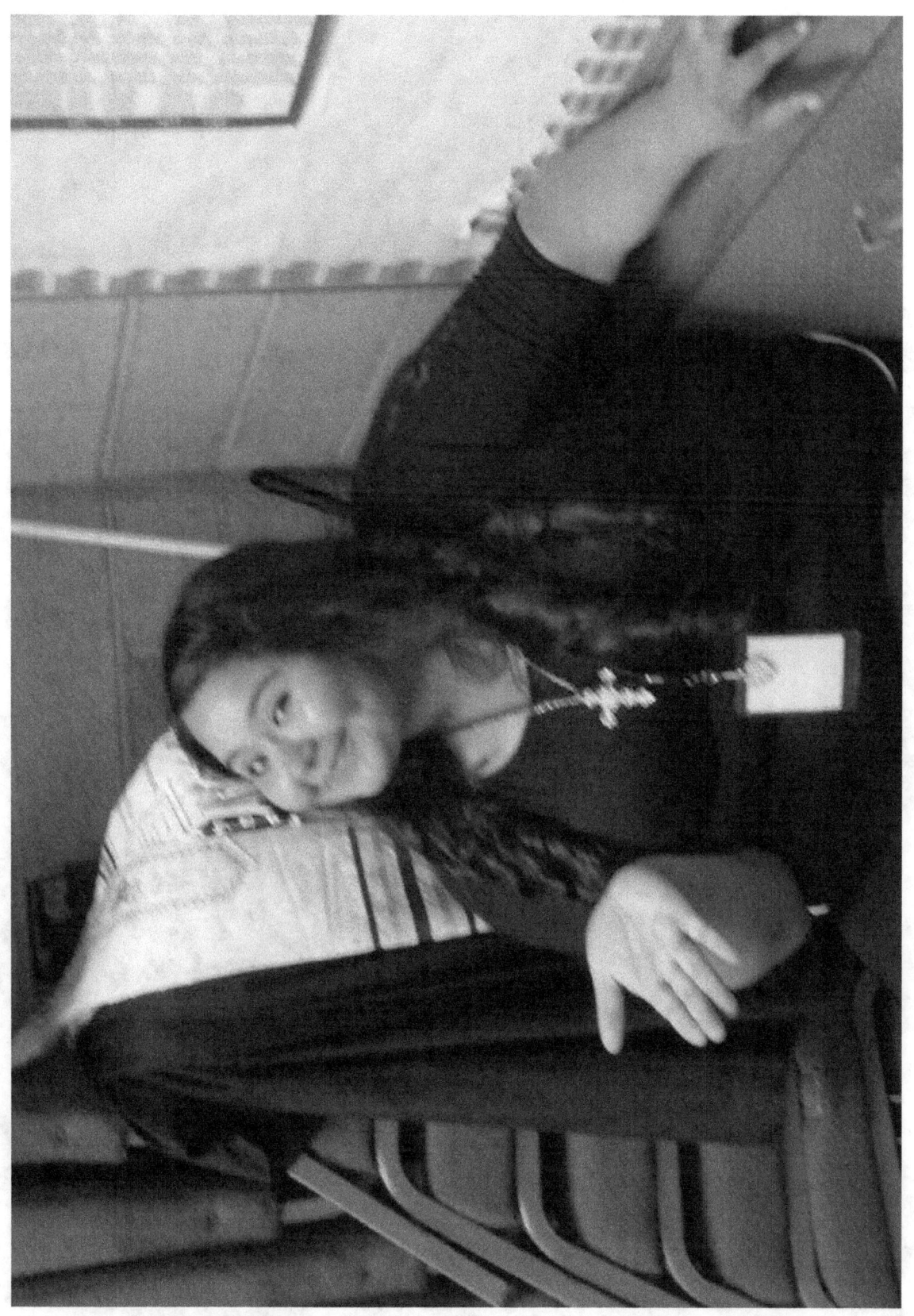

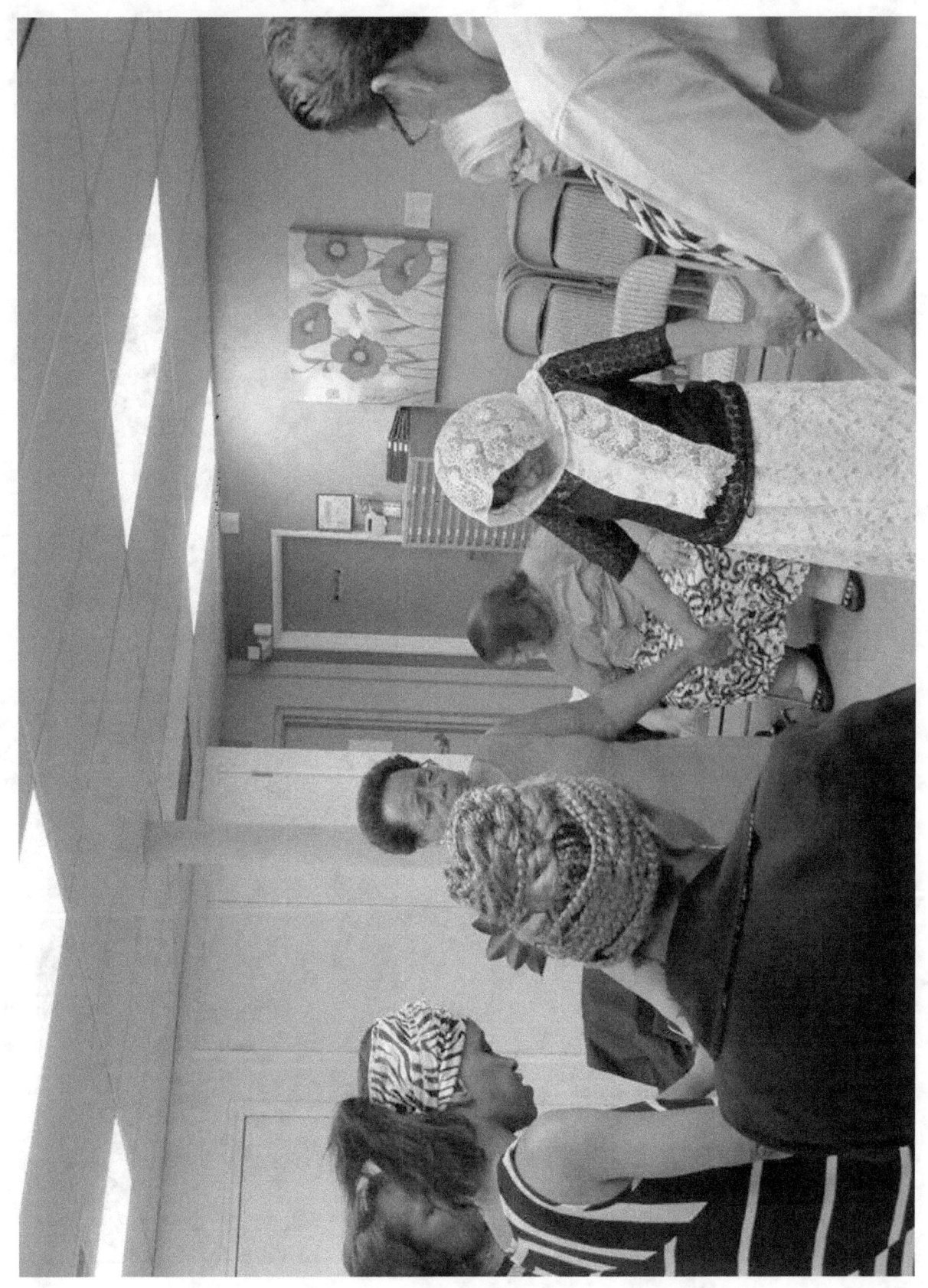

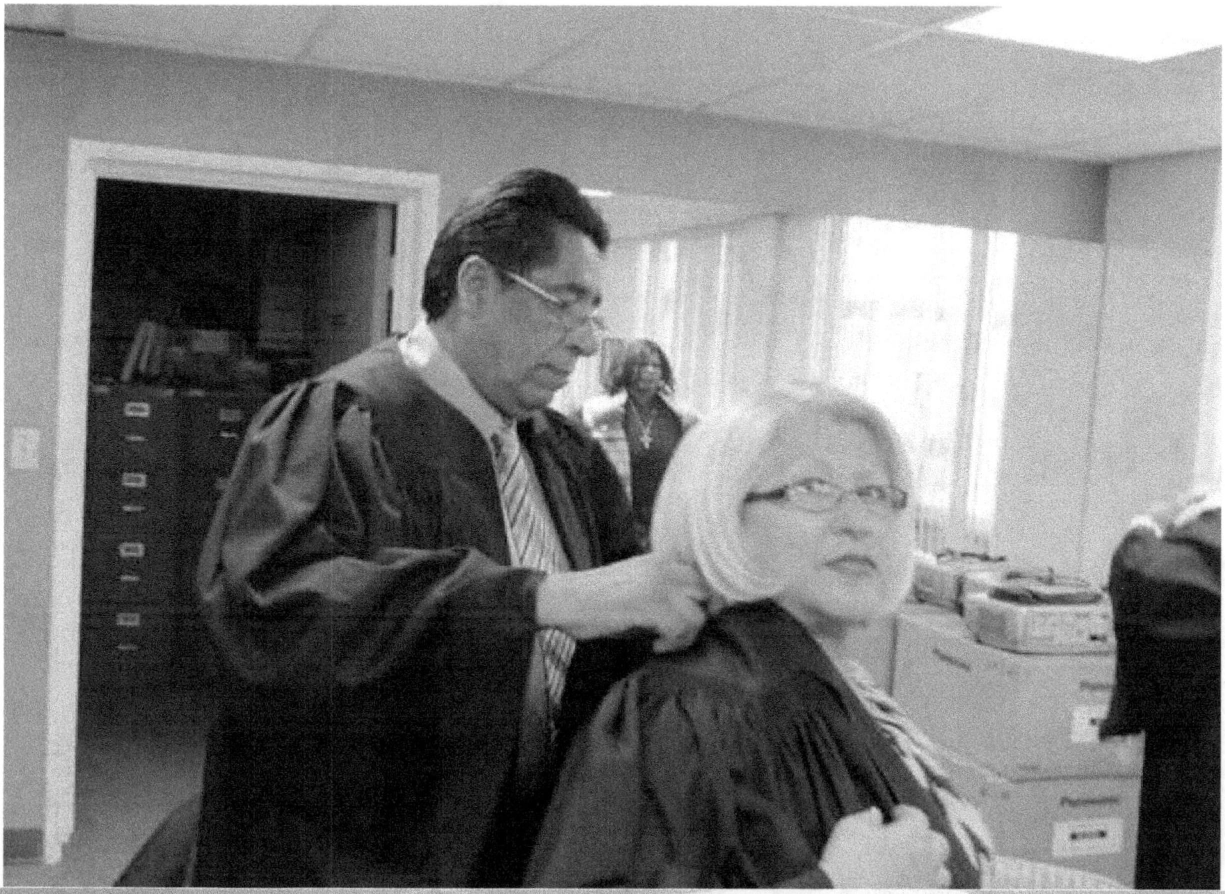

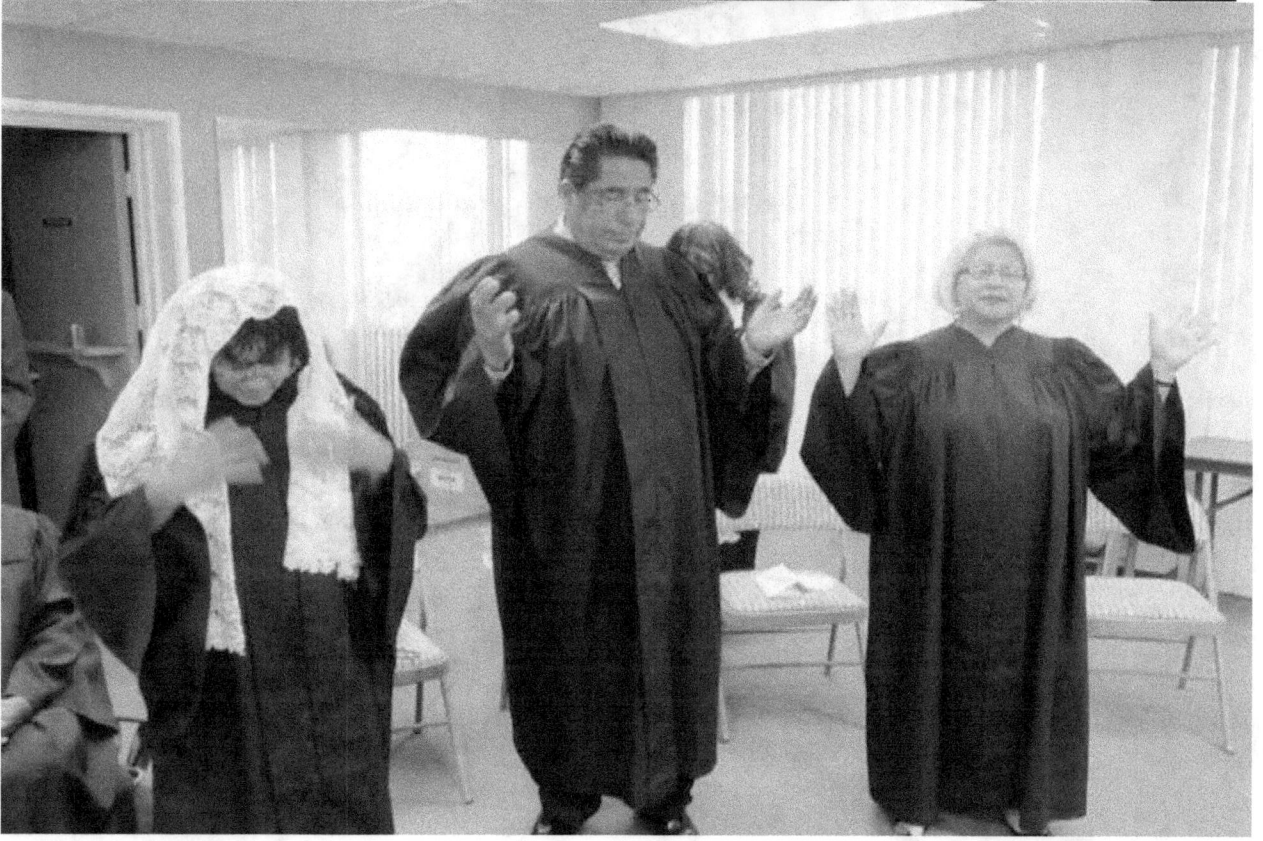

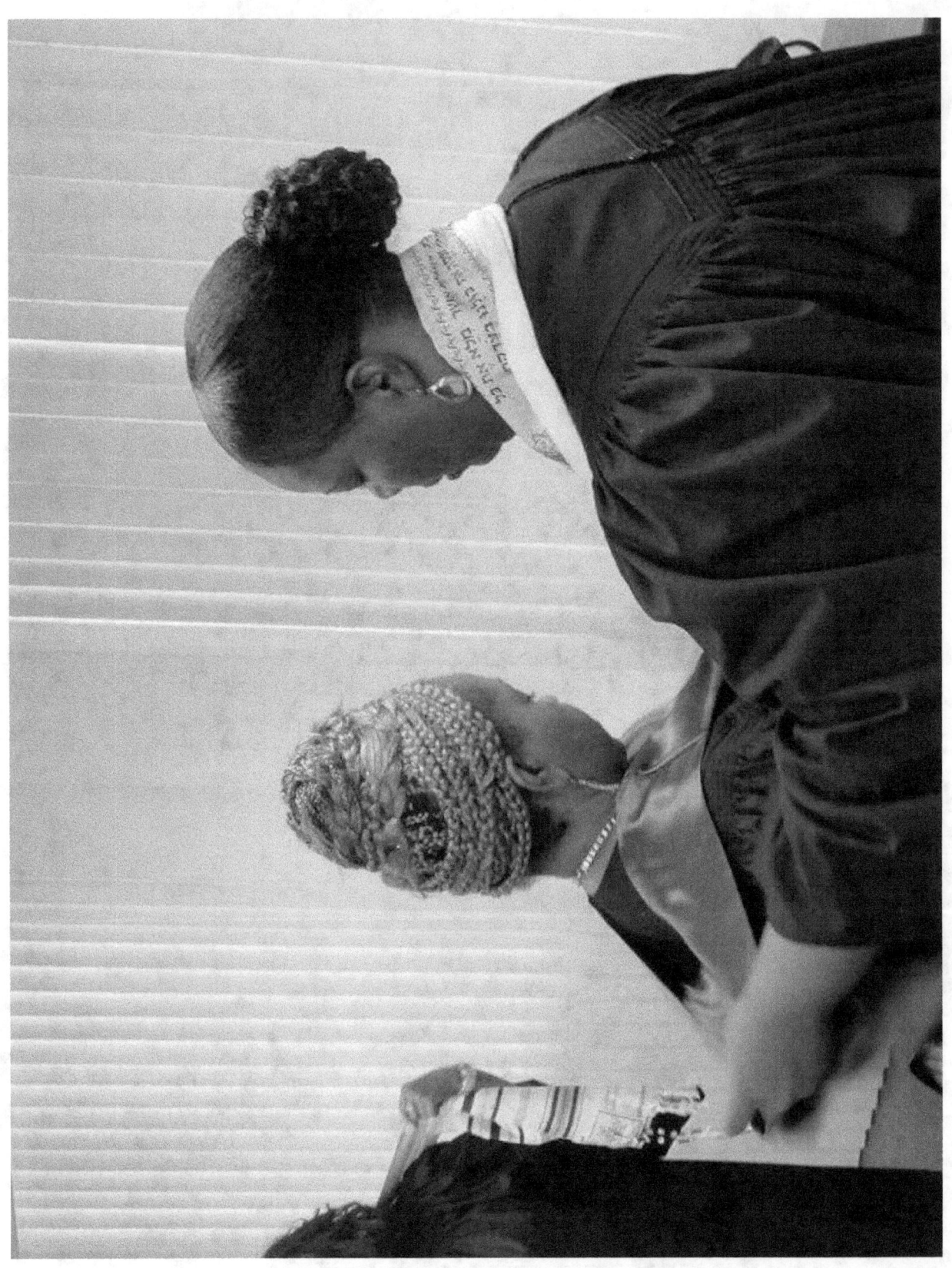

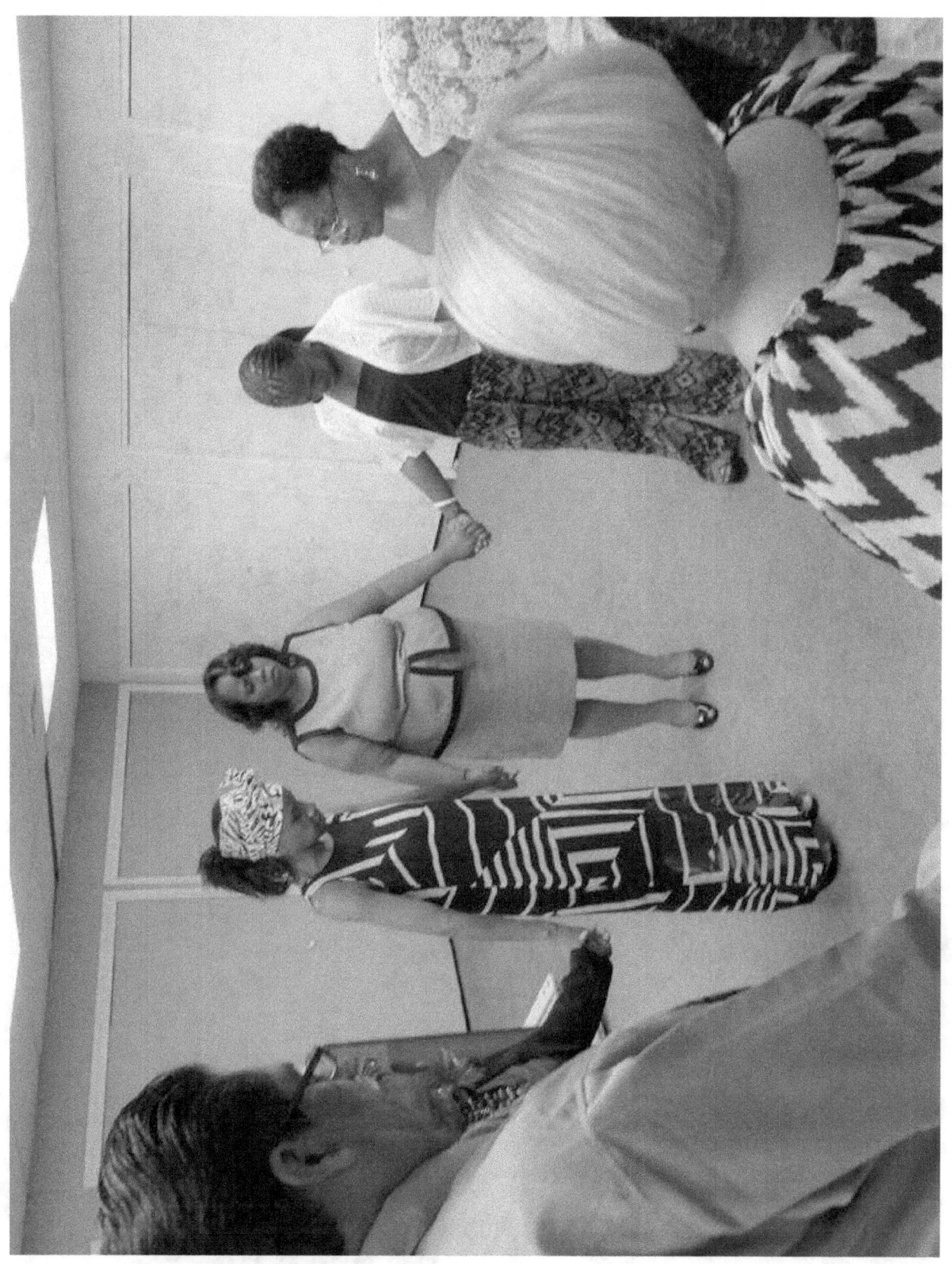

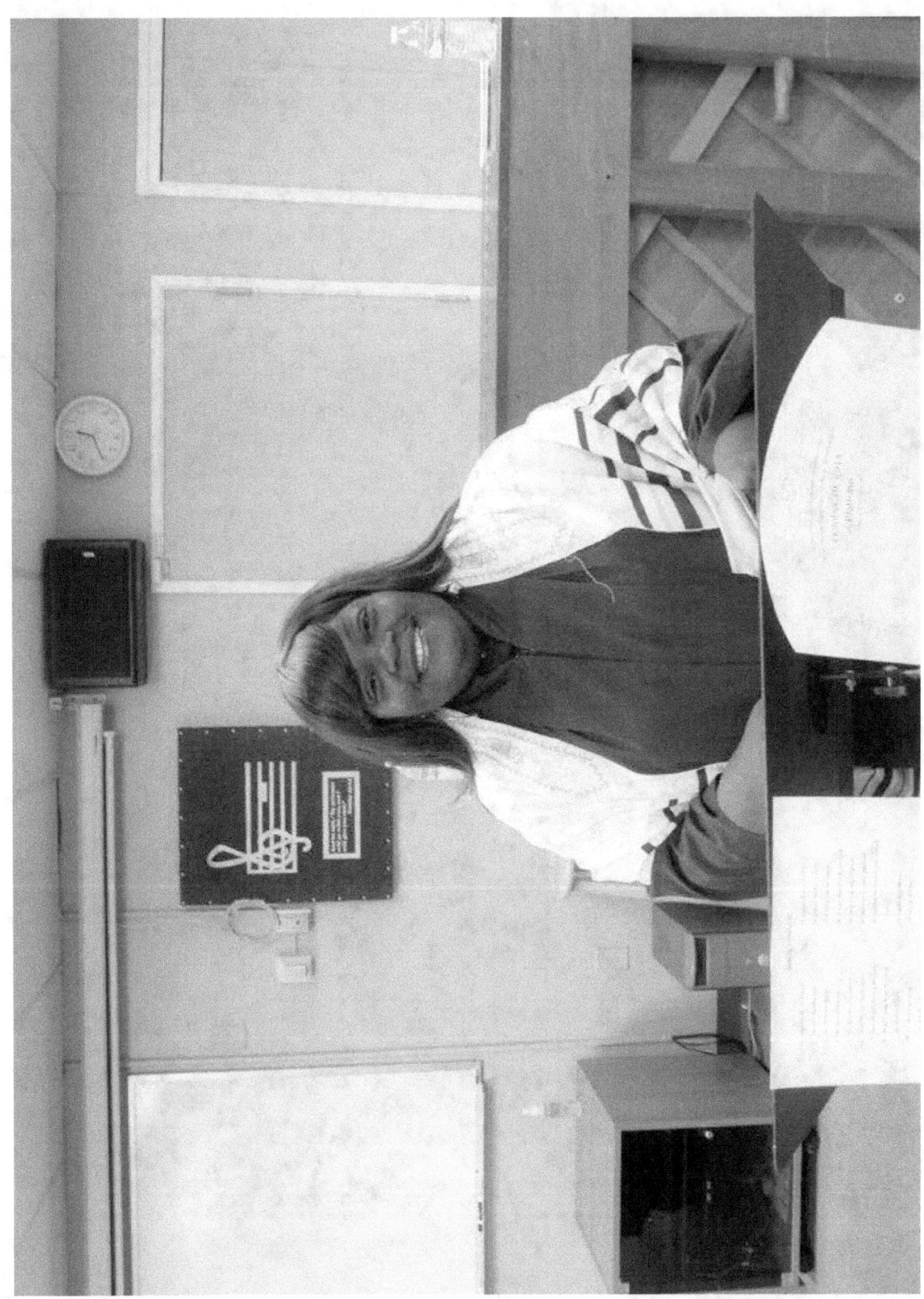

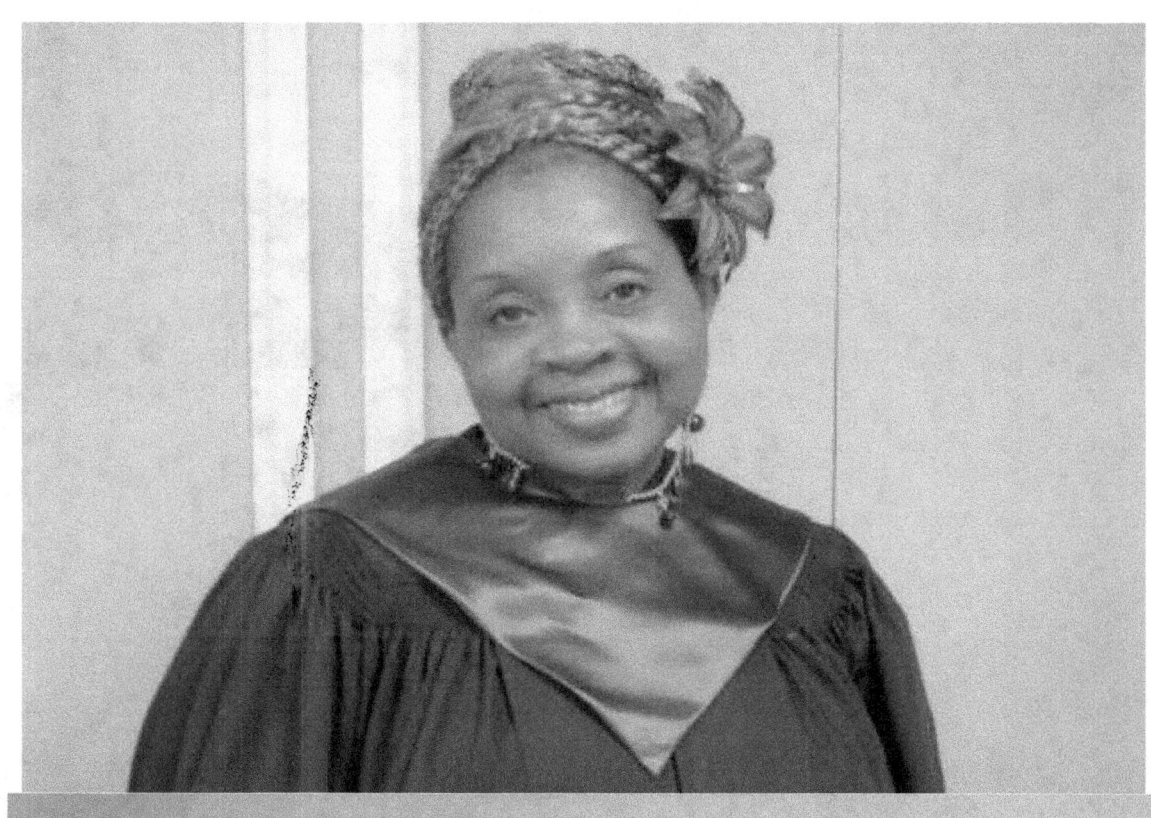

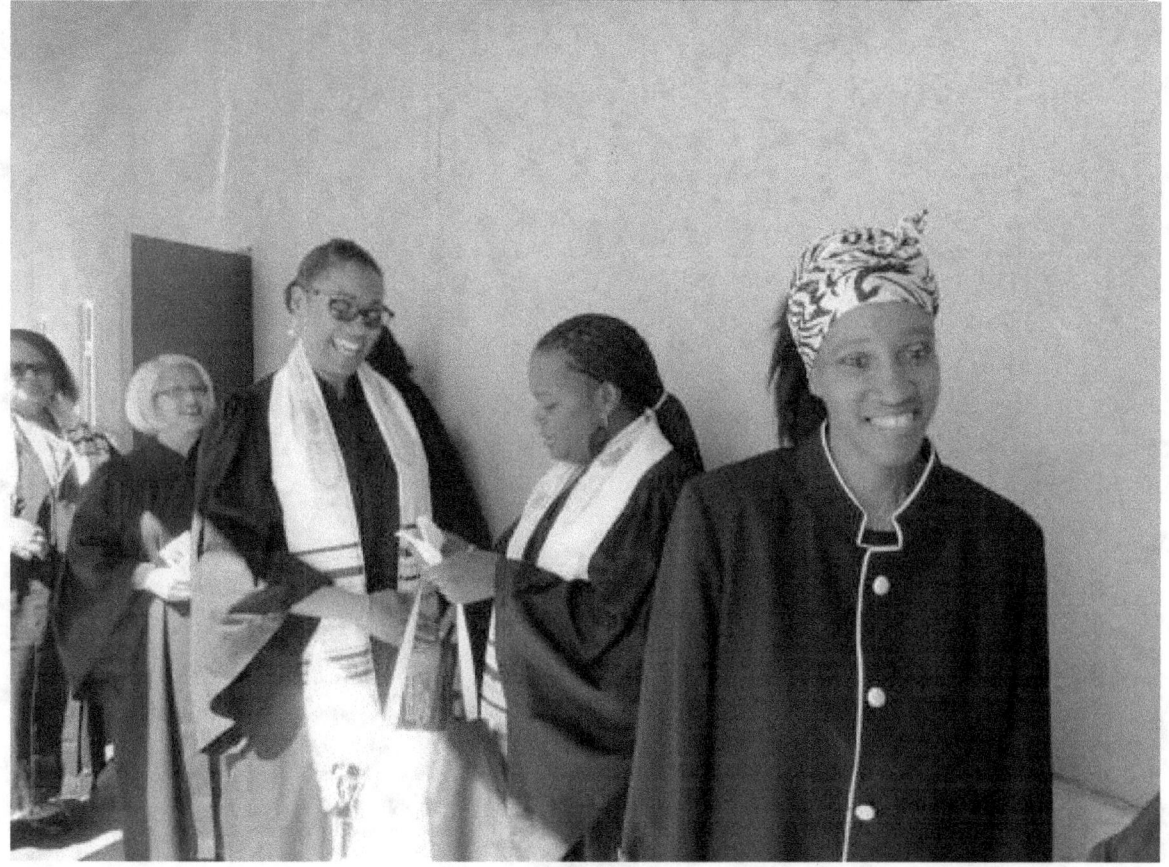

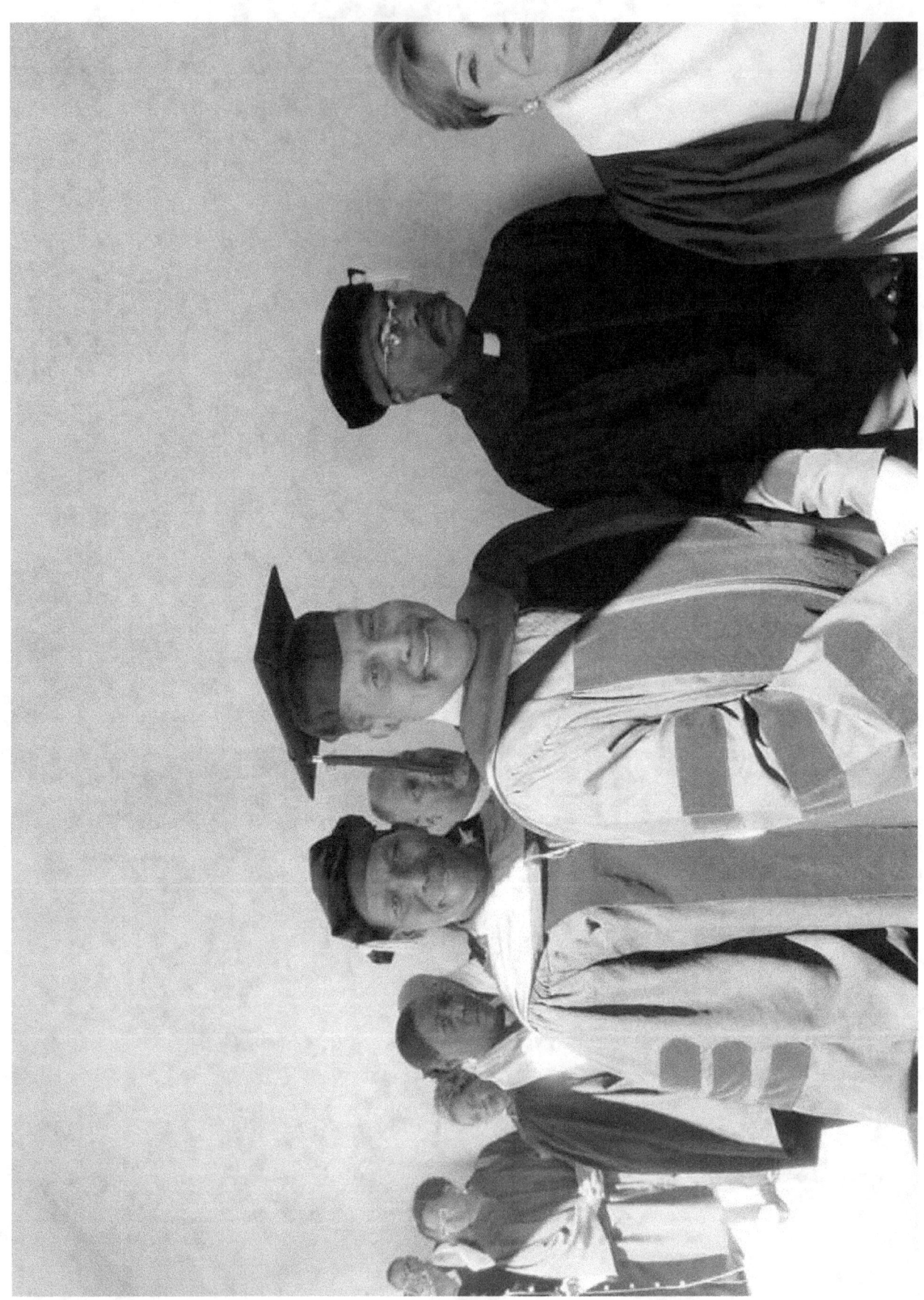

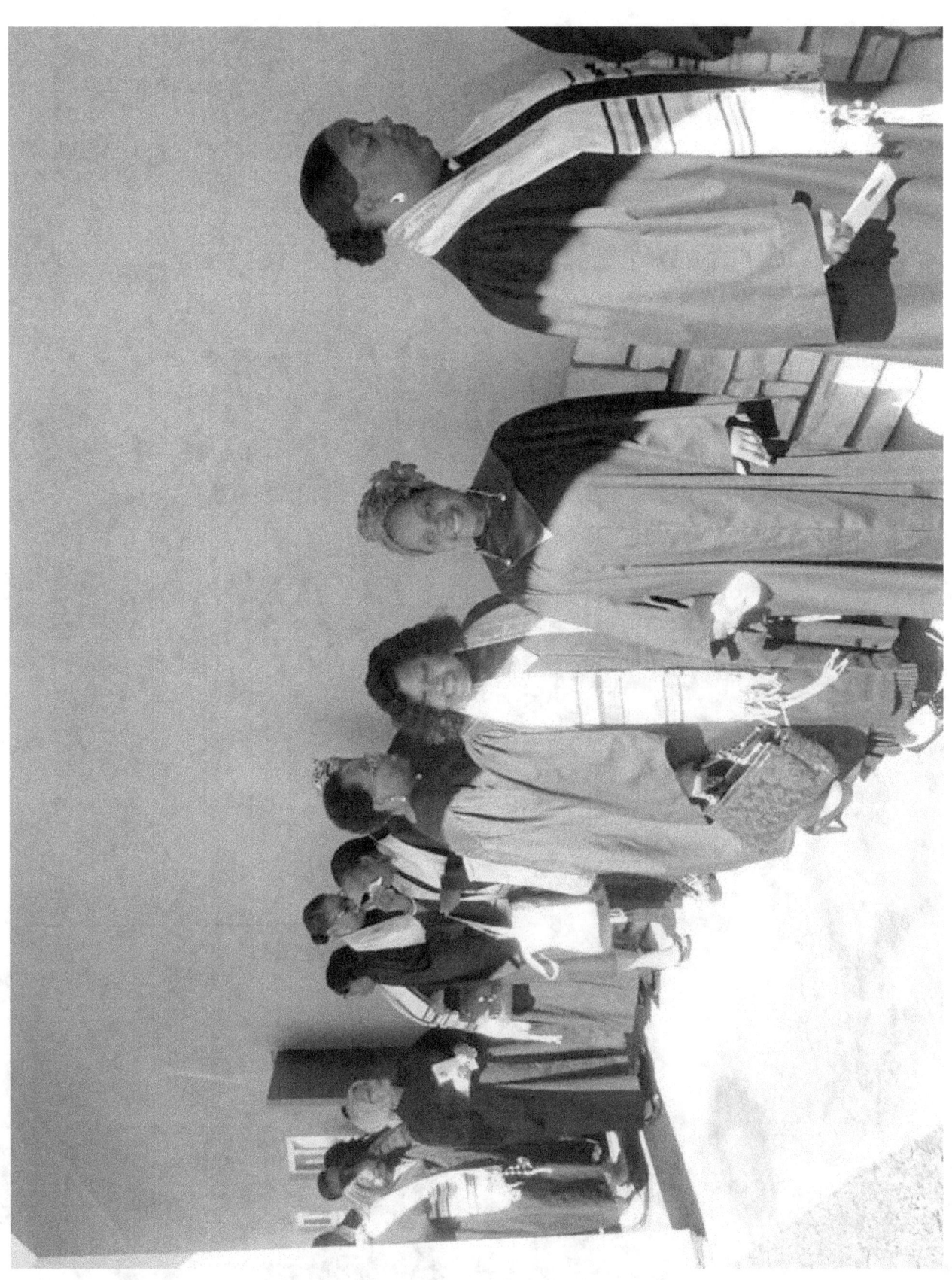

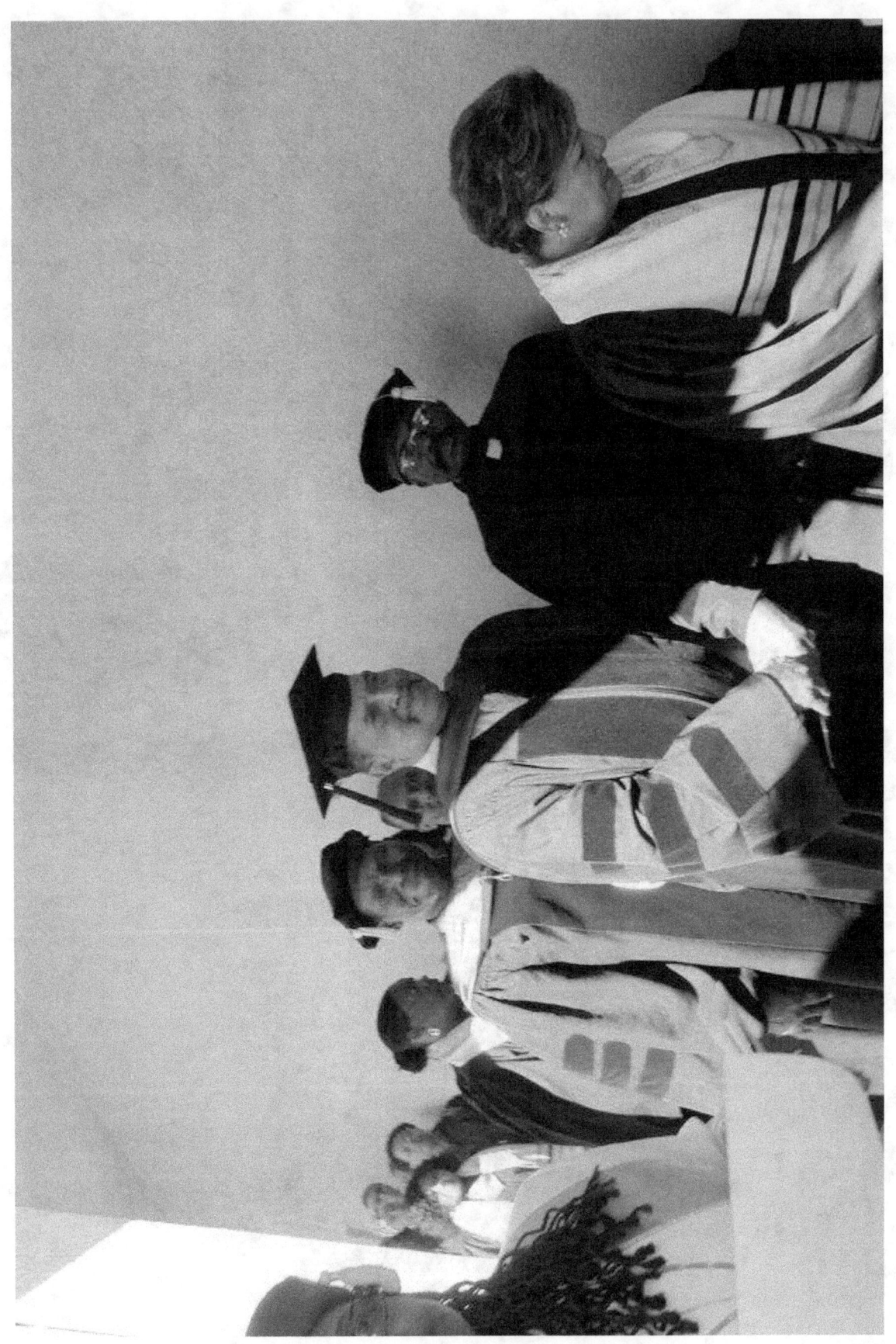

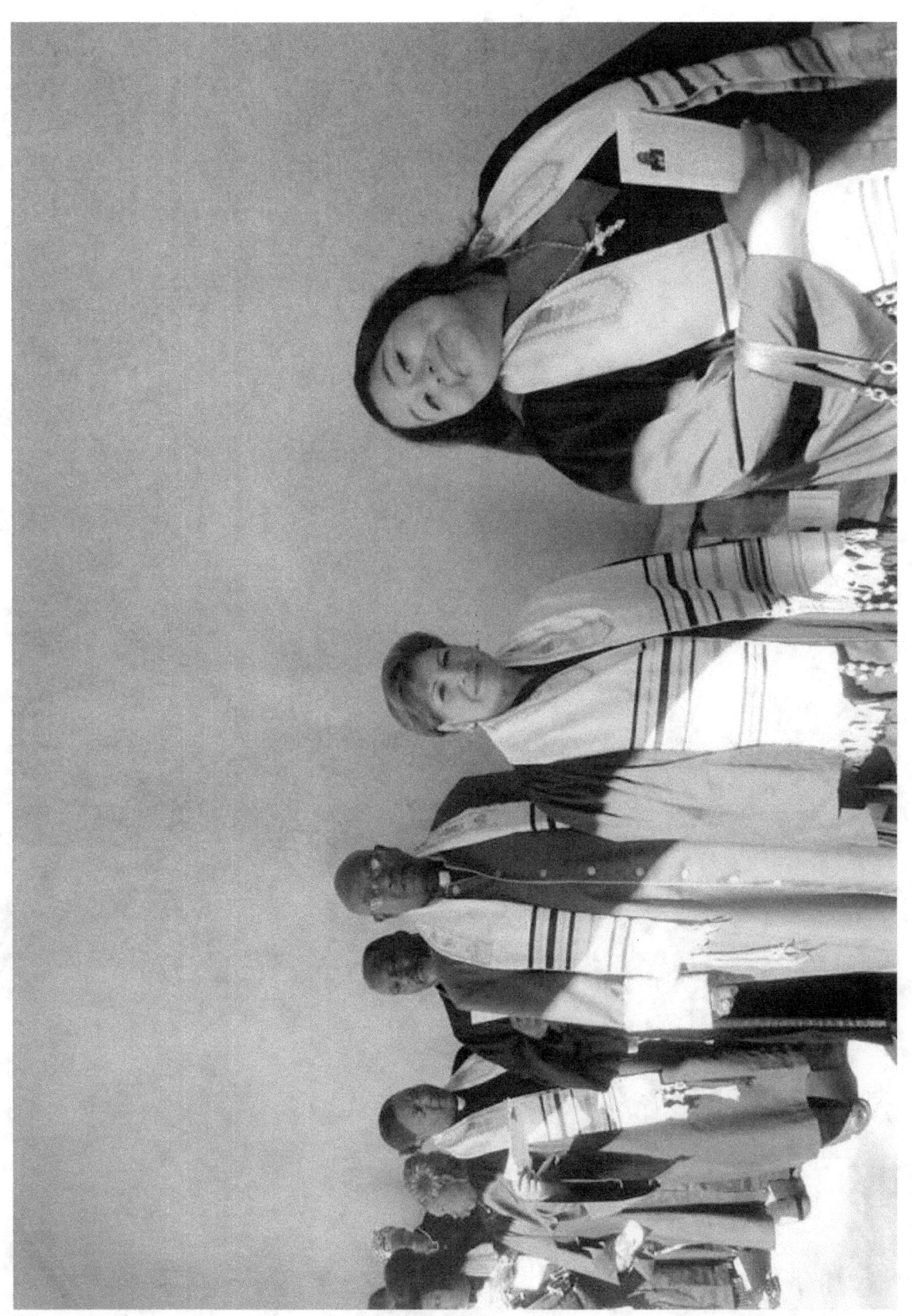

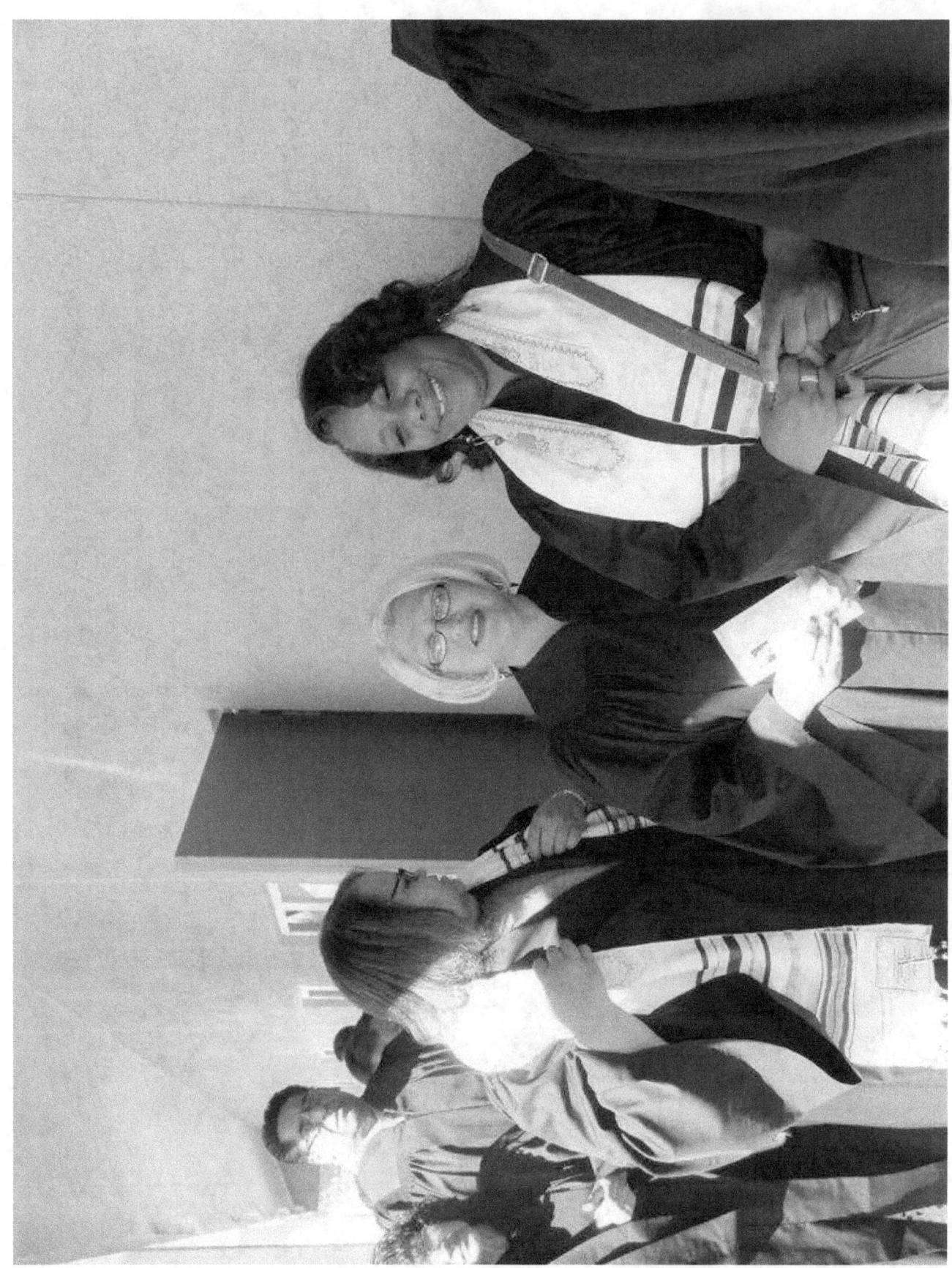

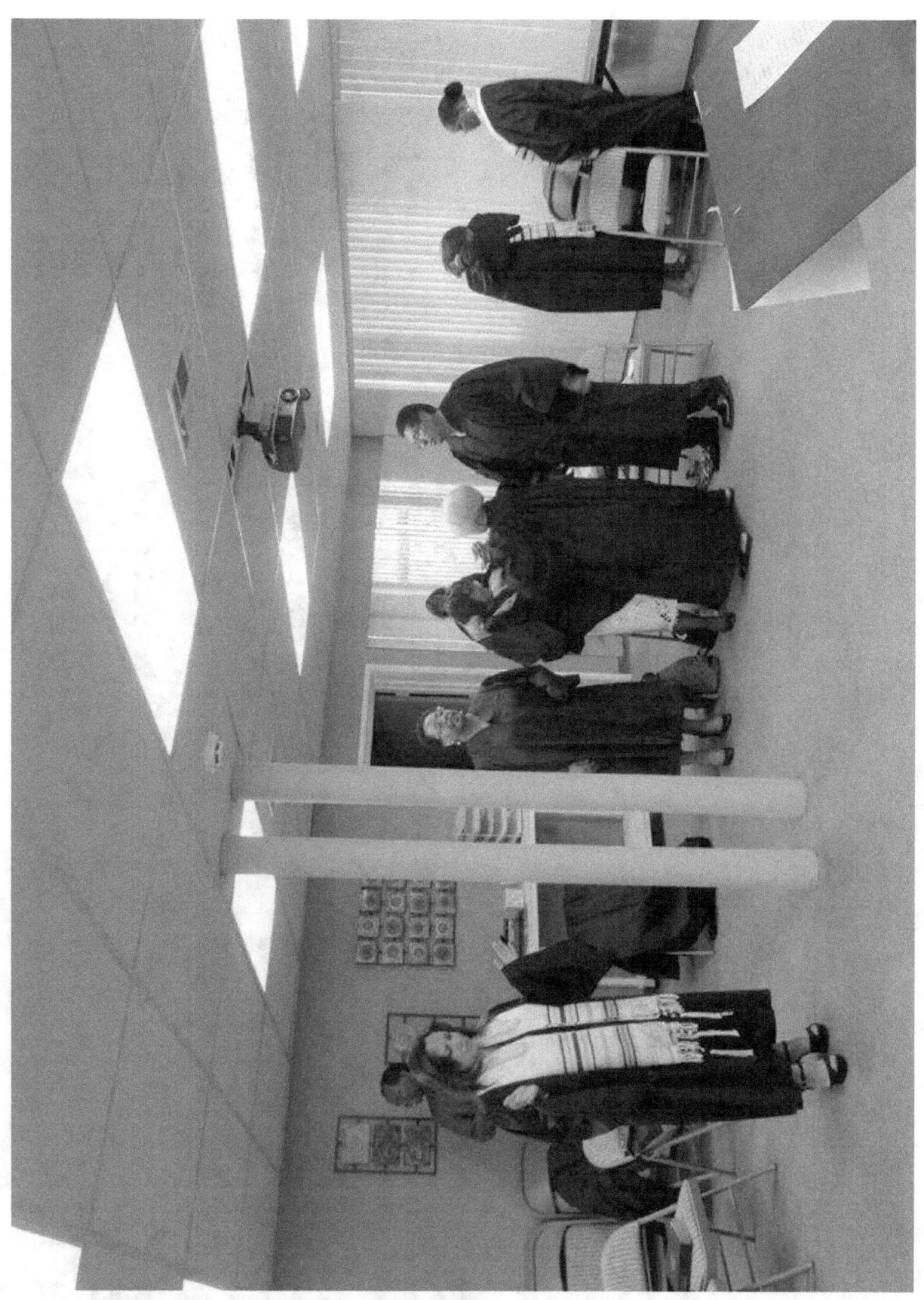

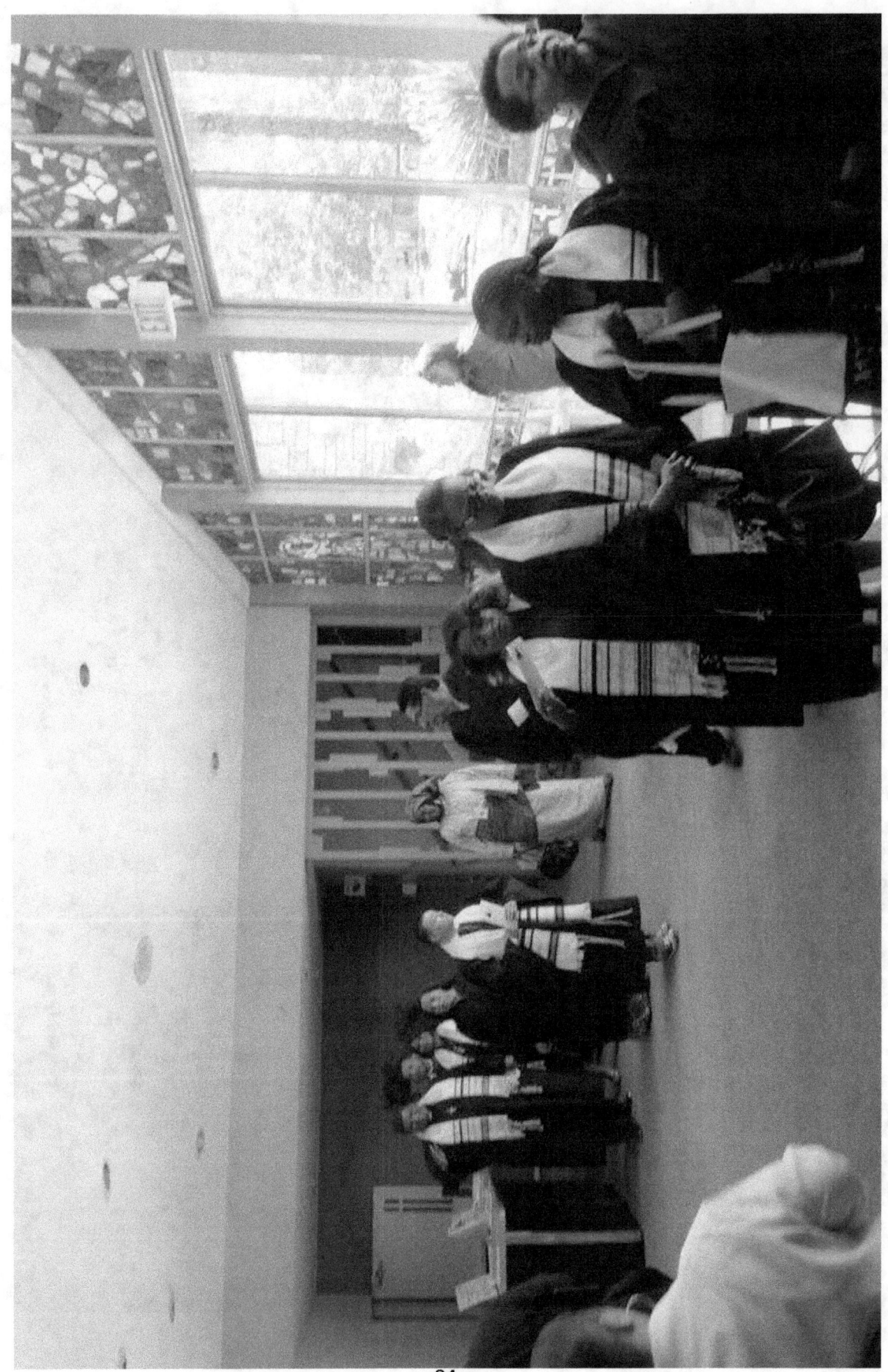

84

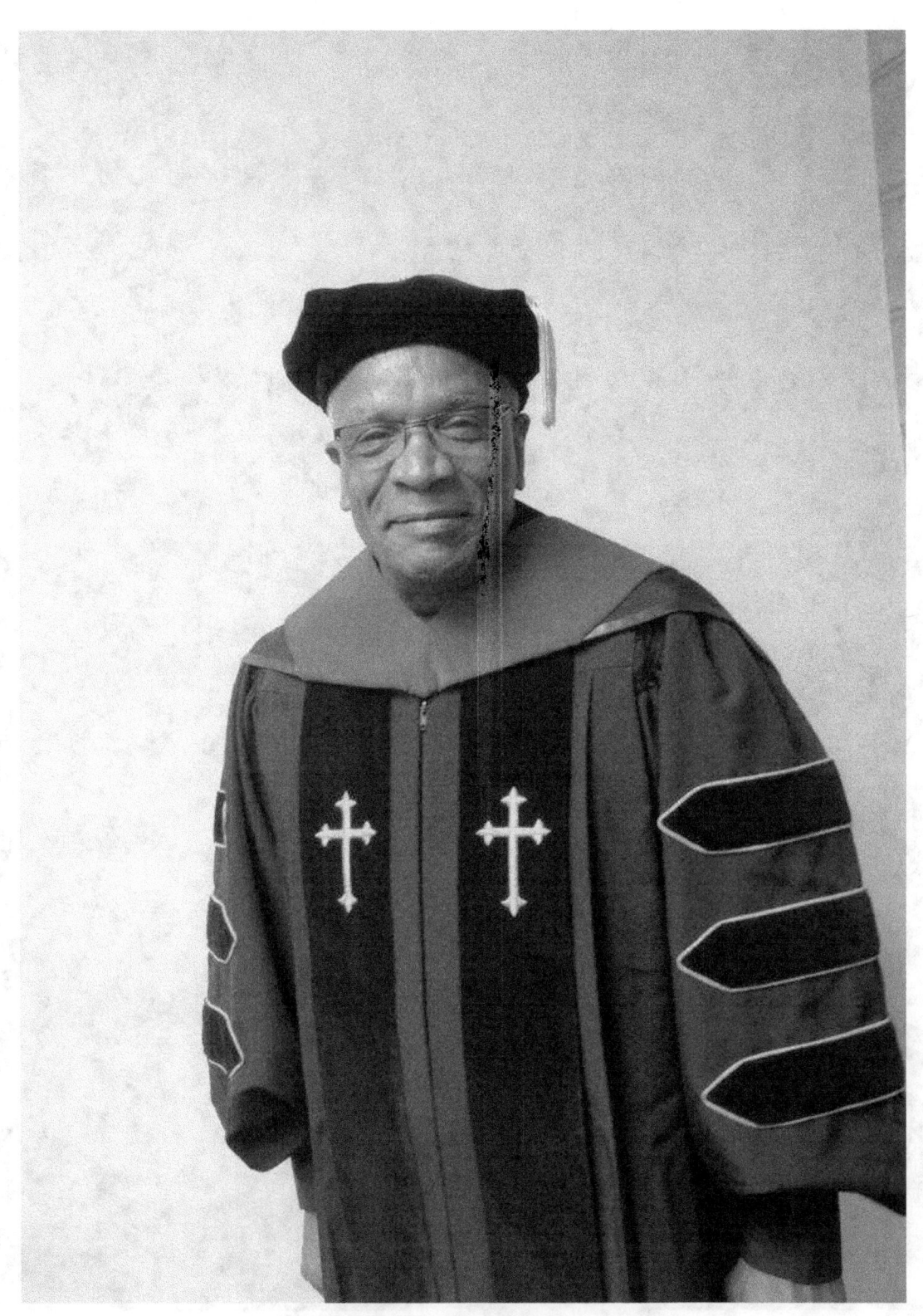

DR. RON ROBERSON

DOCTORATE PROGRAM DIRECTOR

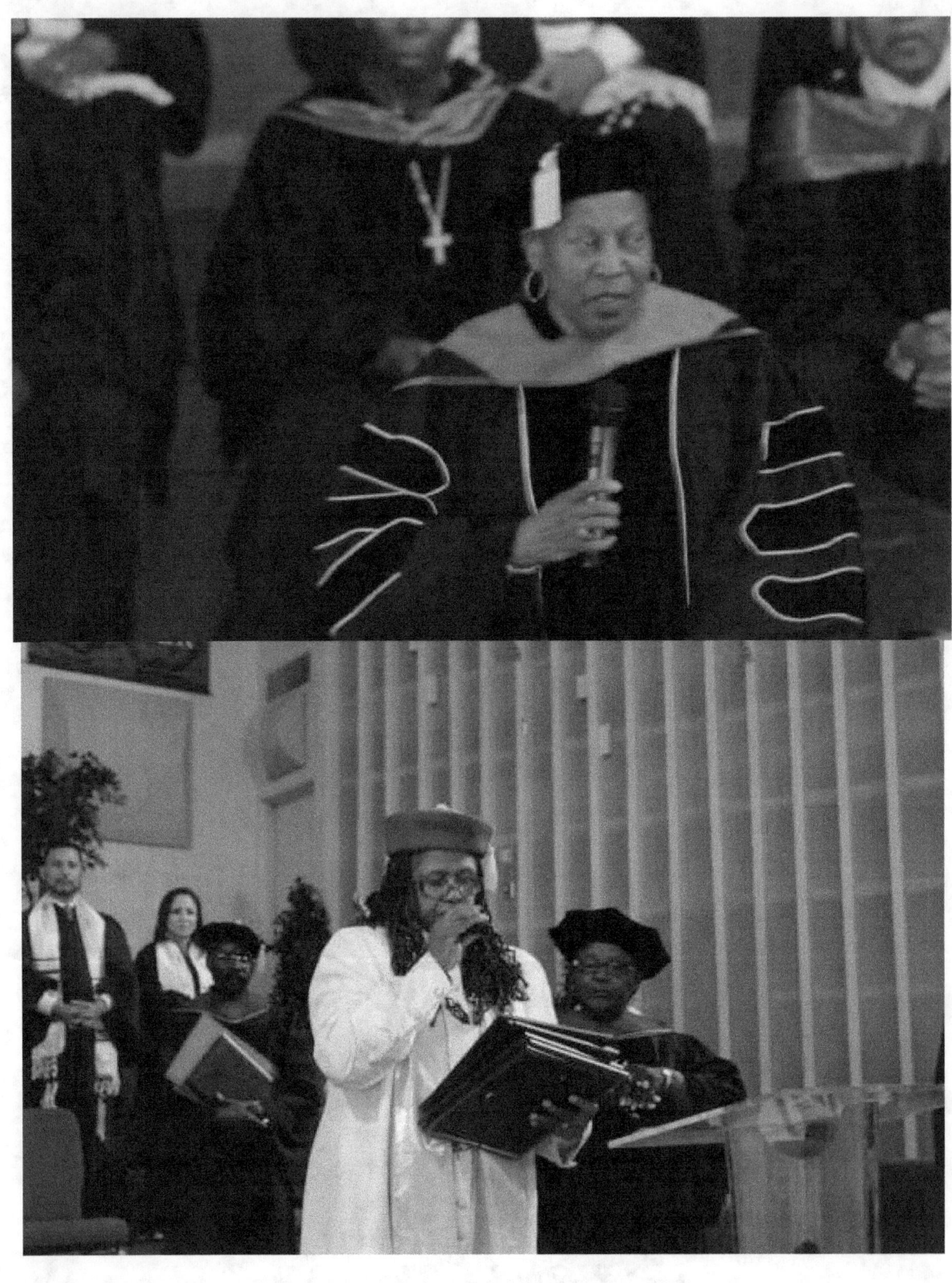

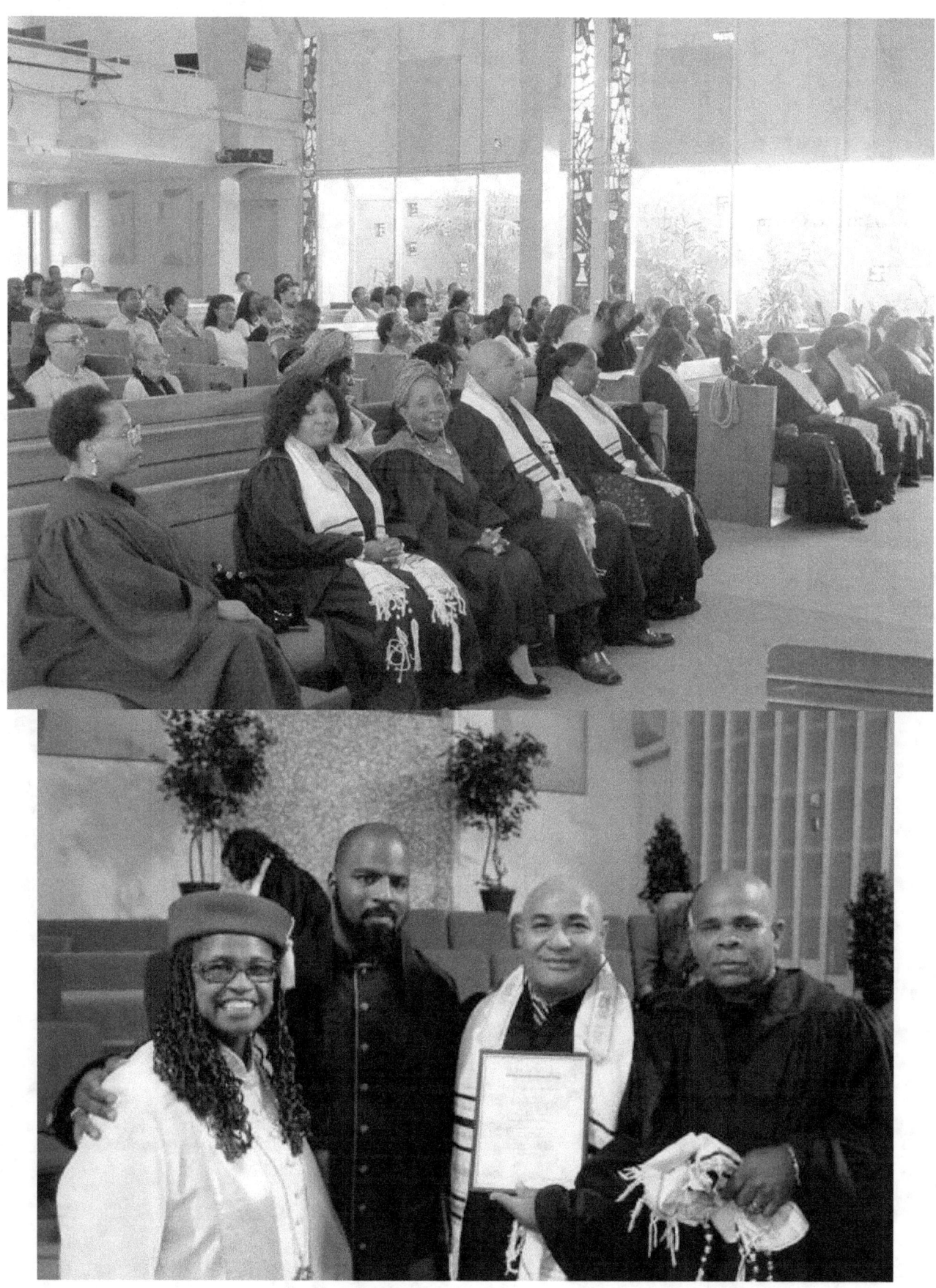

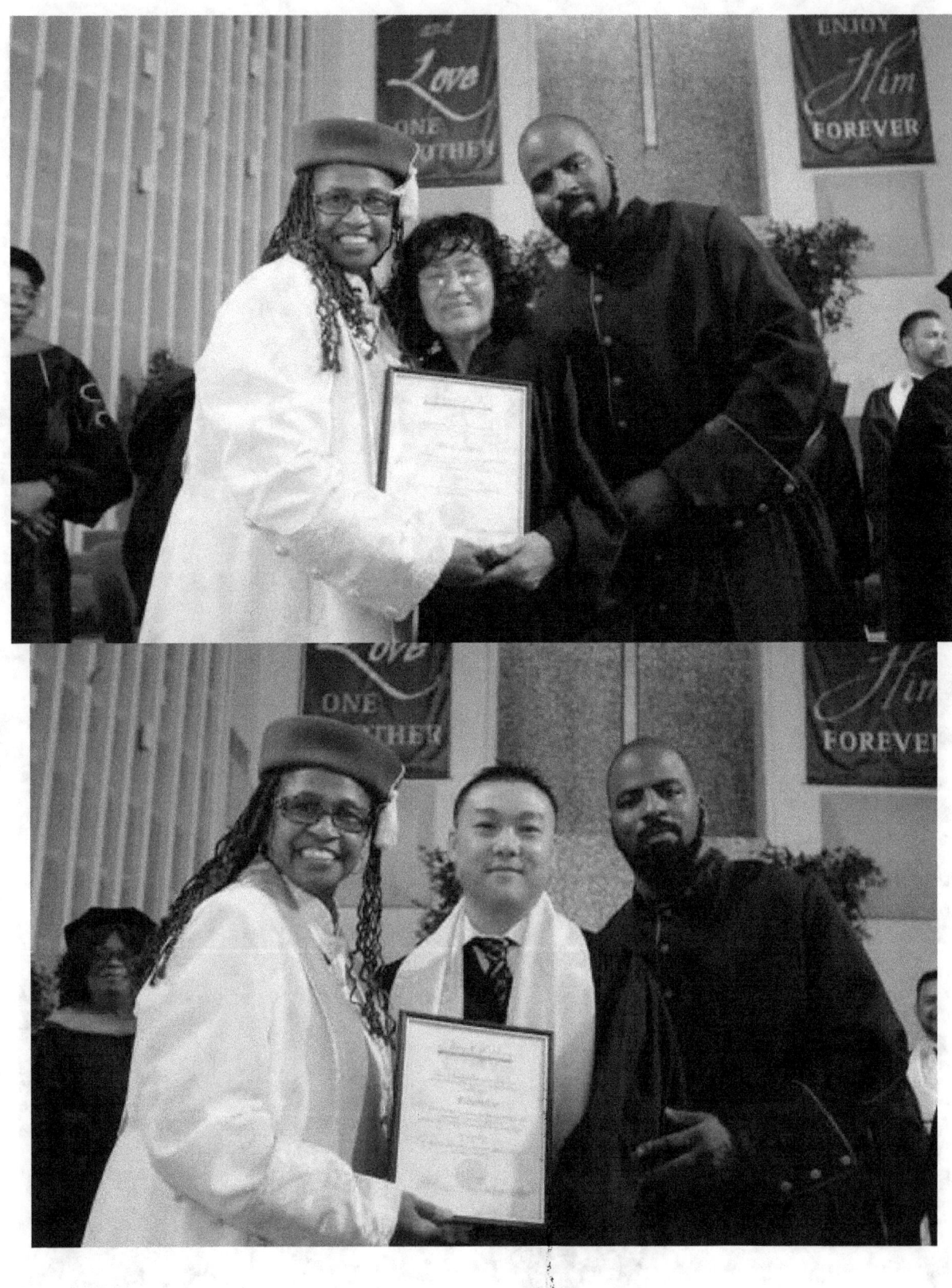

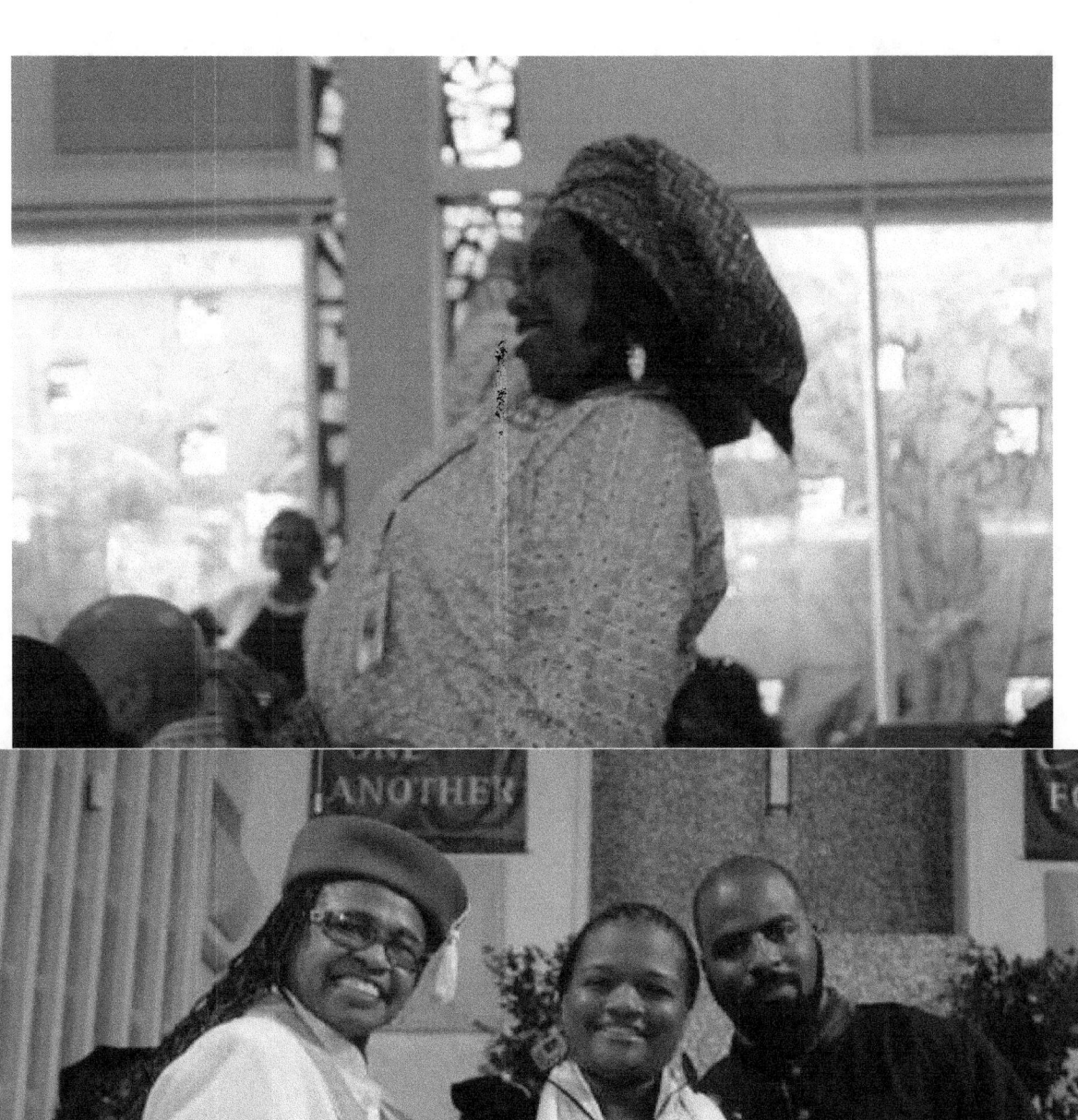

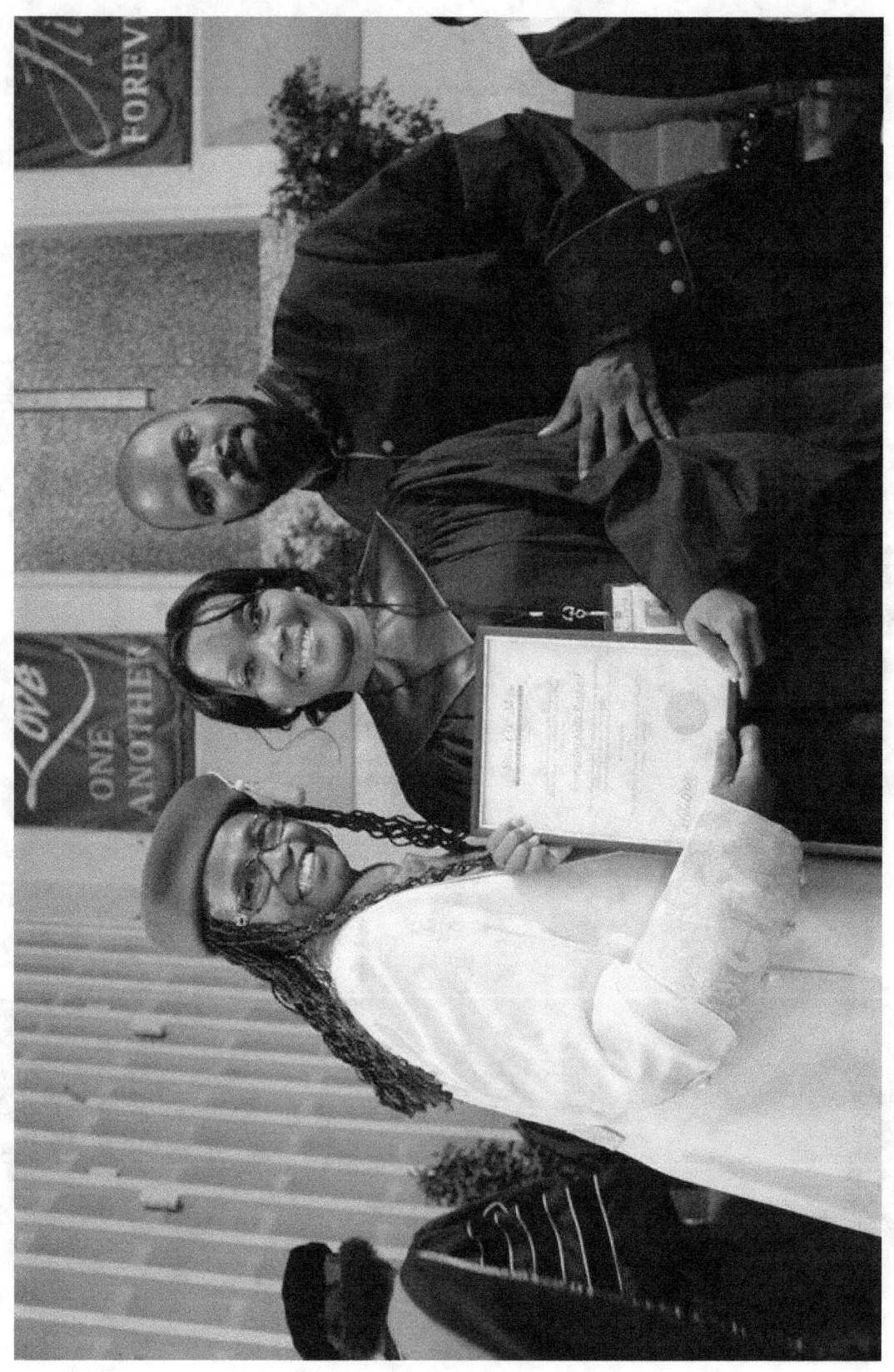

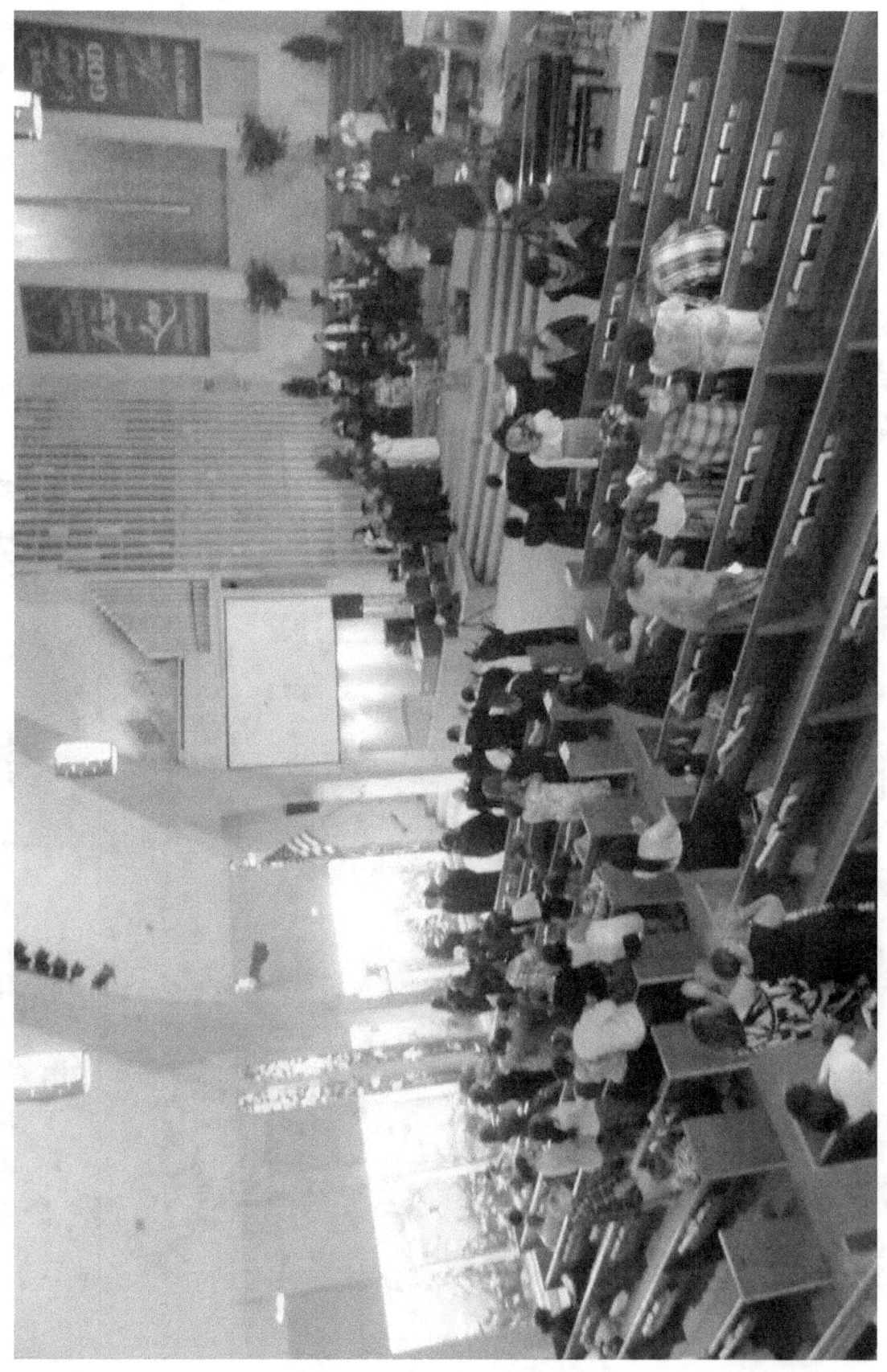

91

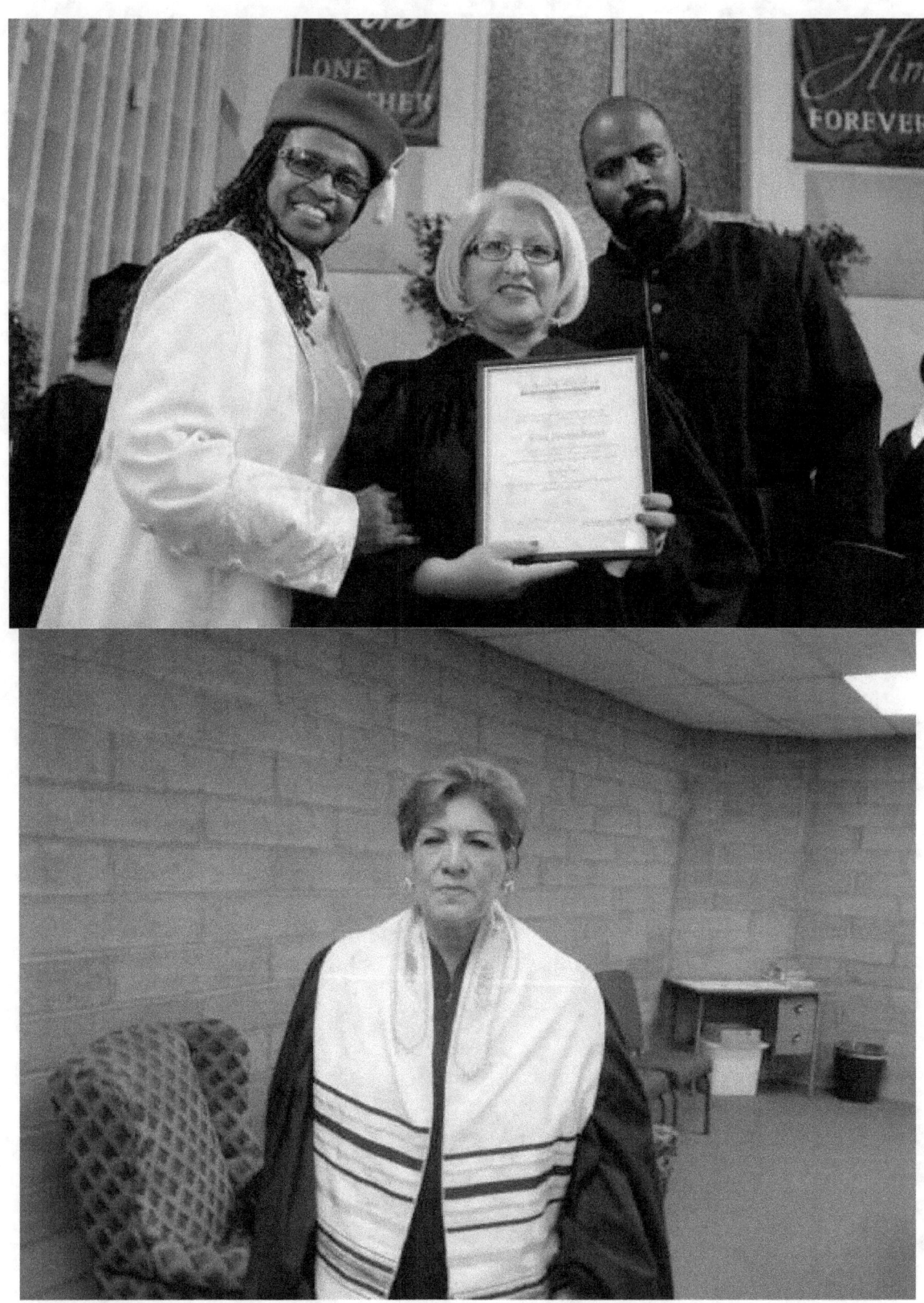

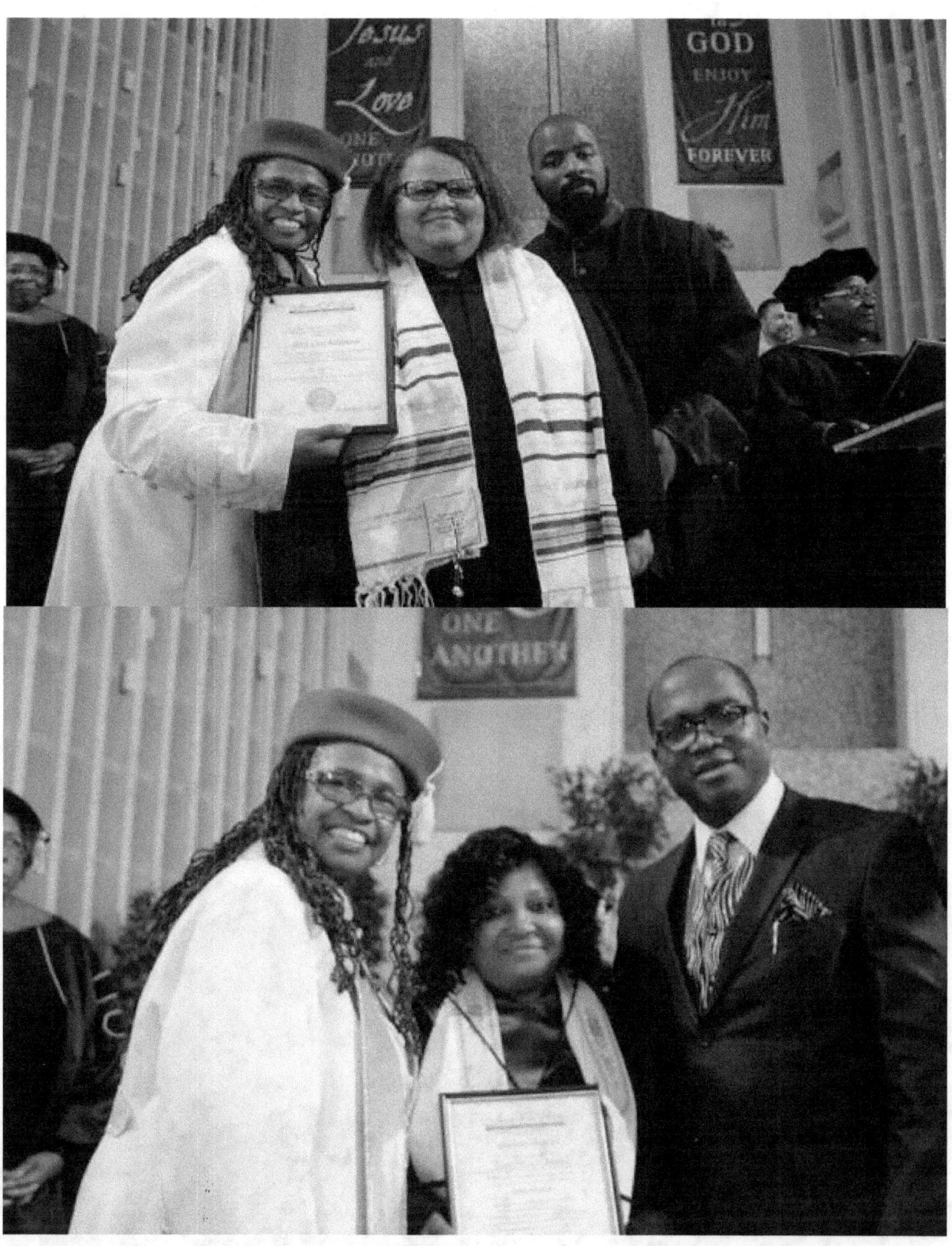

93

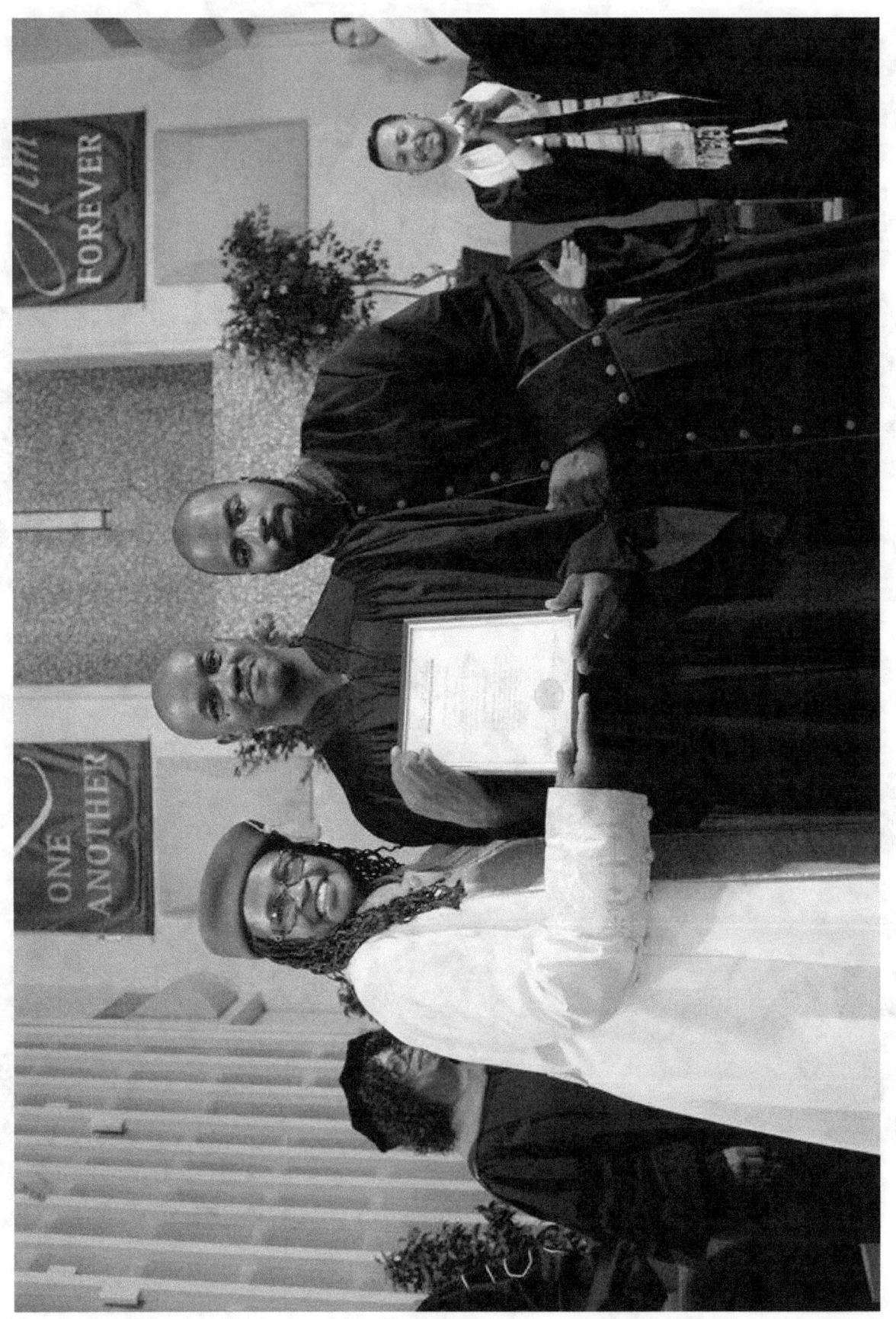

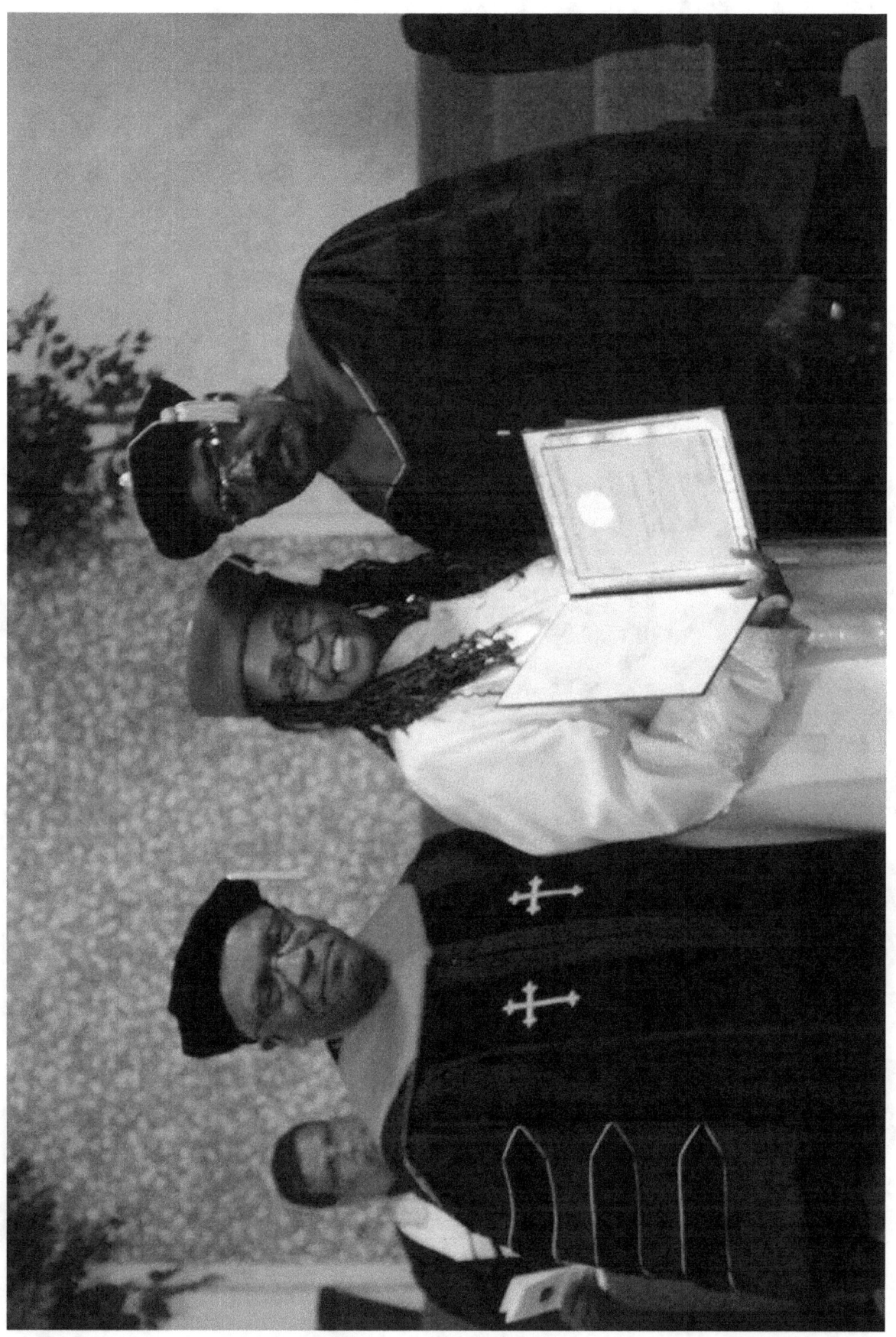

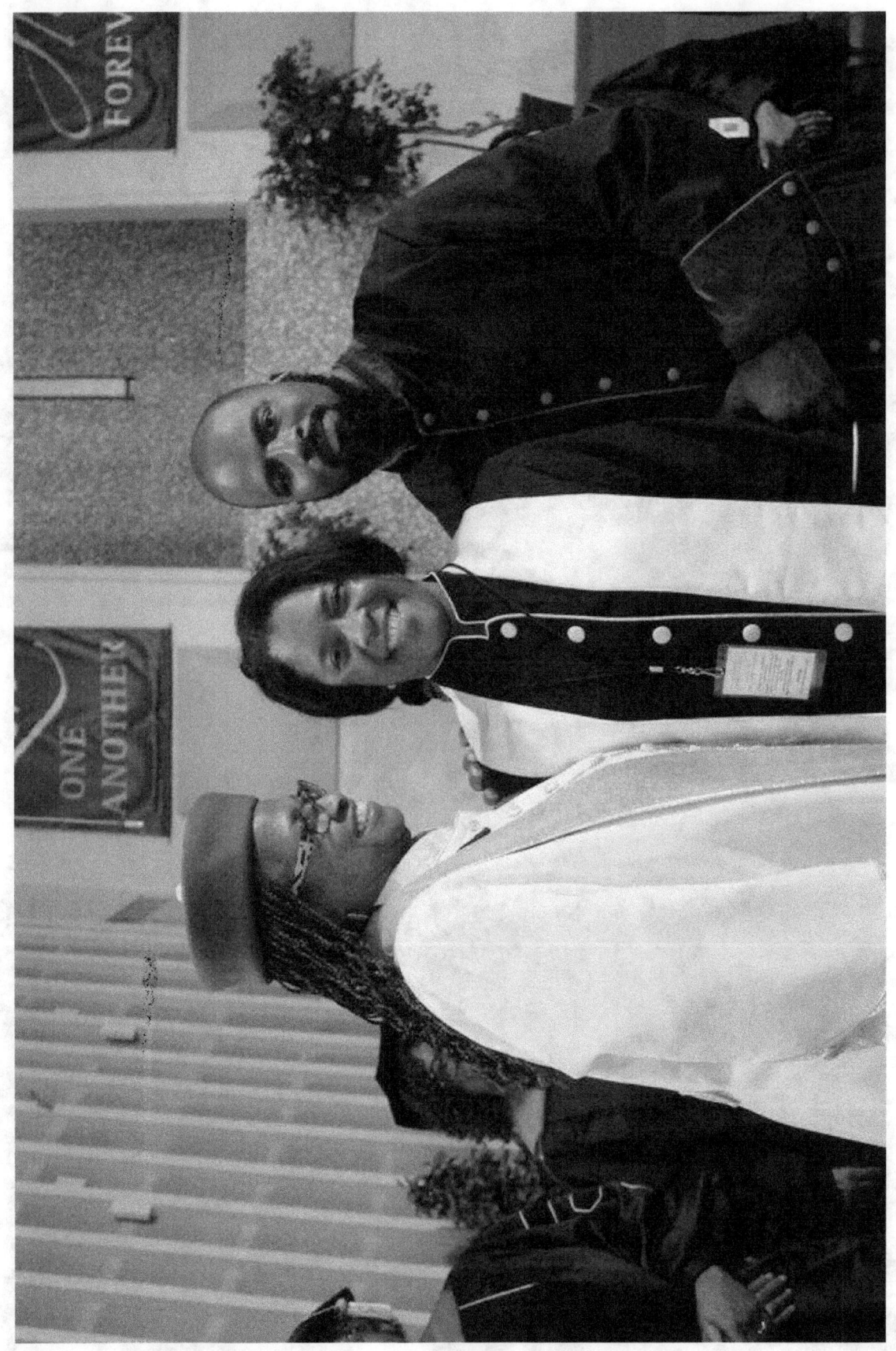

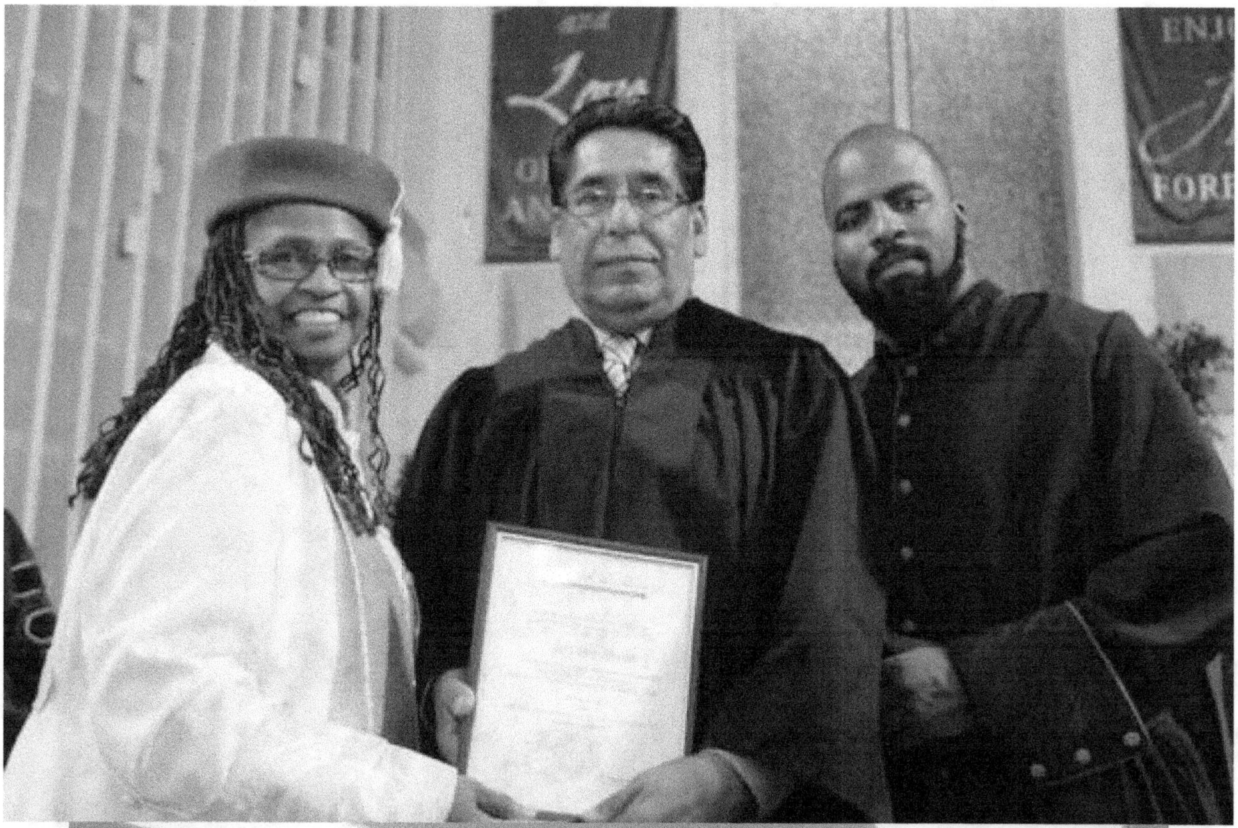

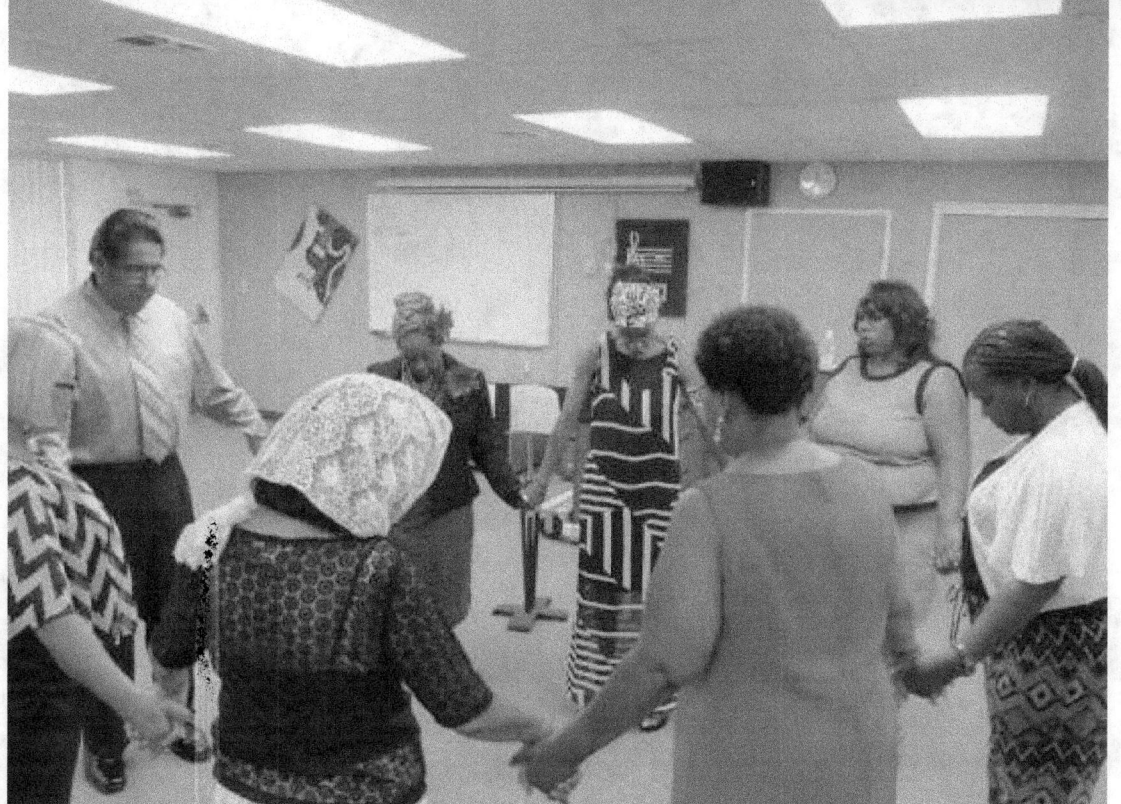

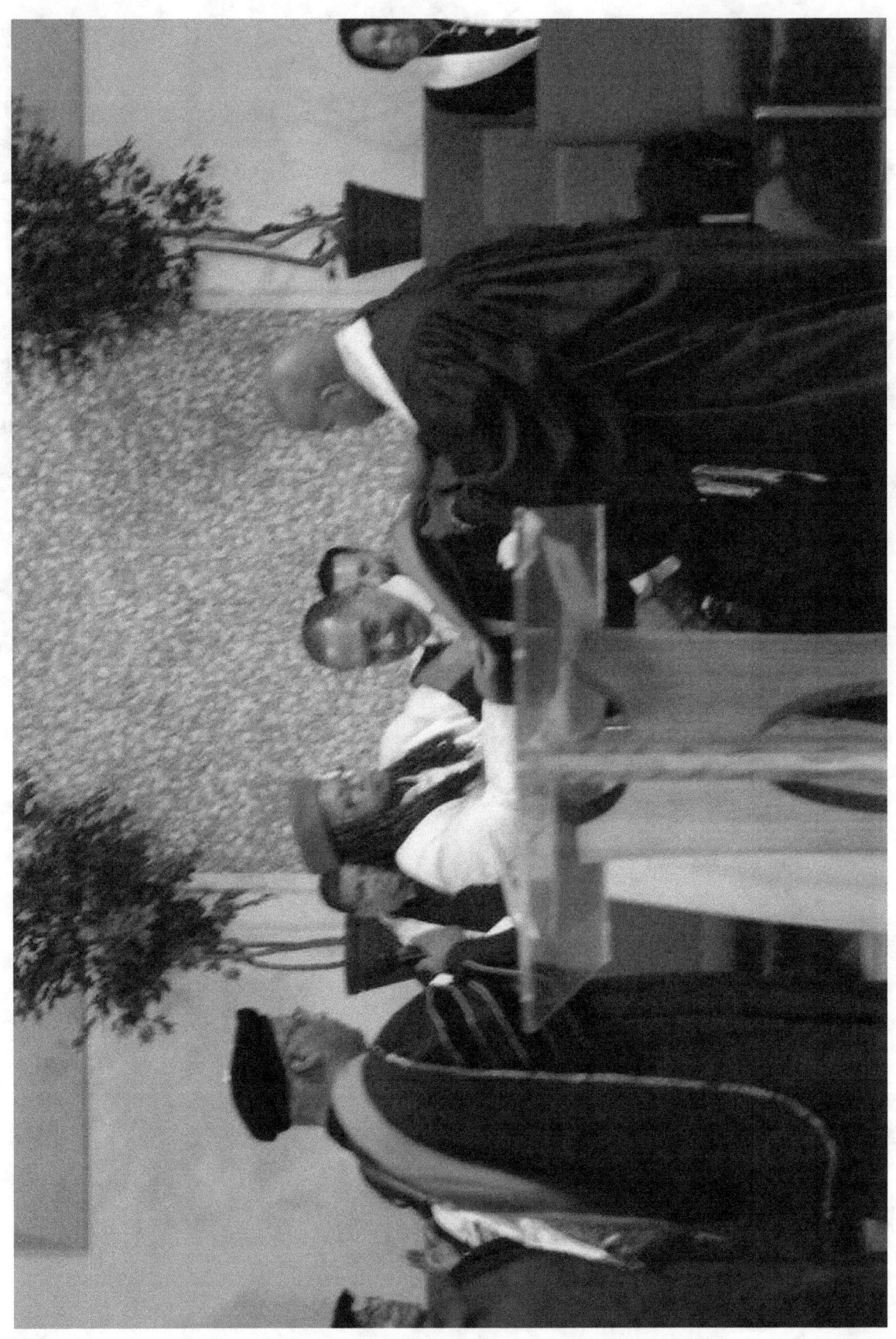

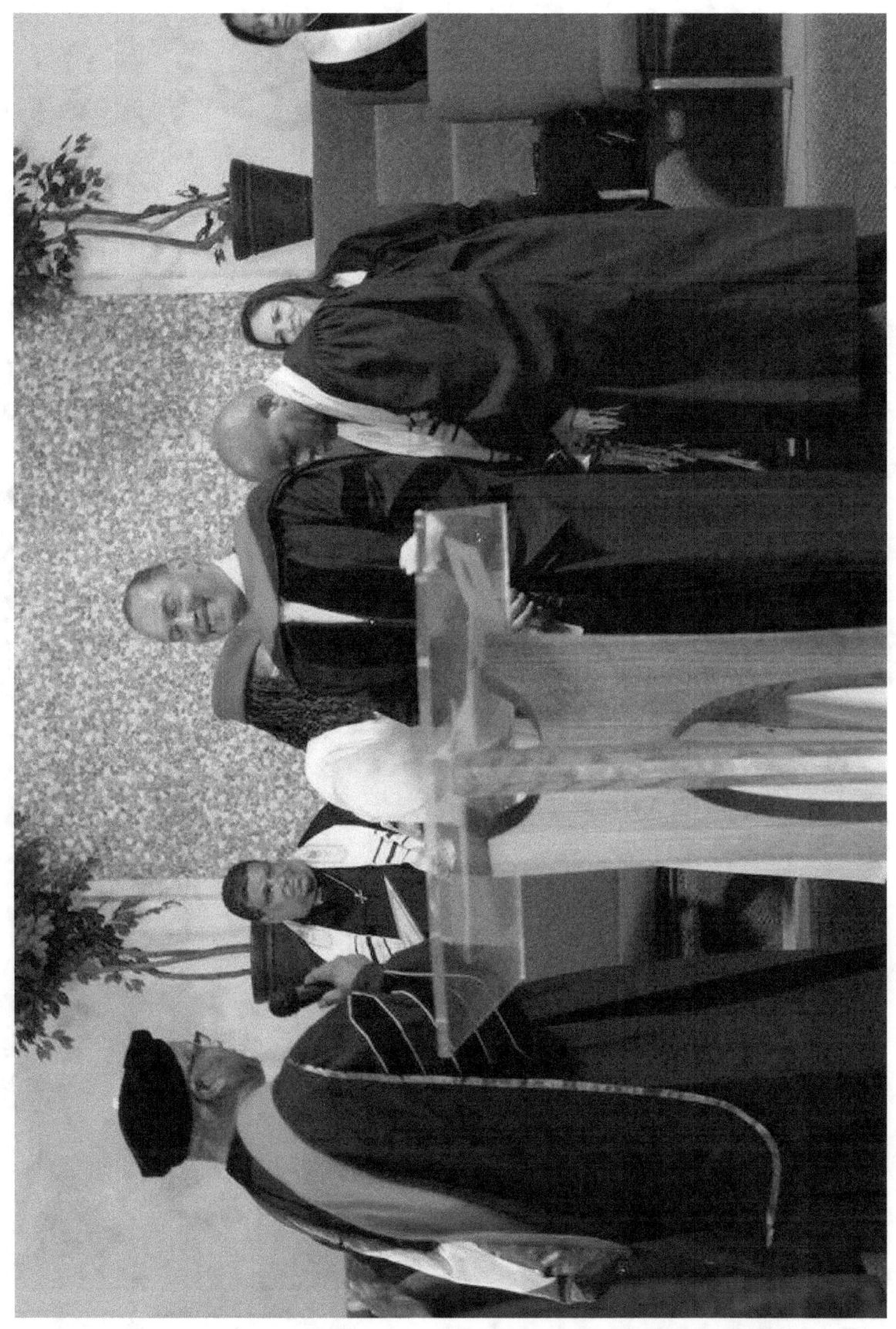

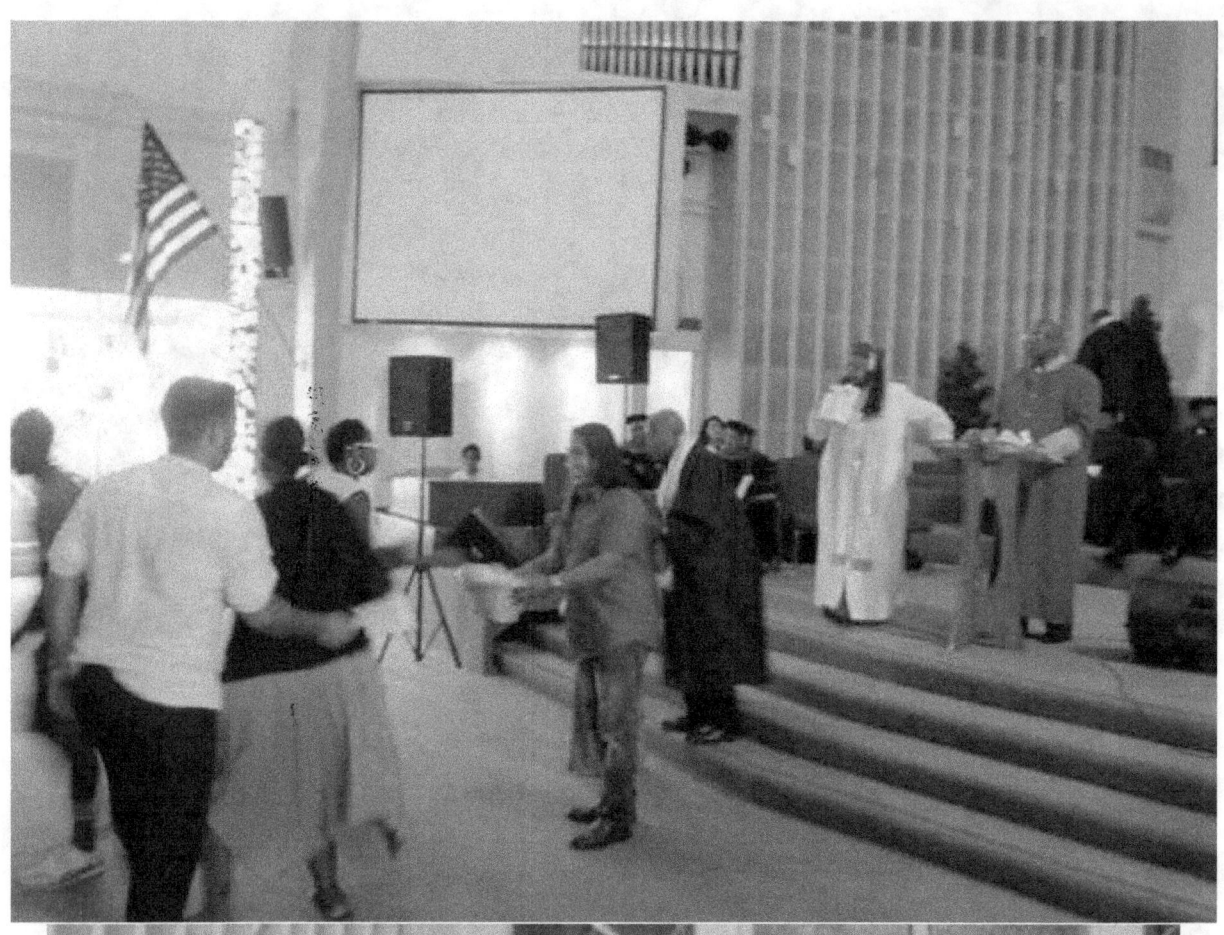

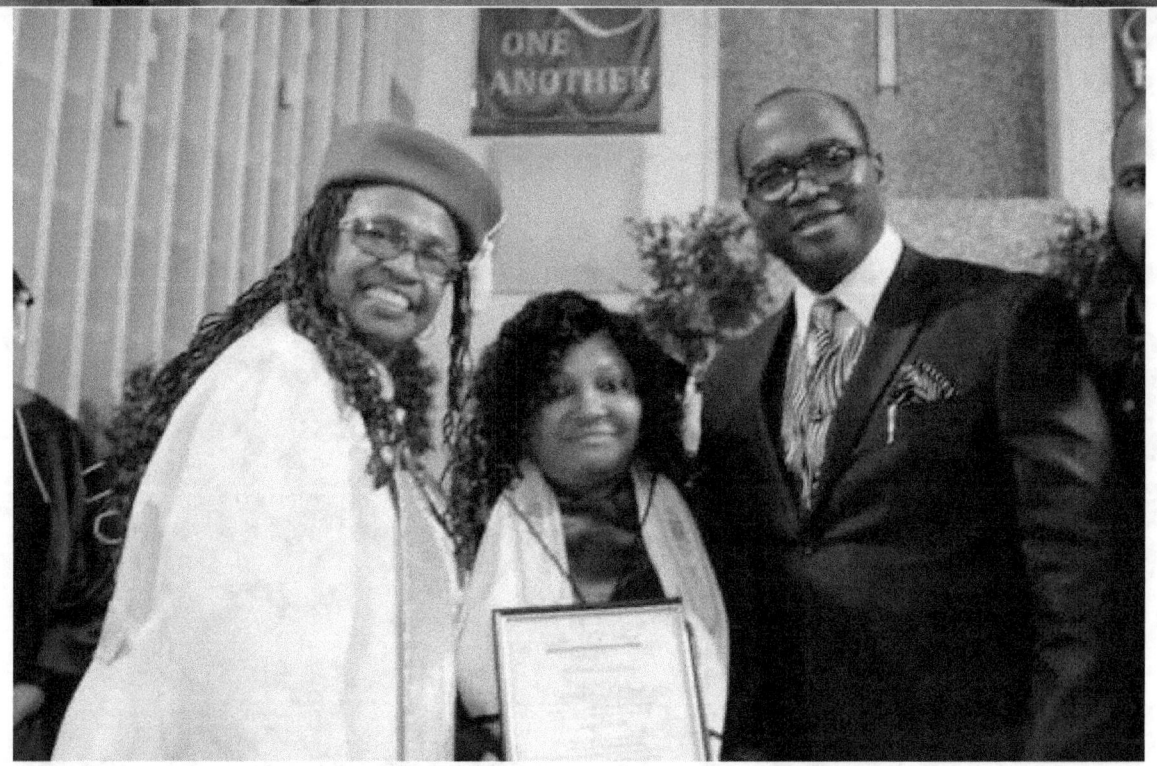

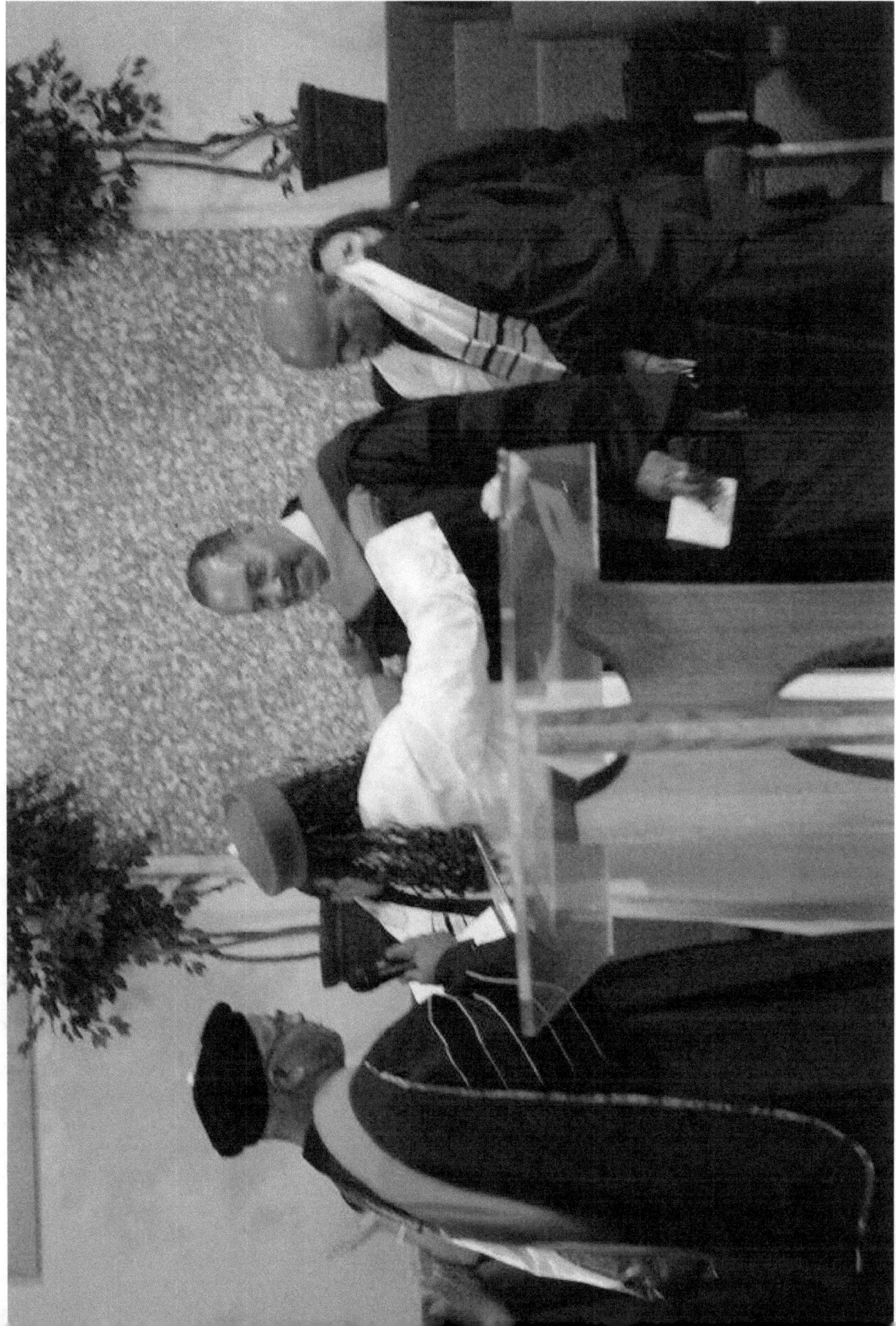

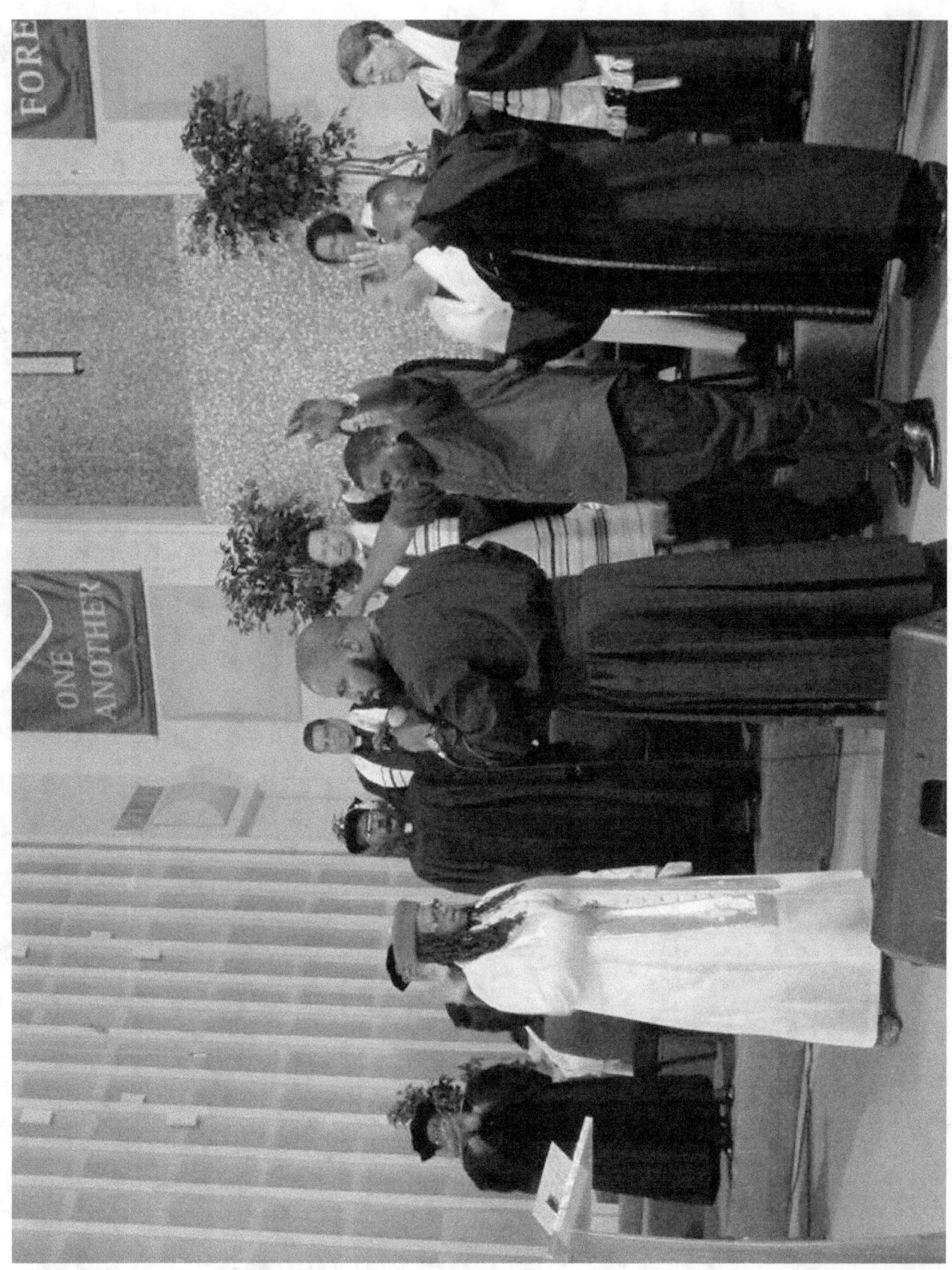

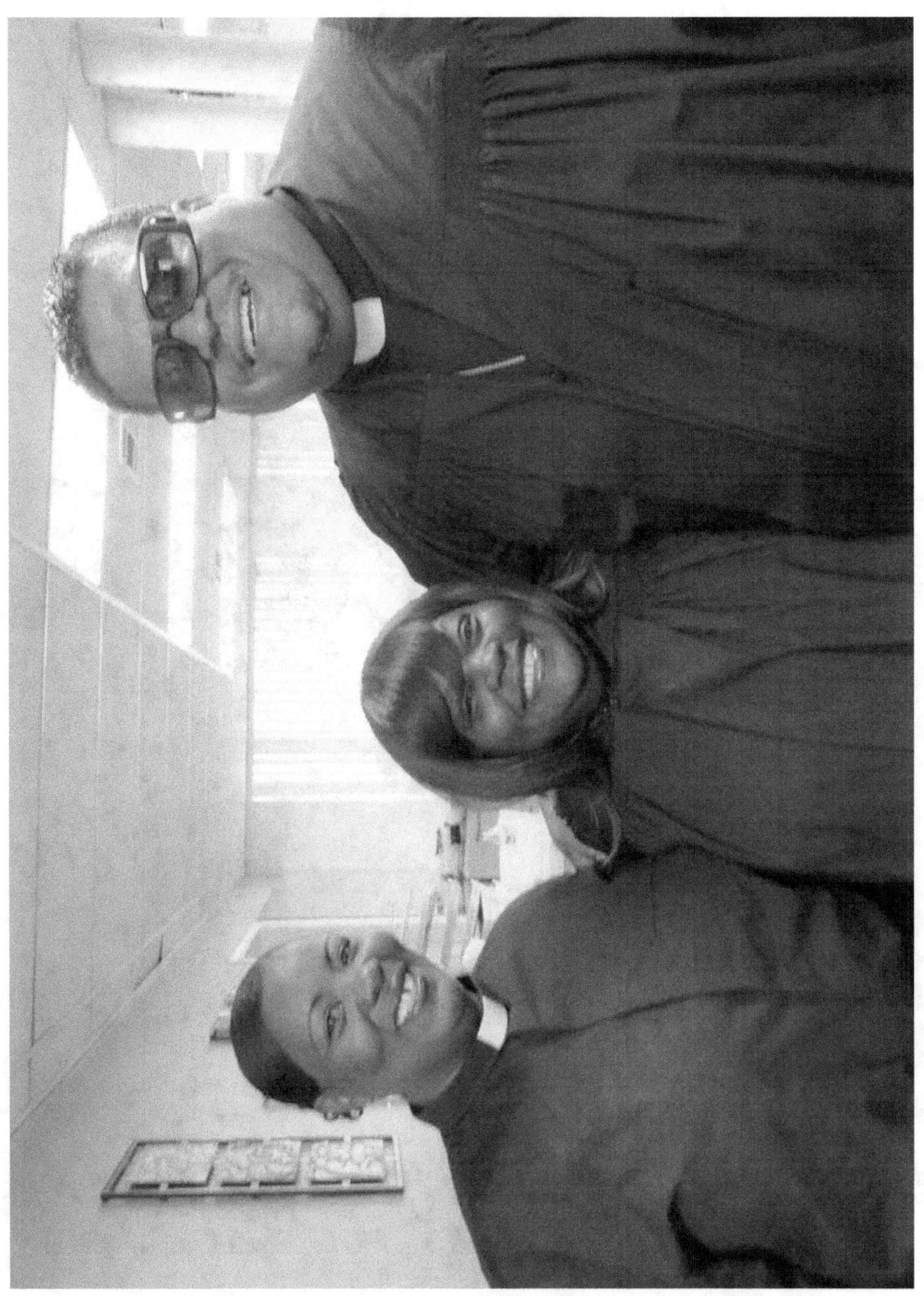

103

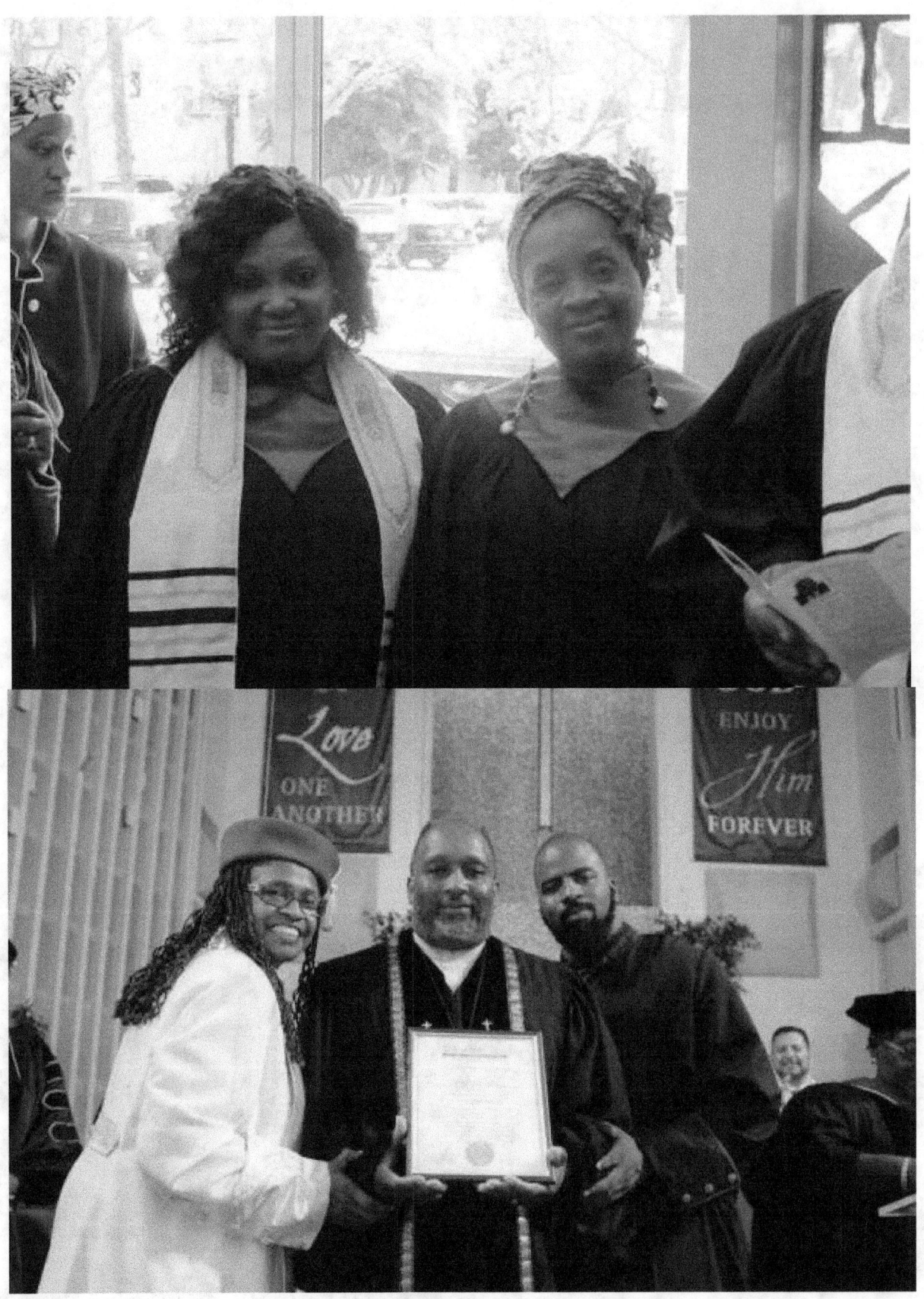

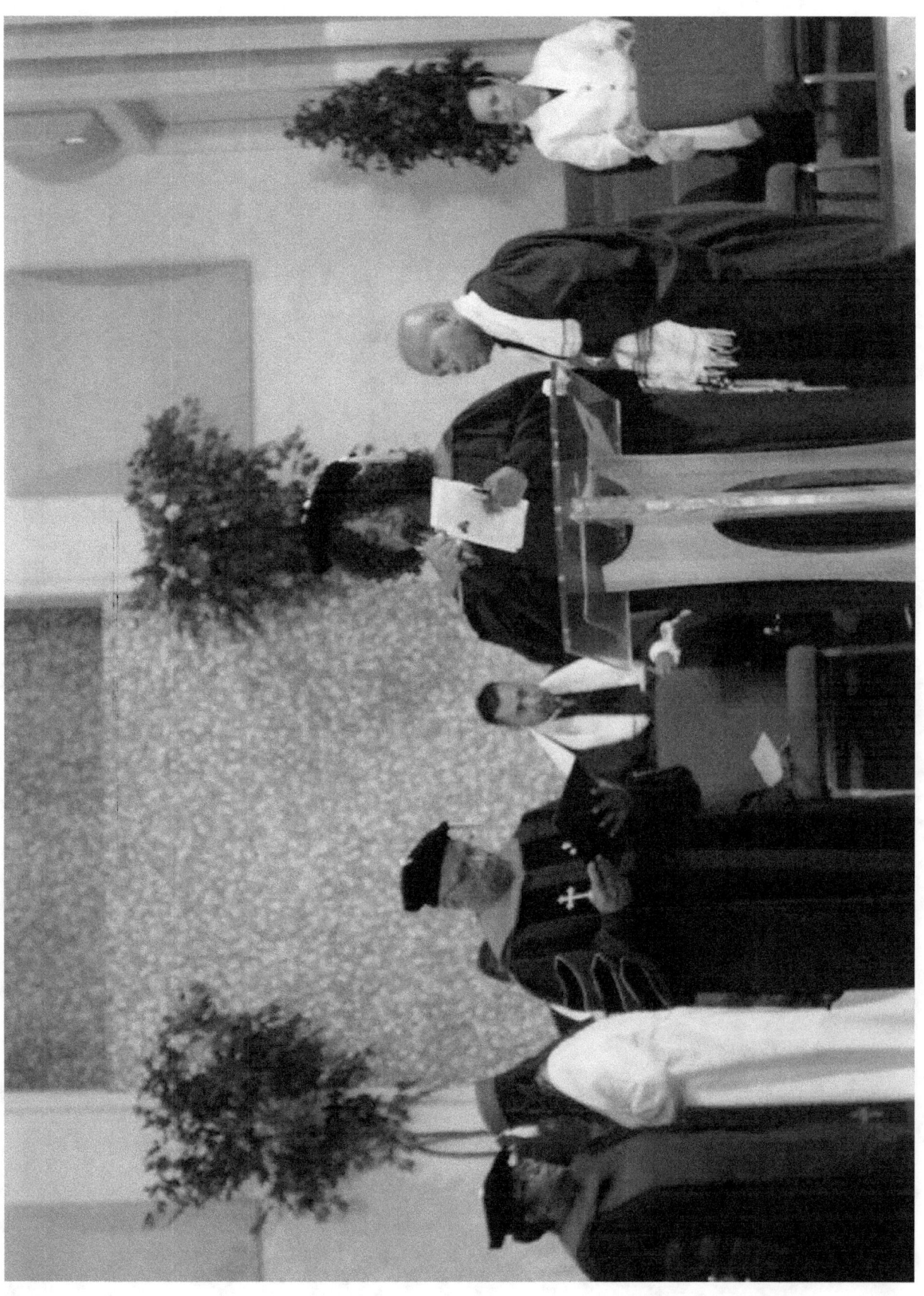

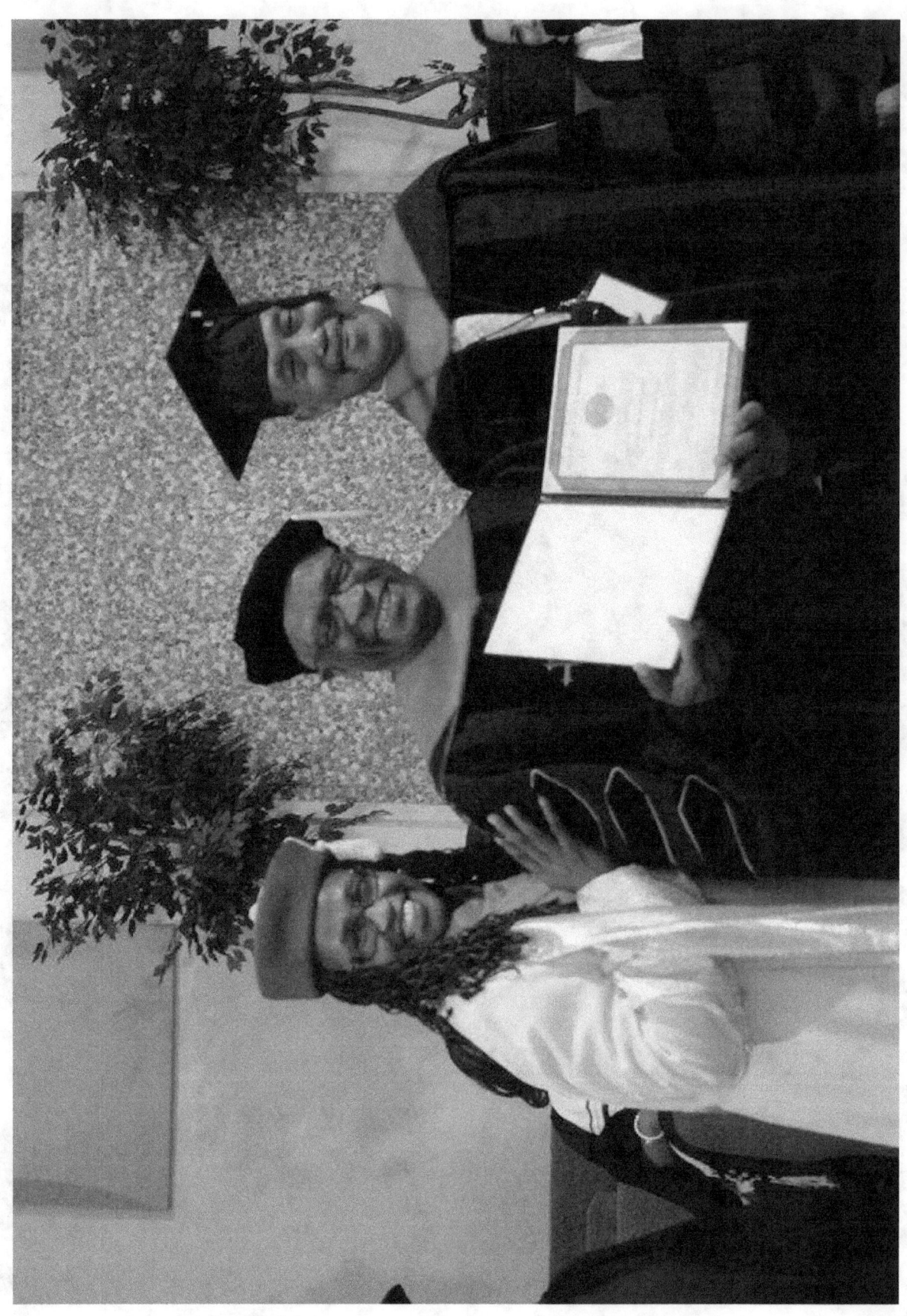

106

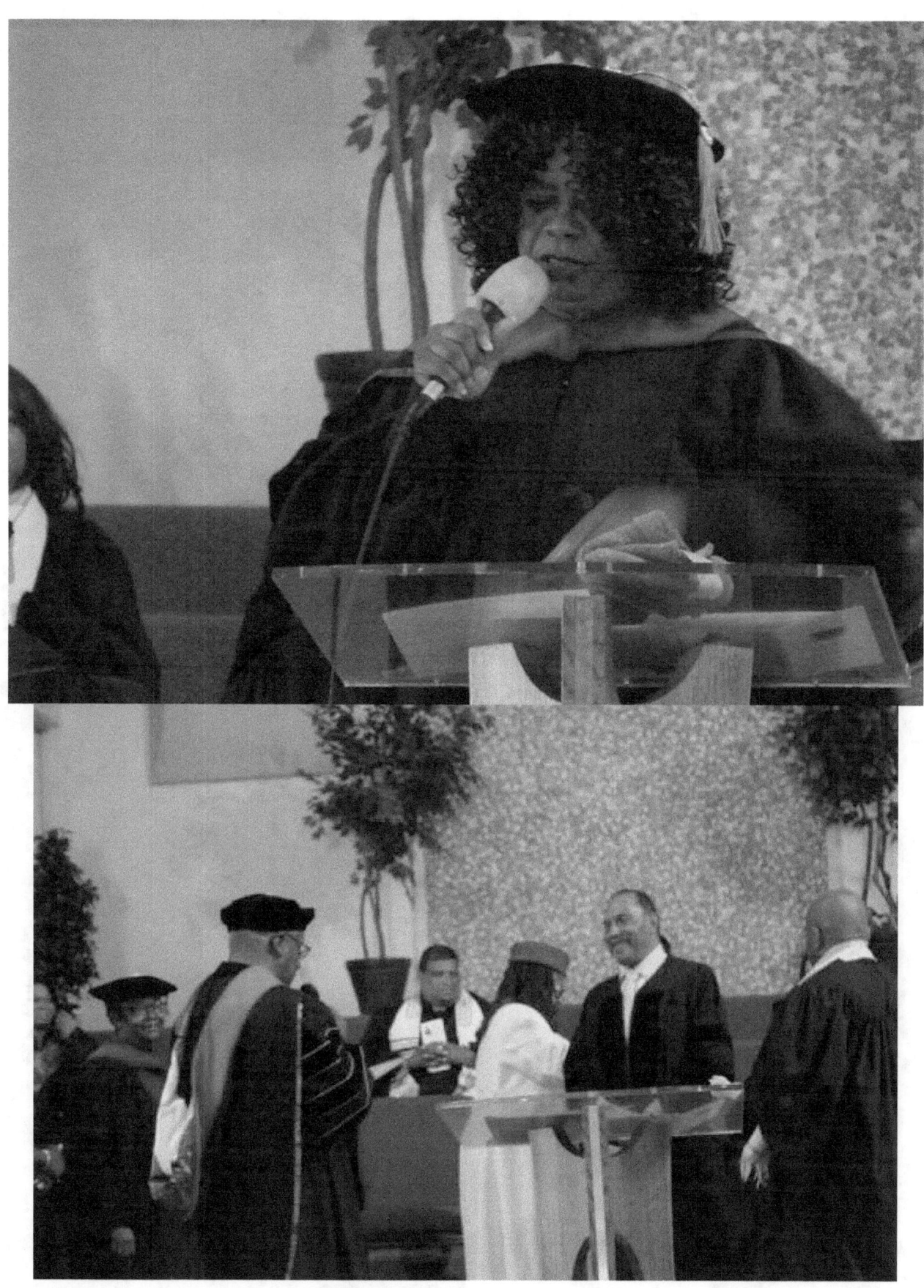

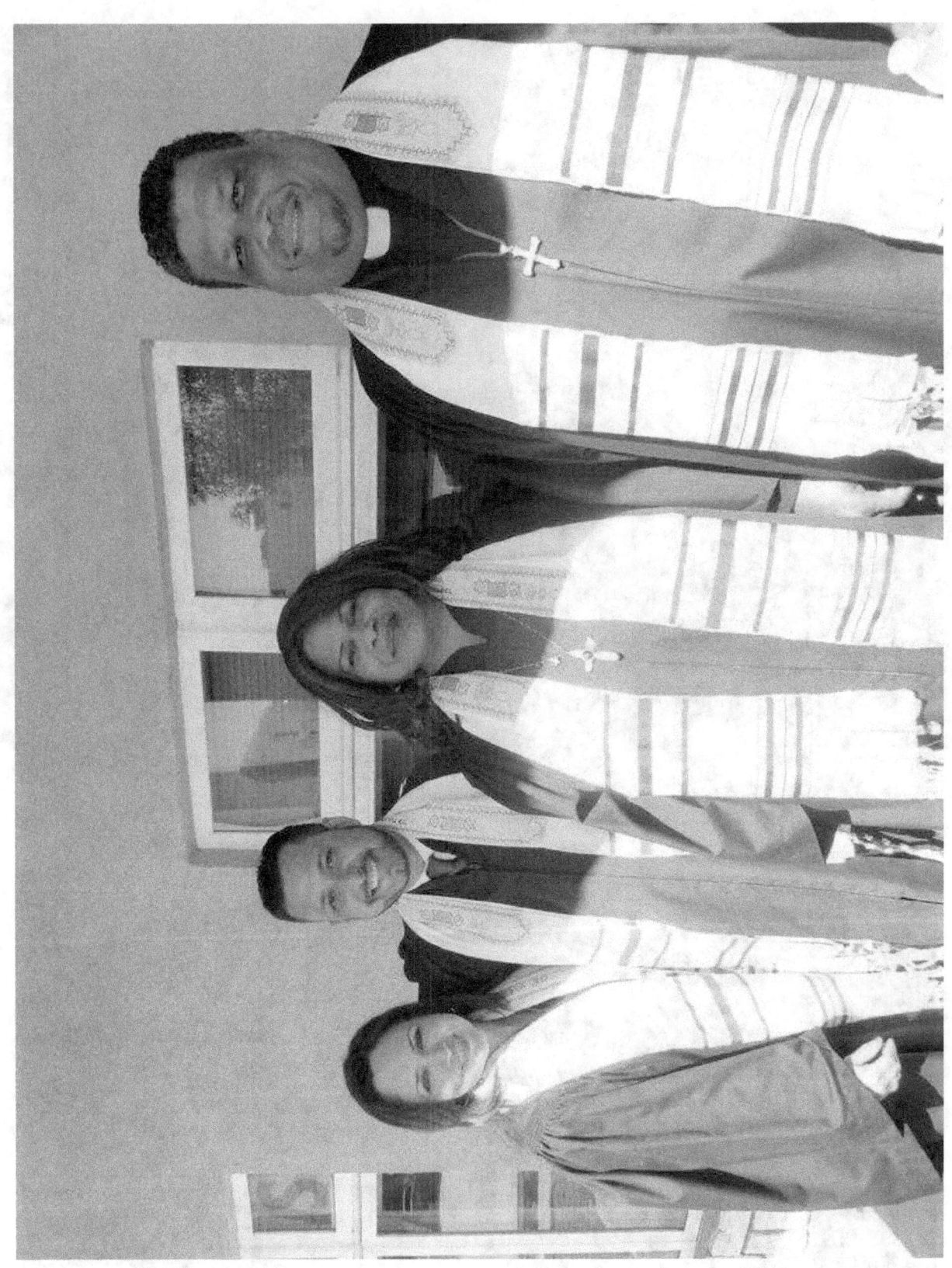

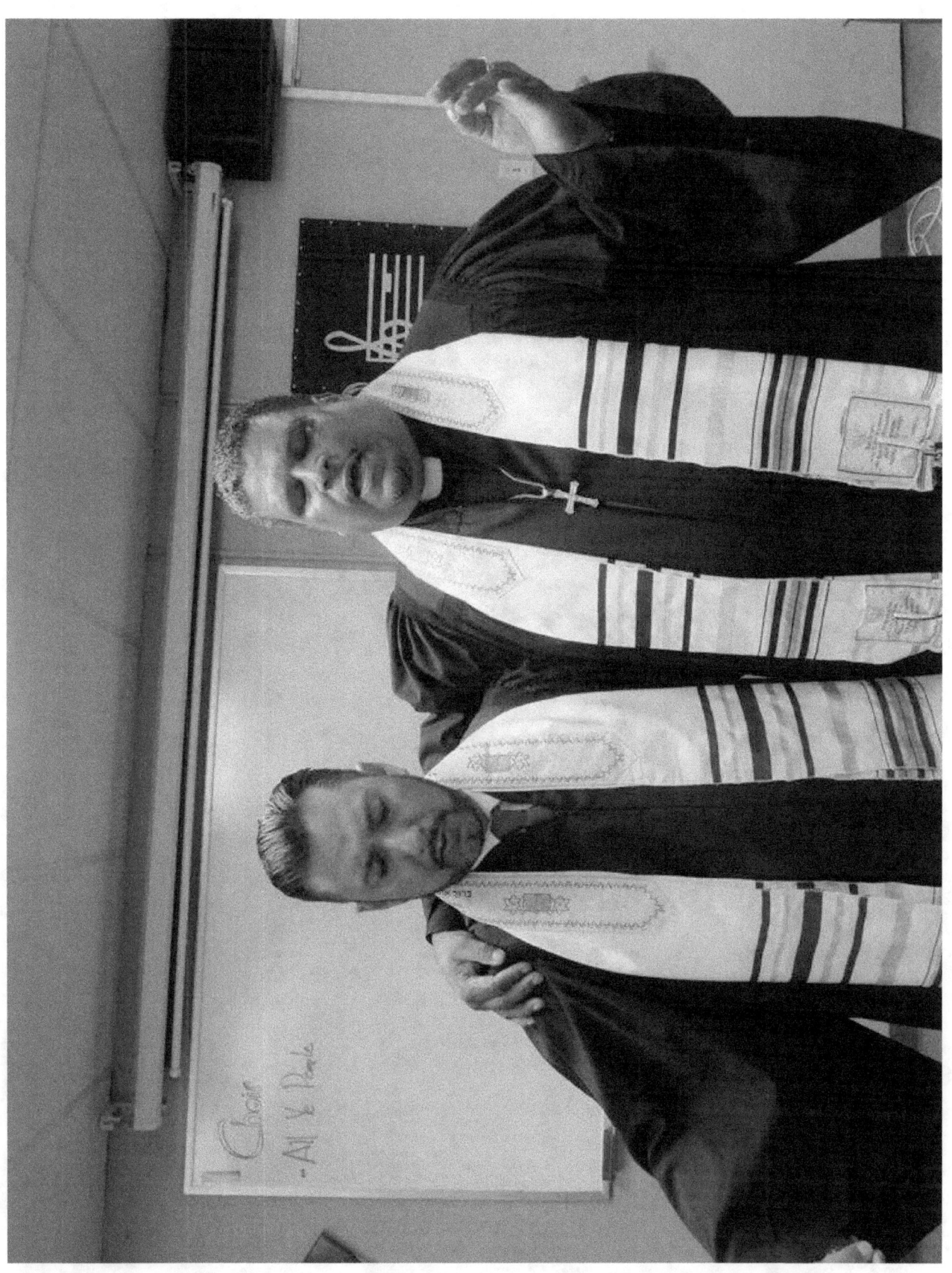

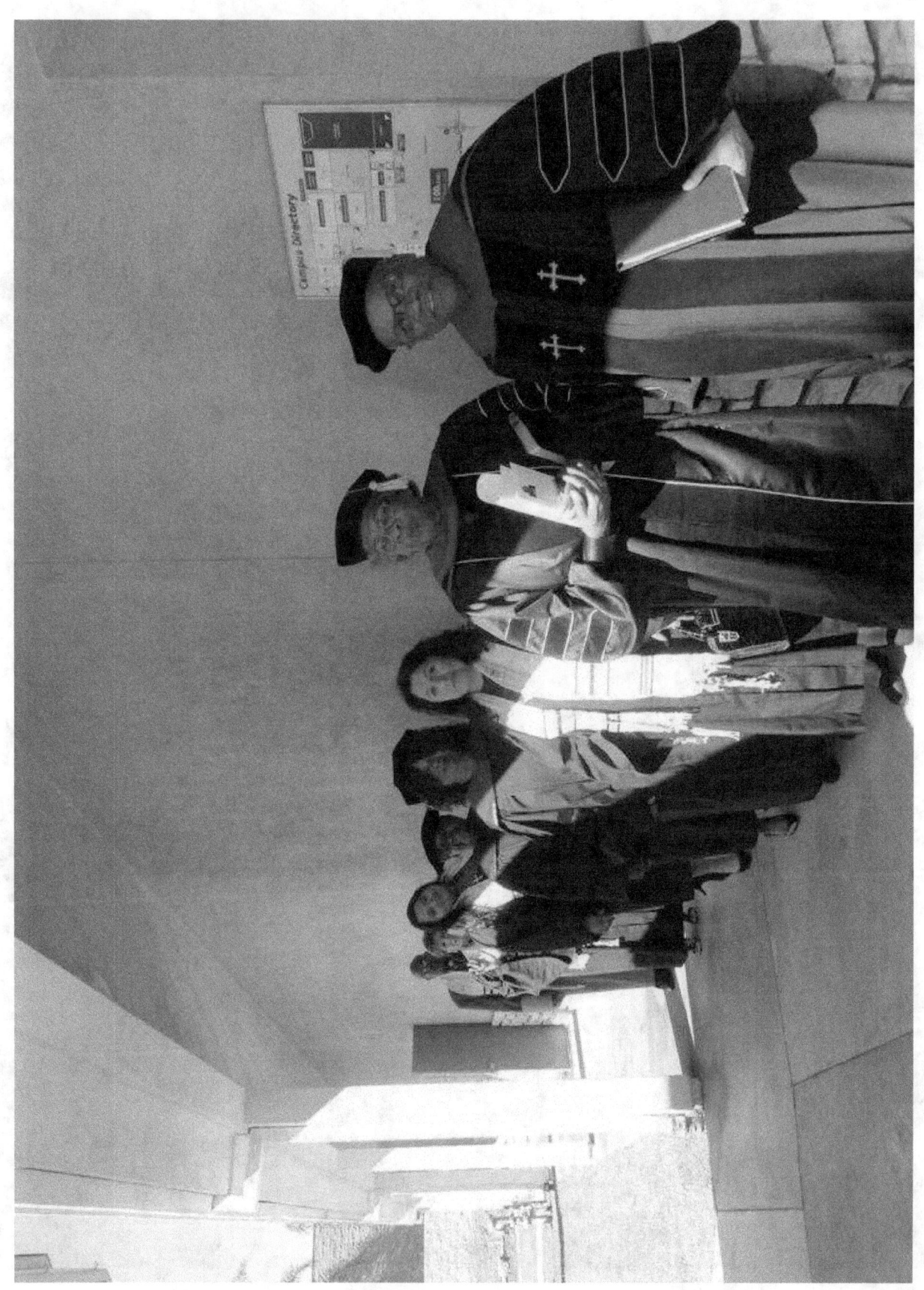

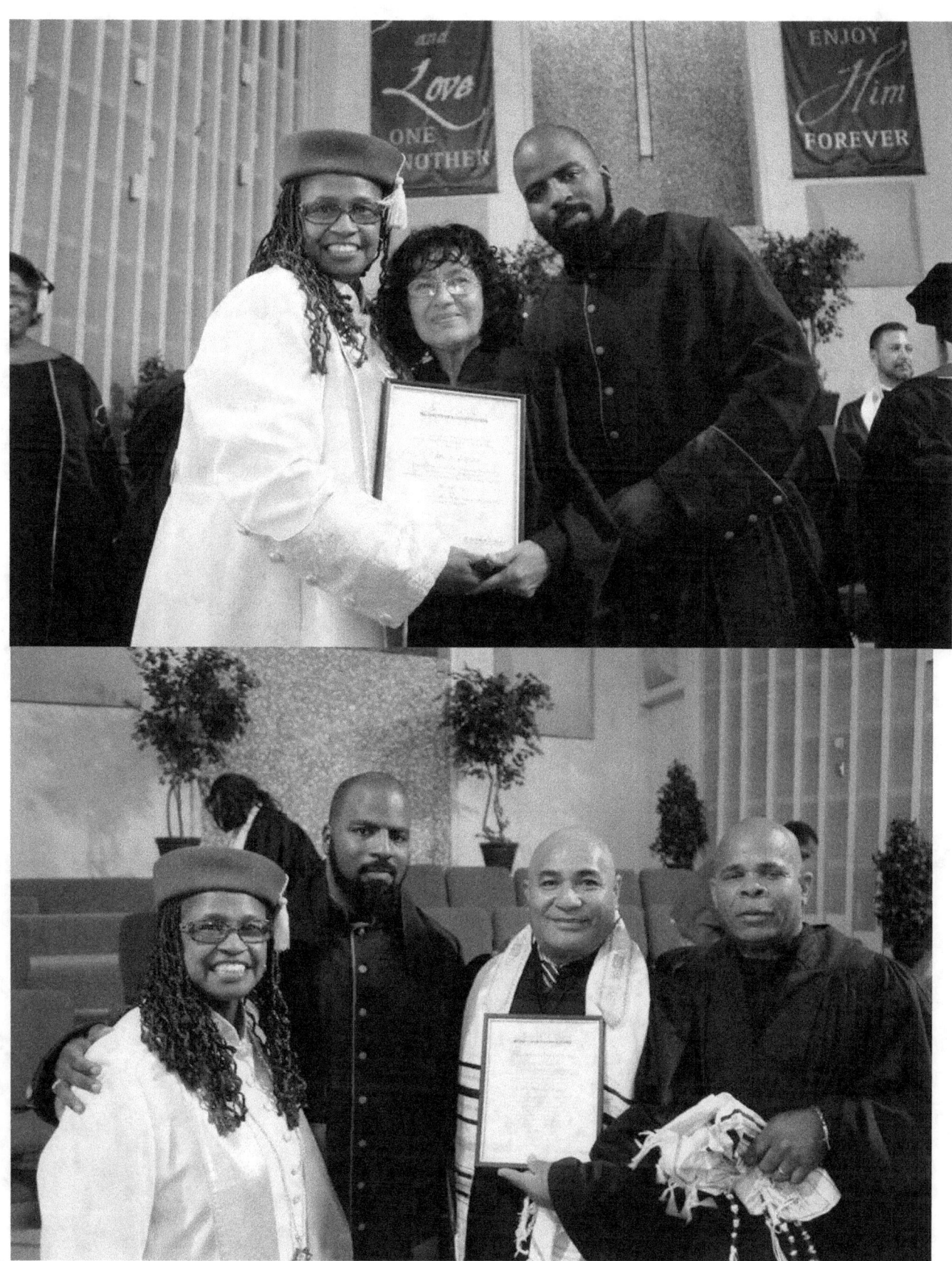

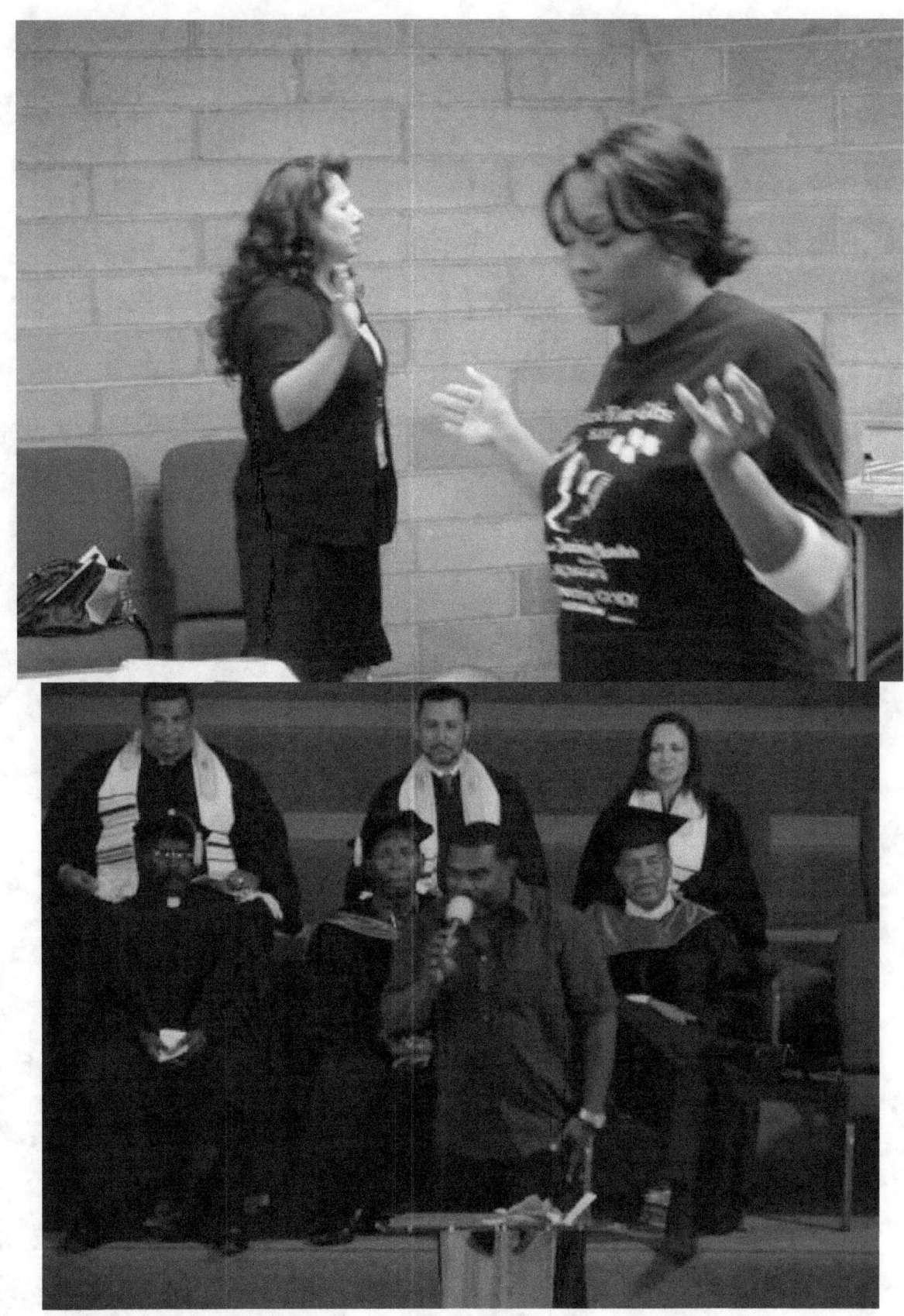

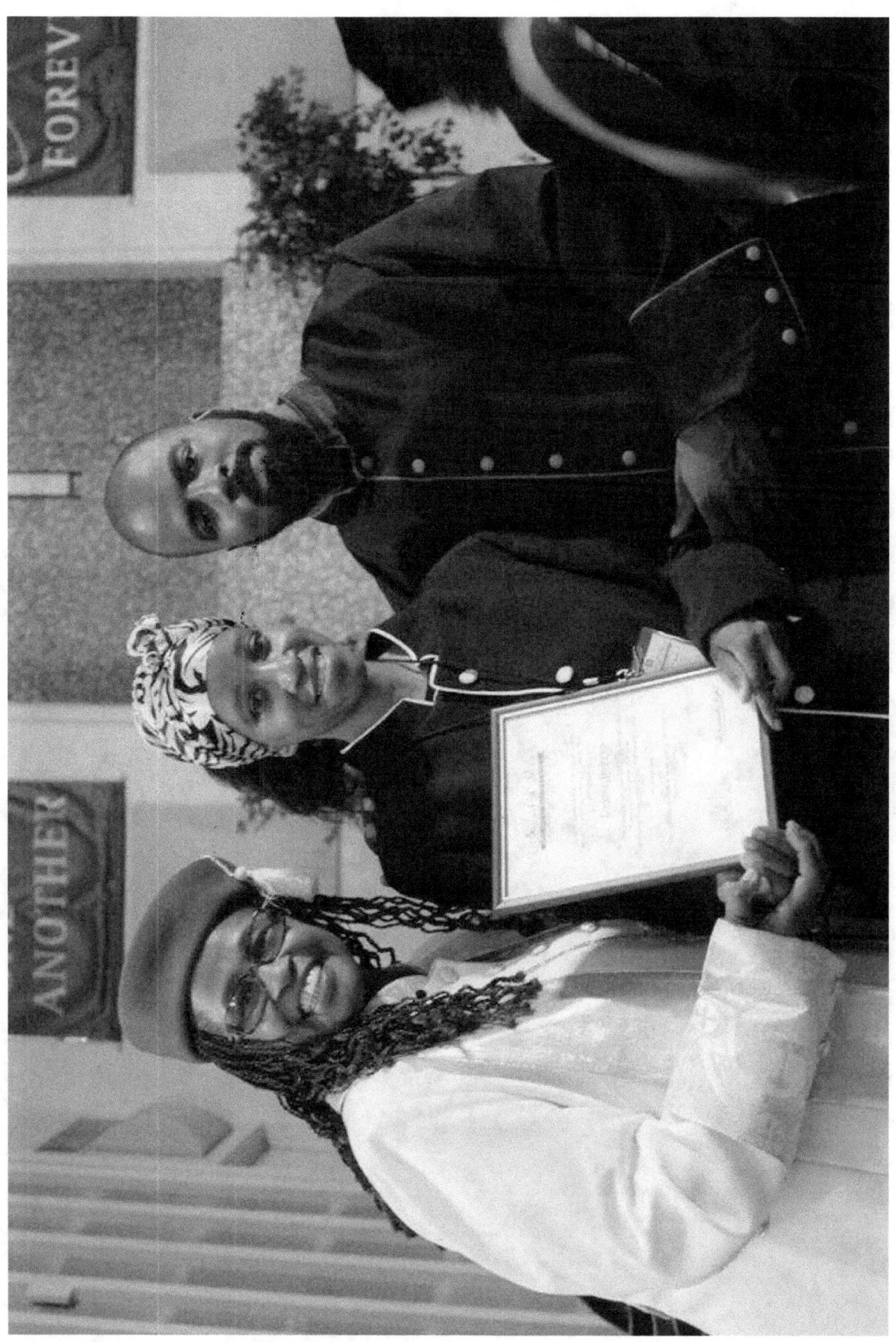

113

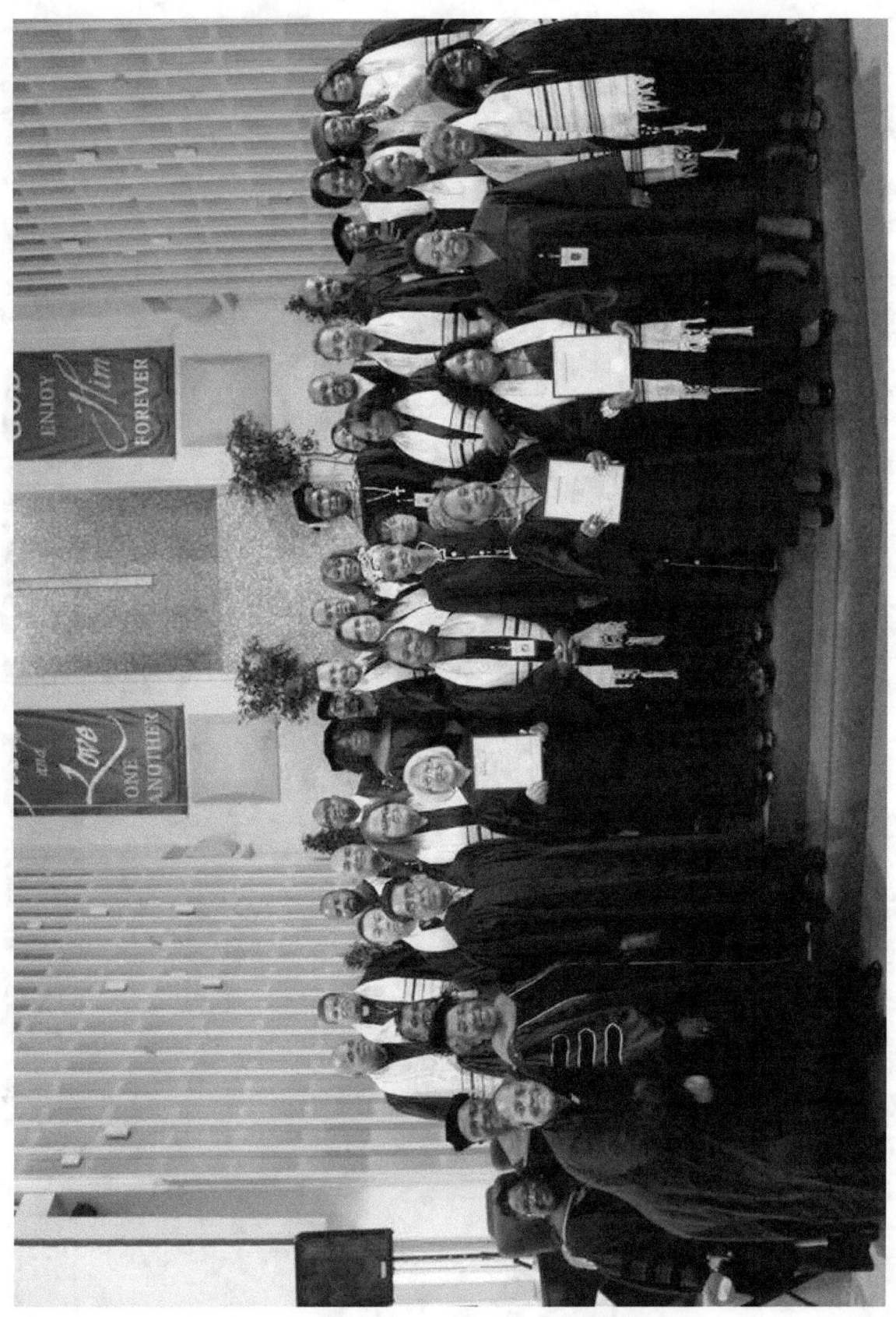

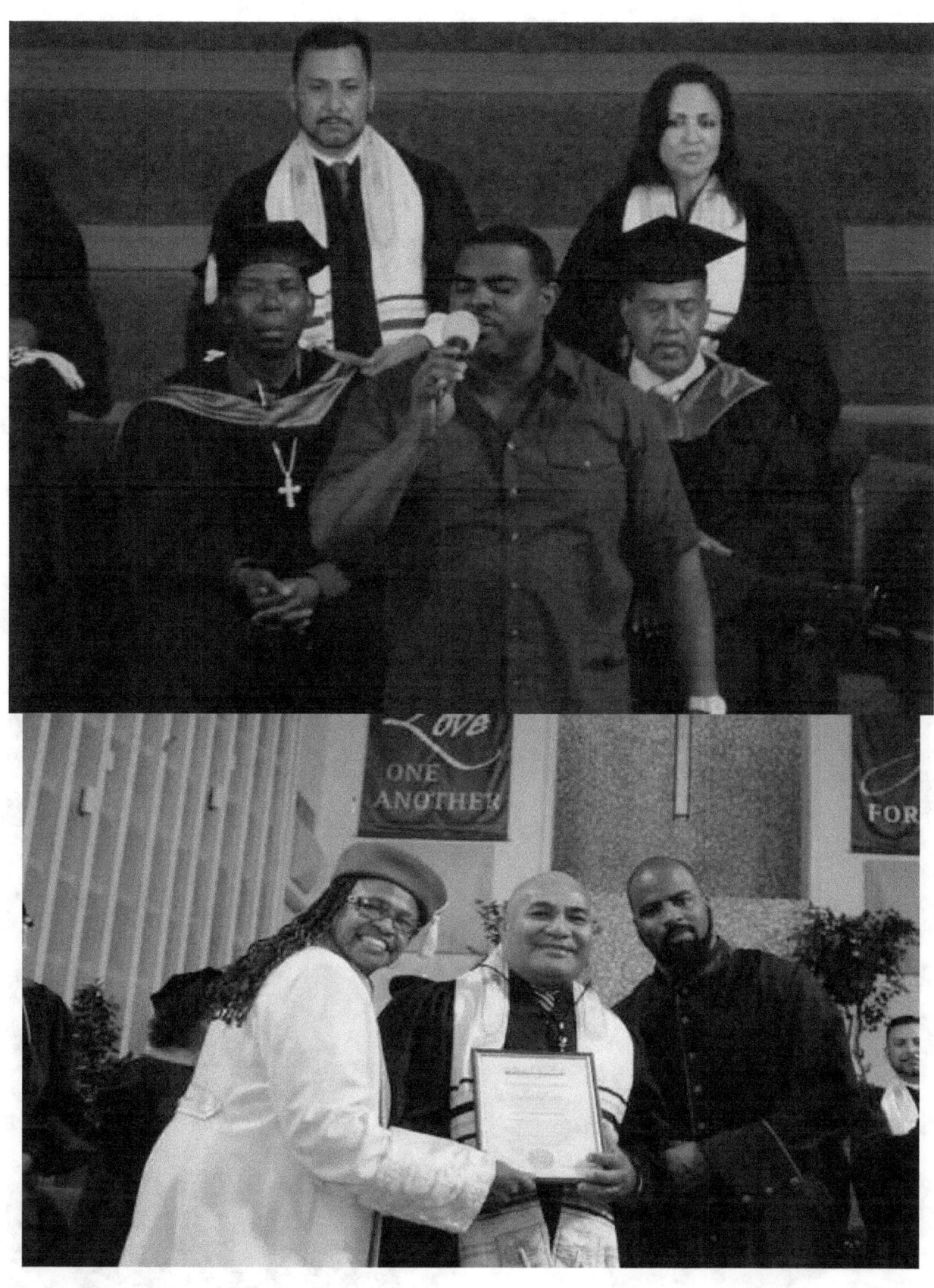

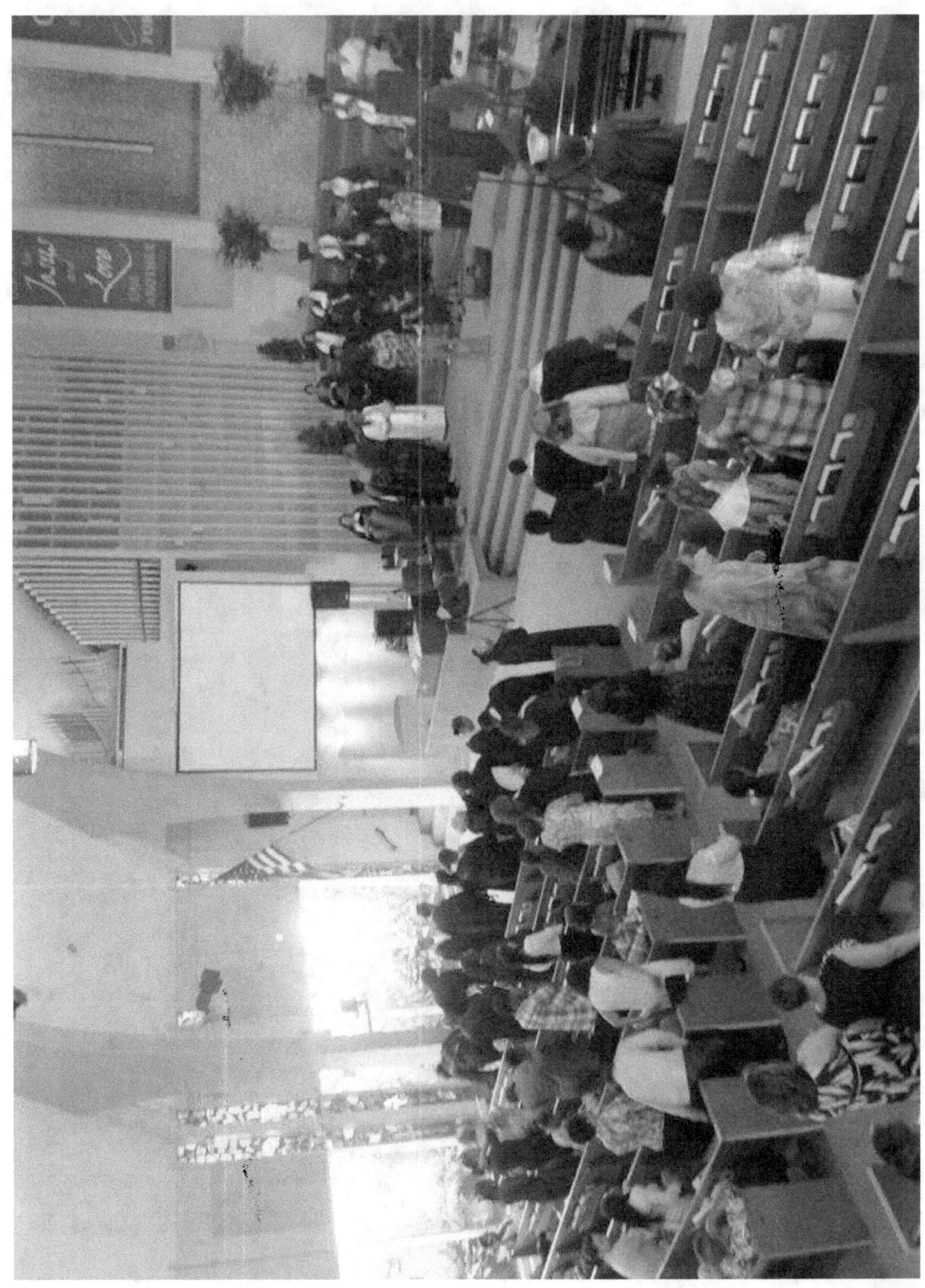

116

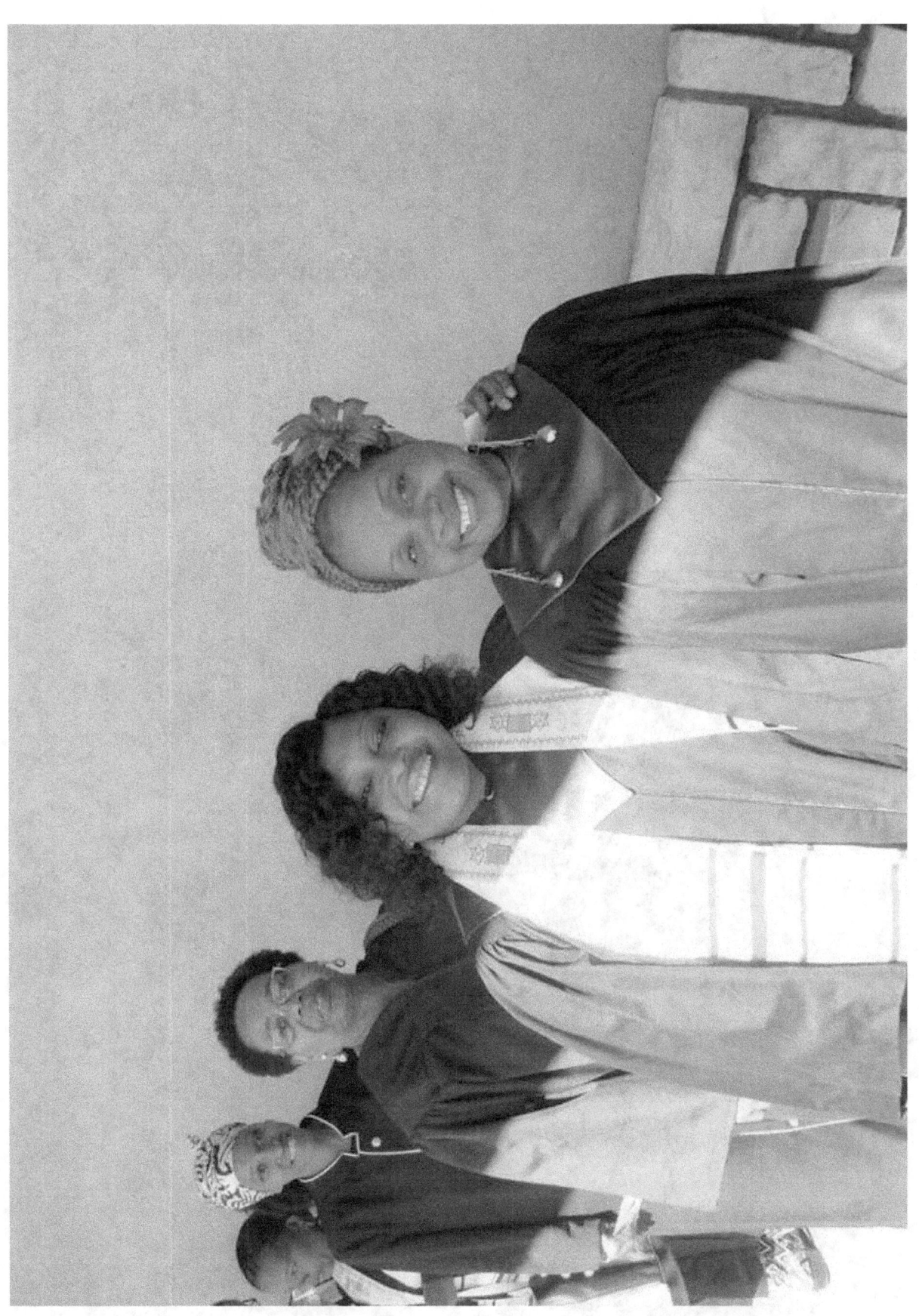

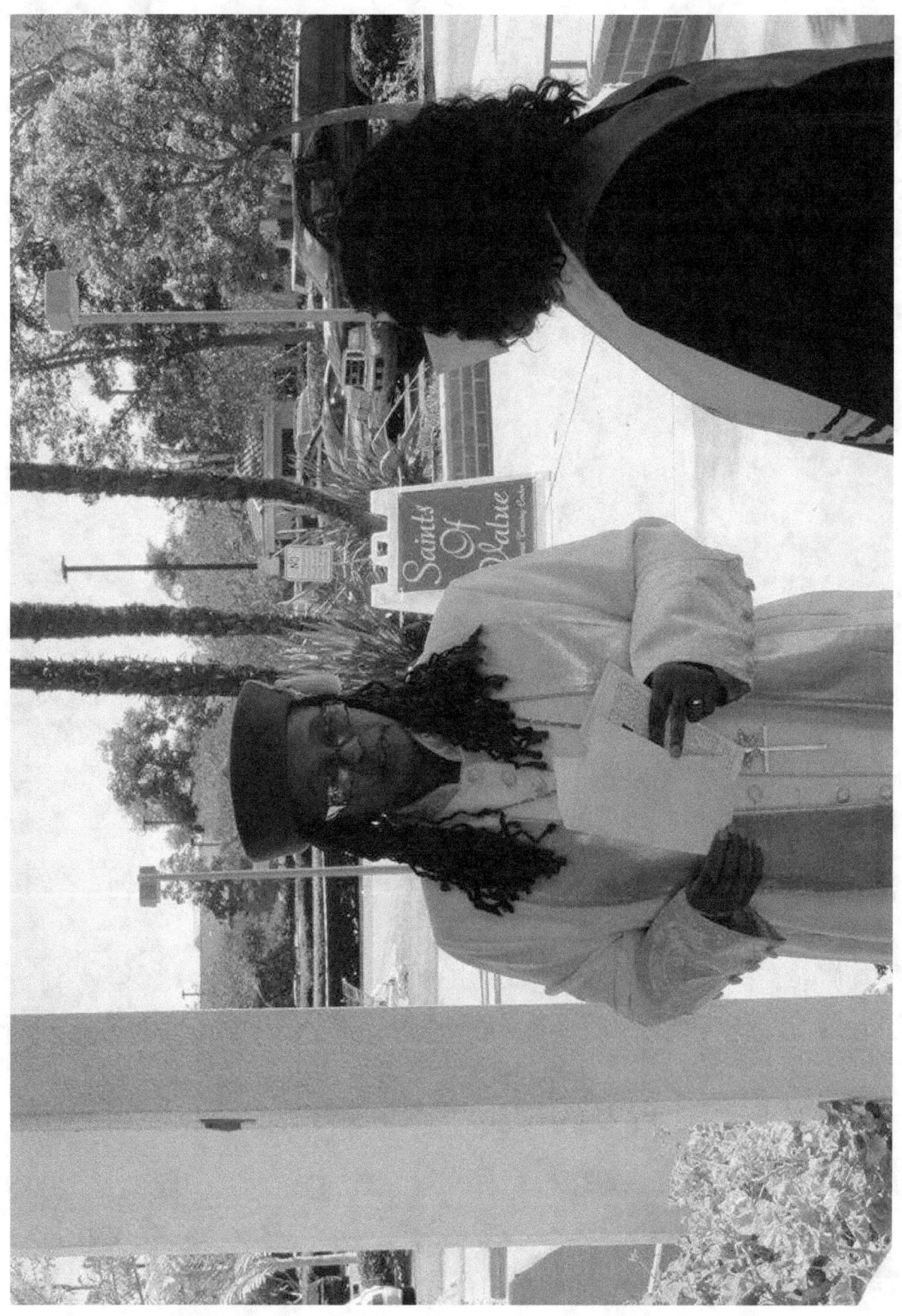

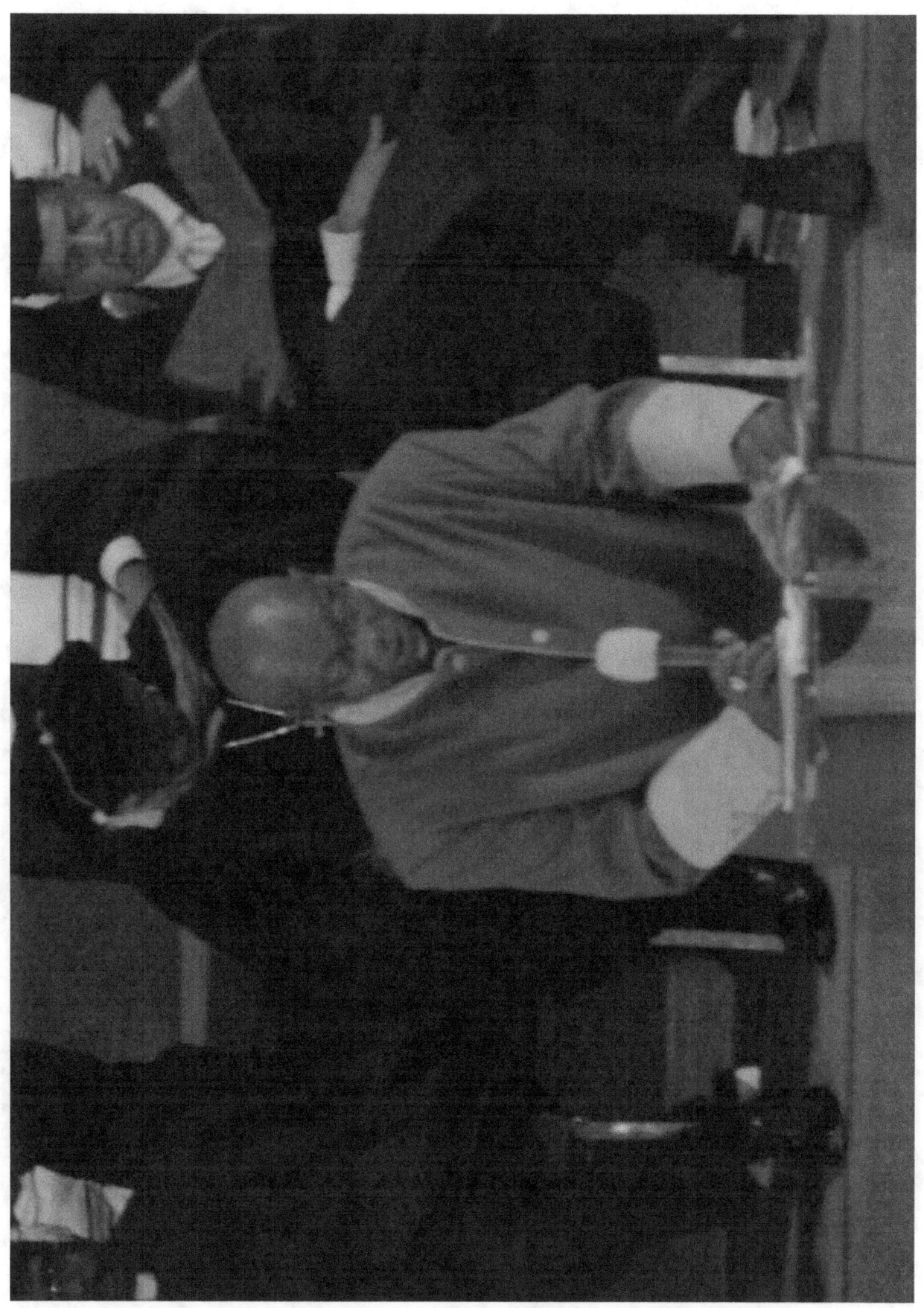

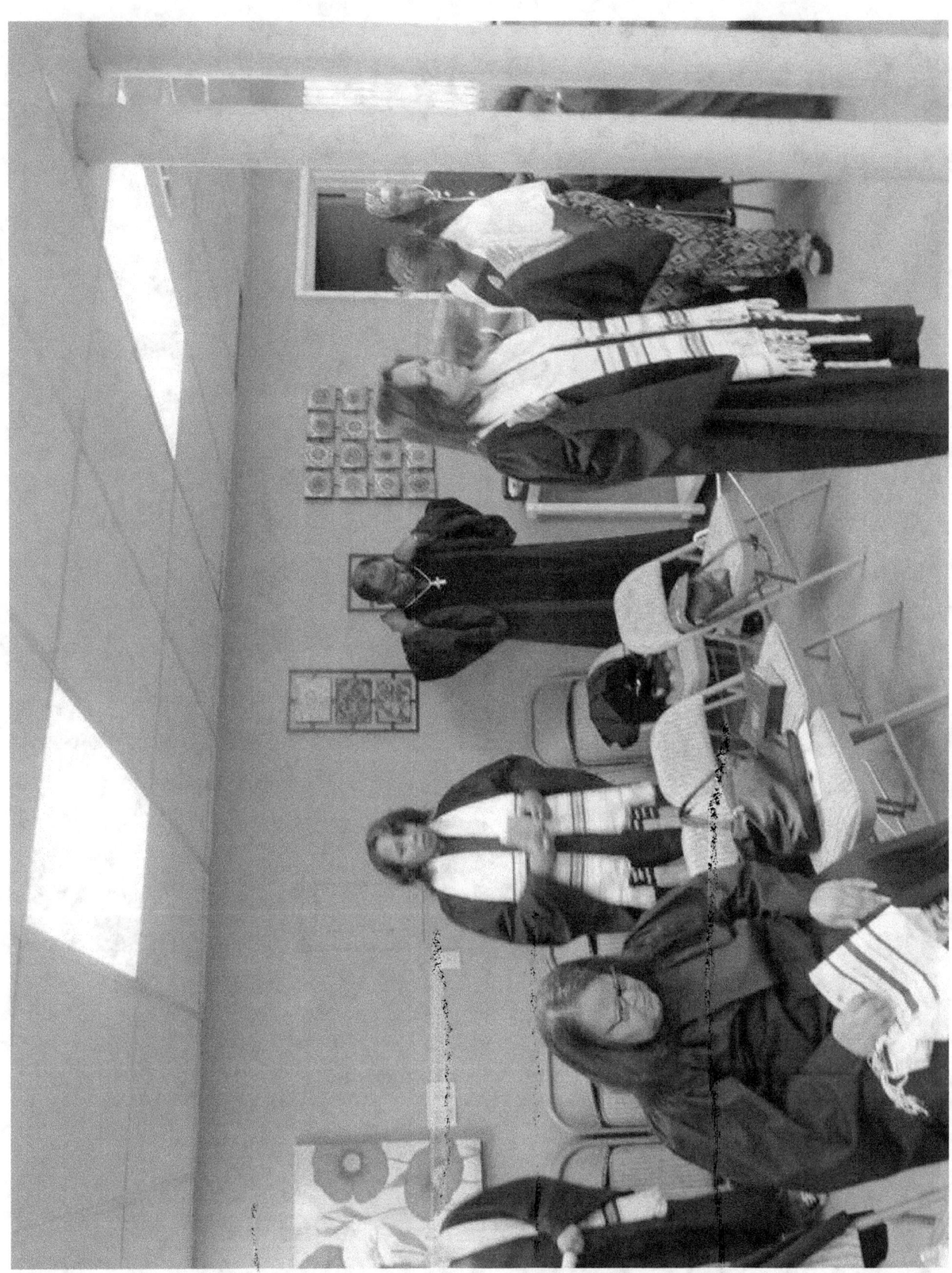

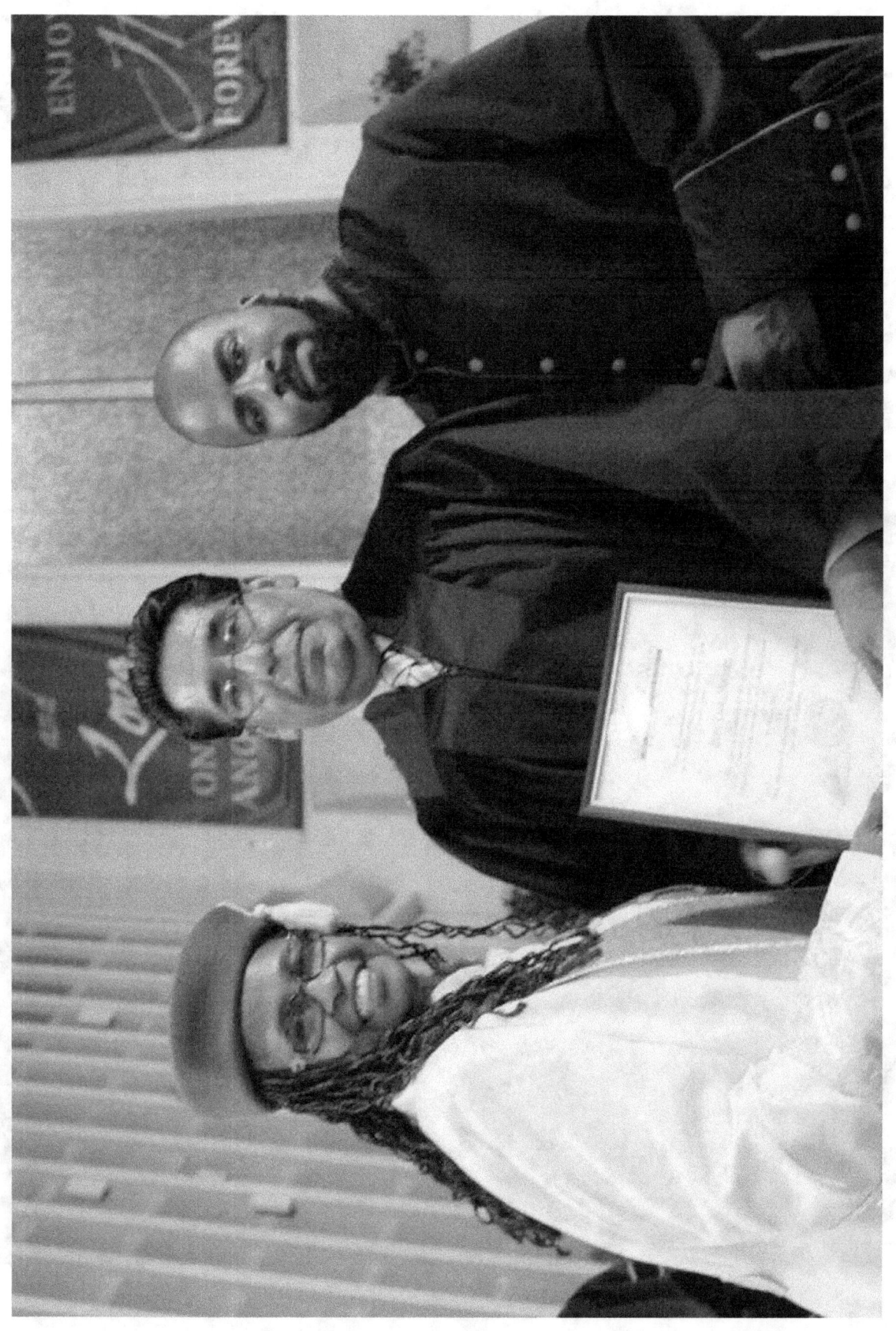

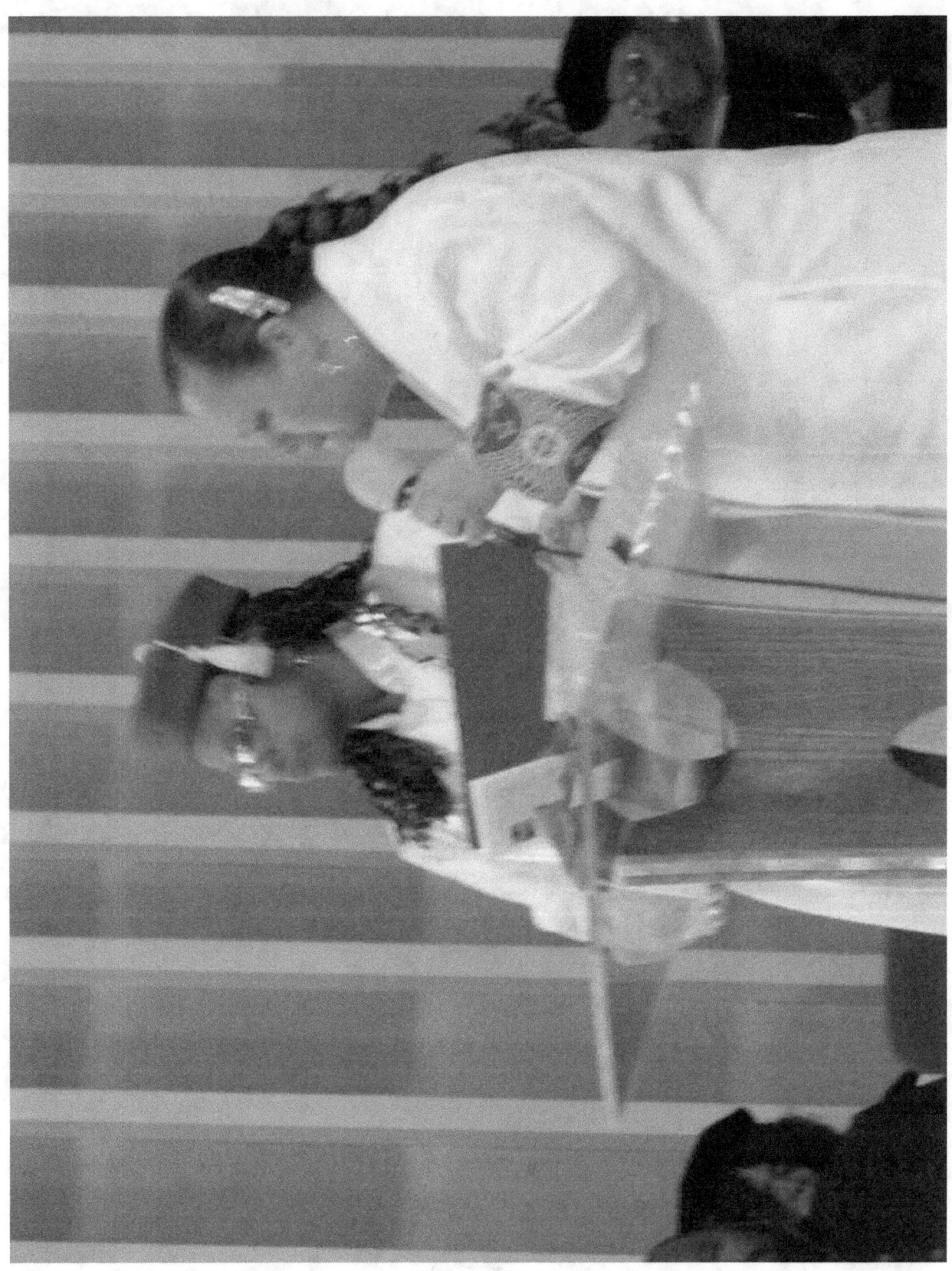

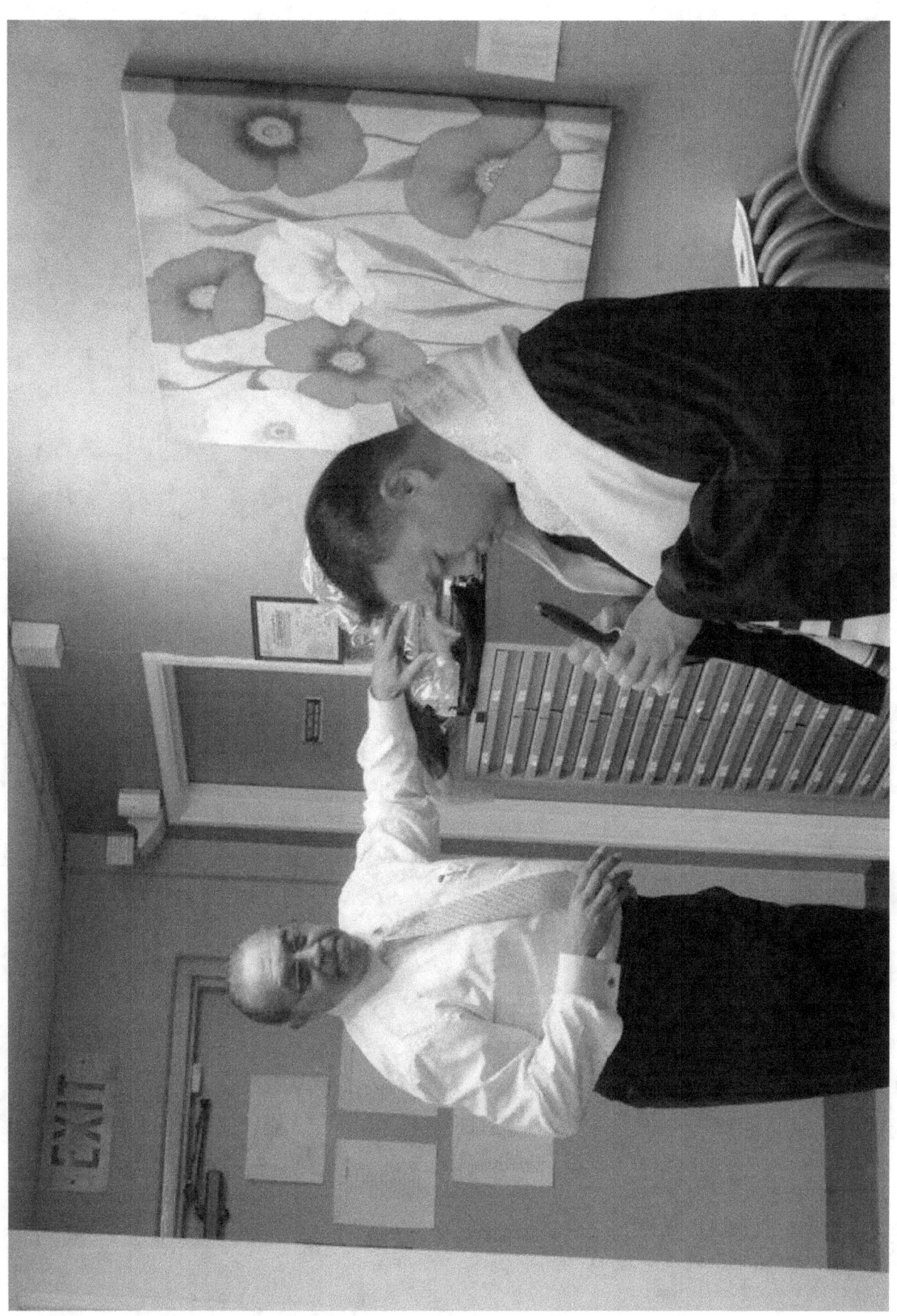

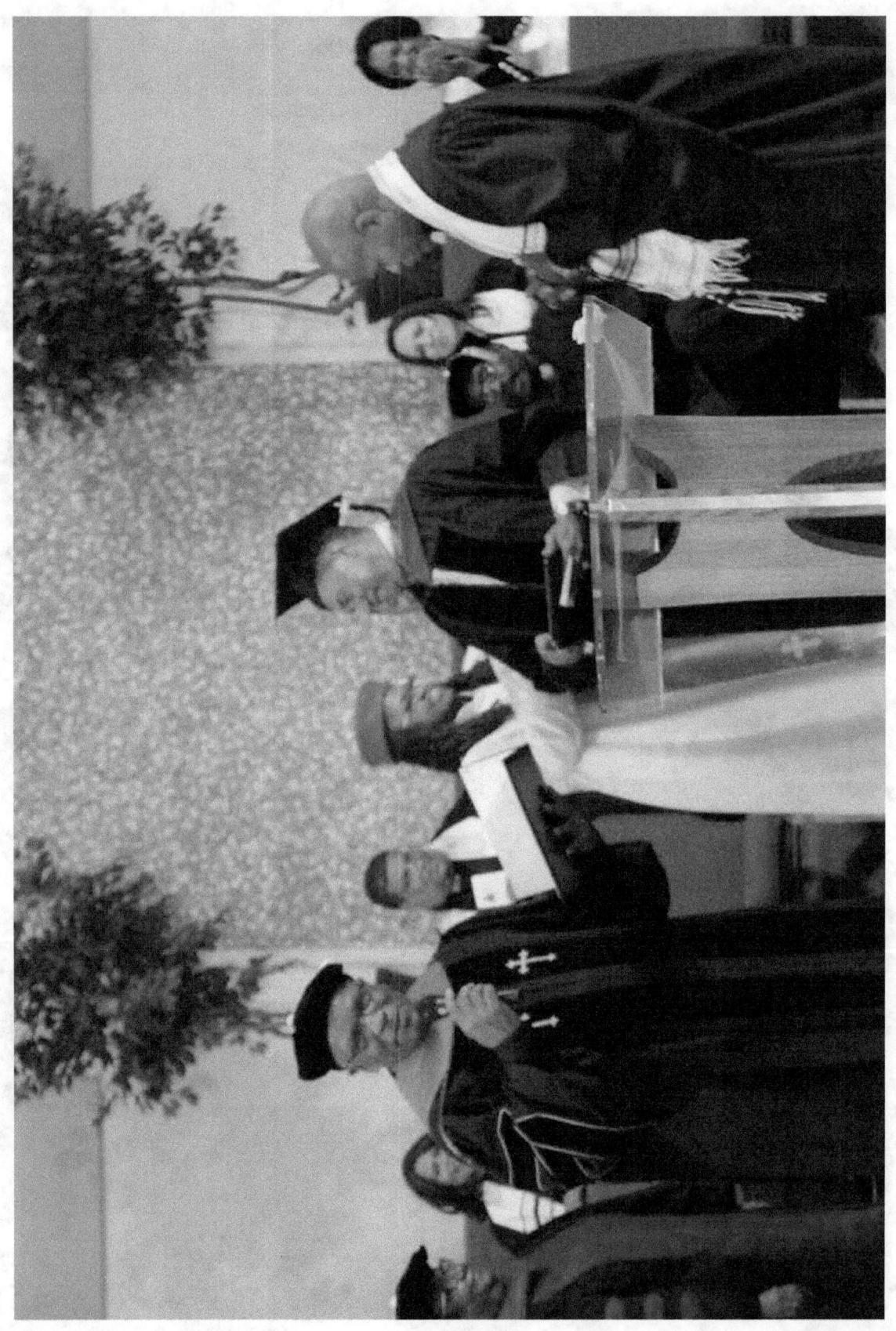

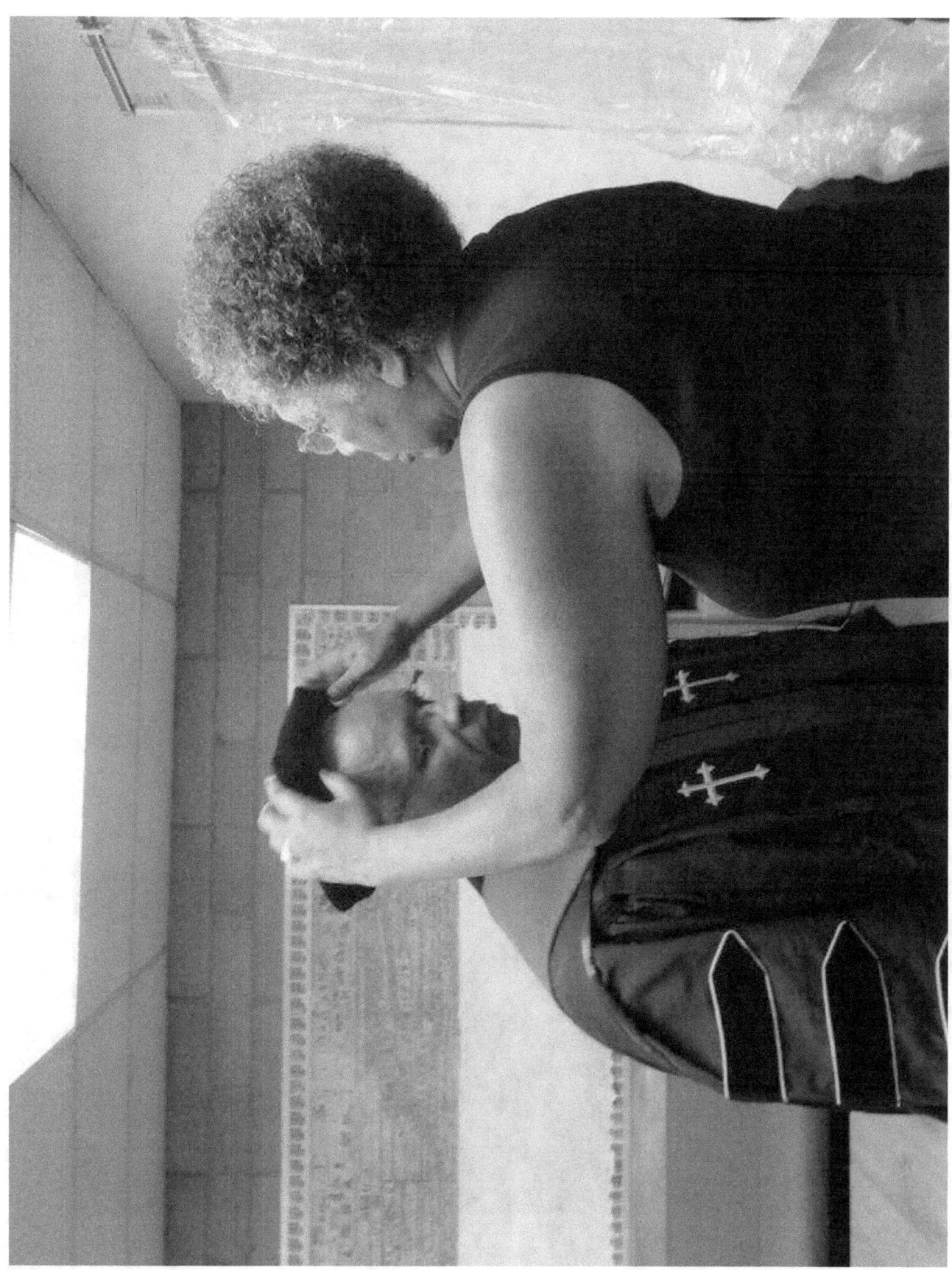

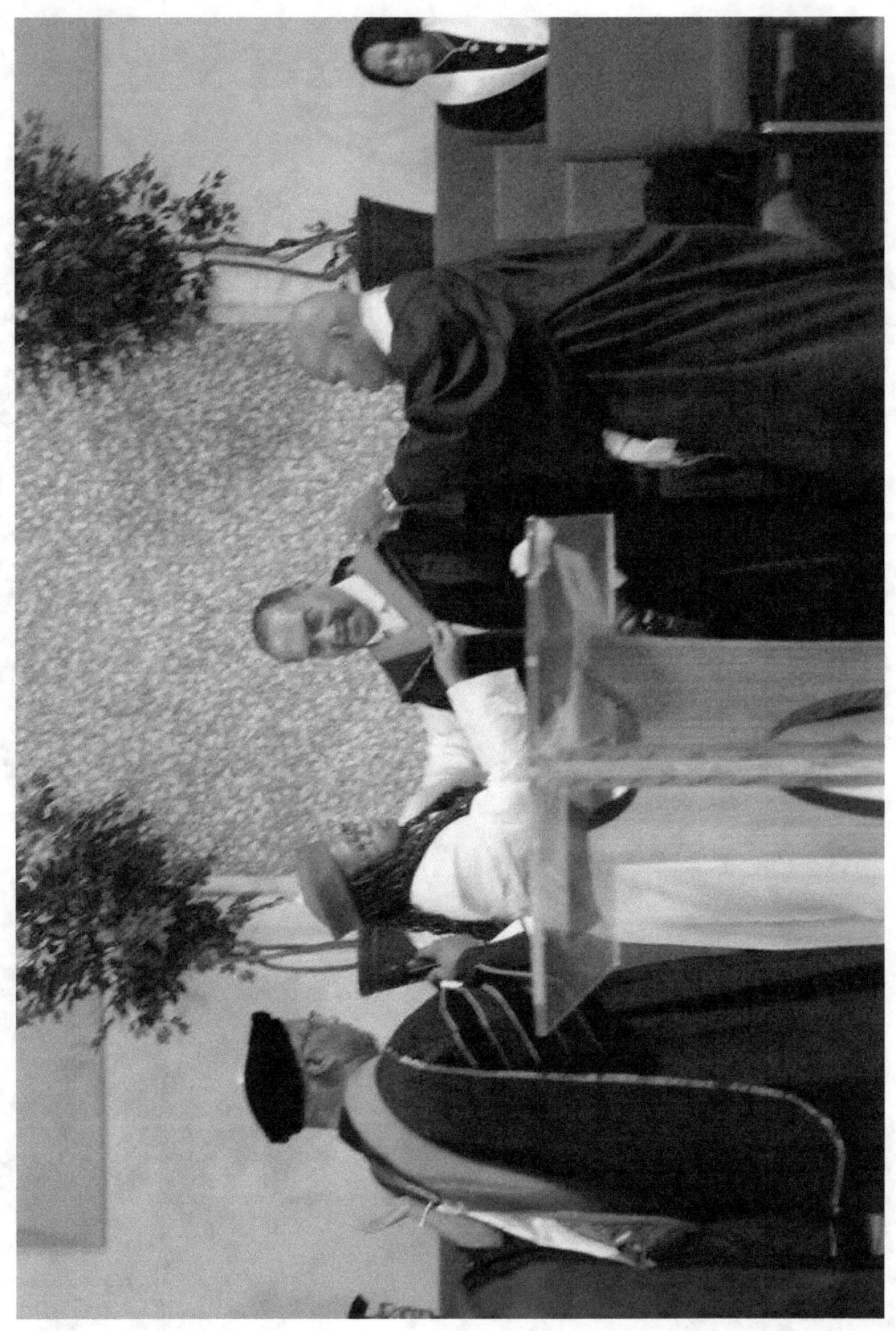

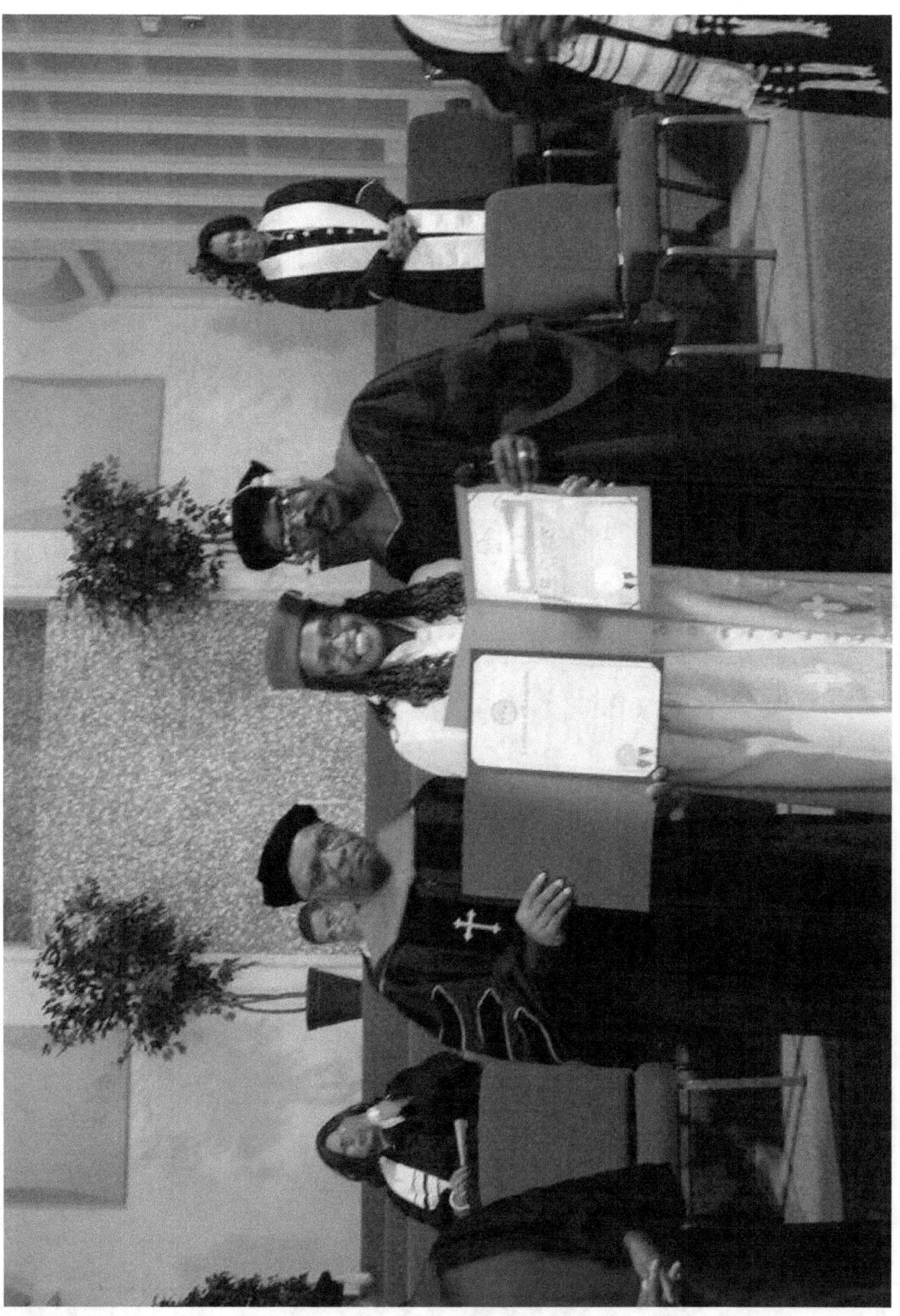

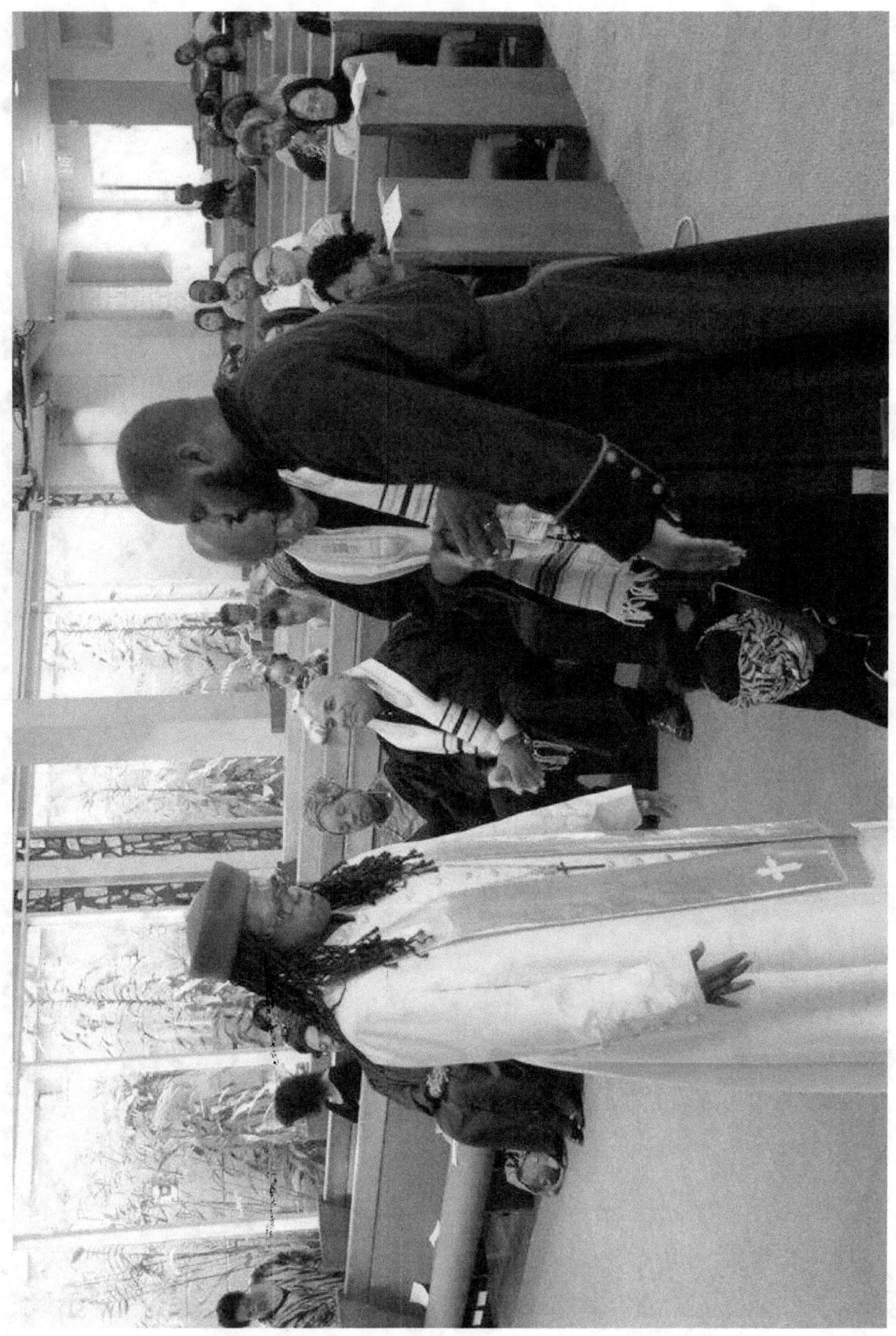

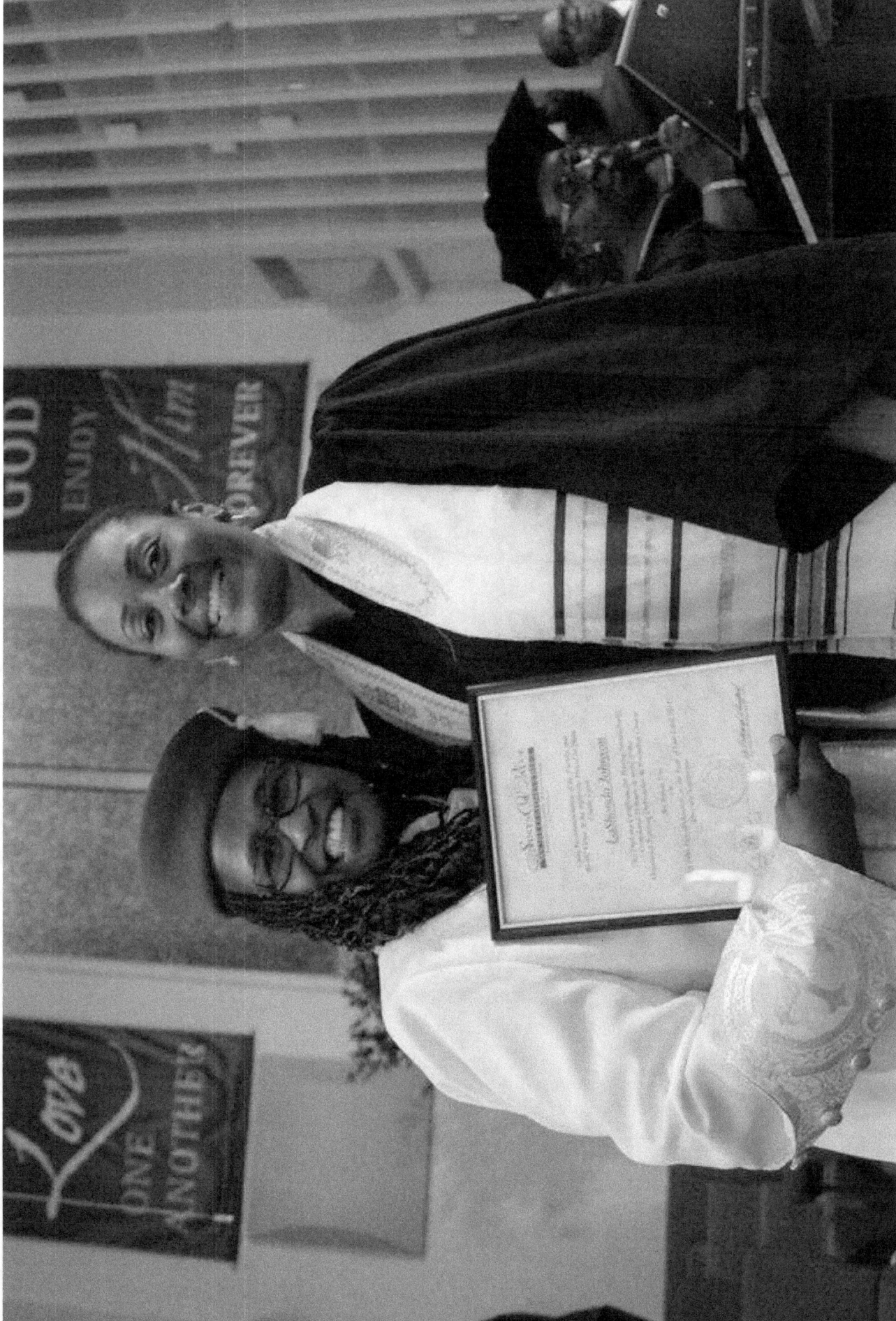

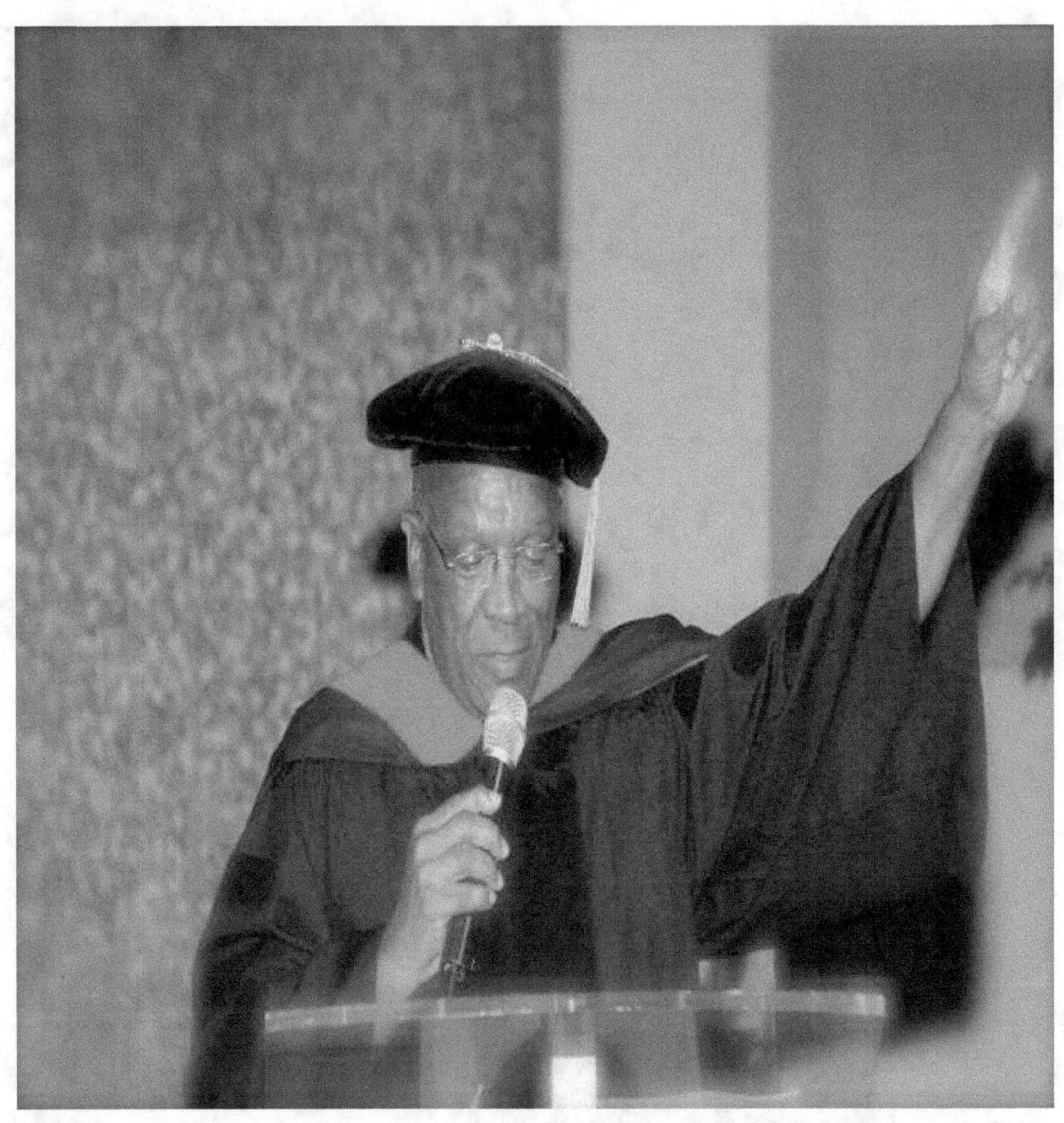

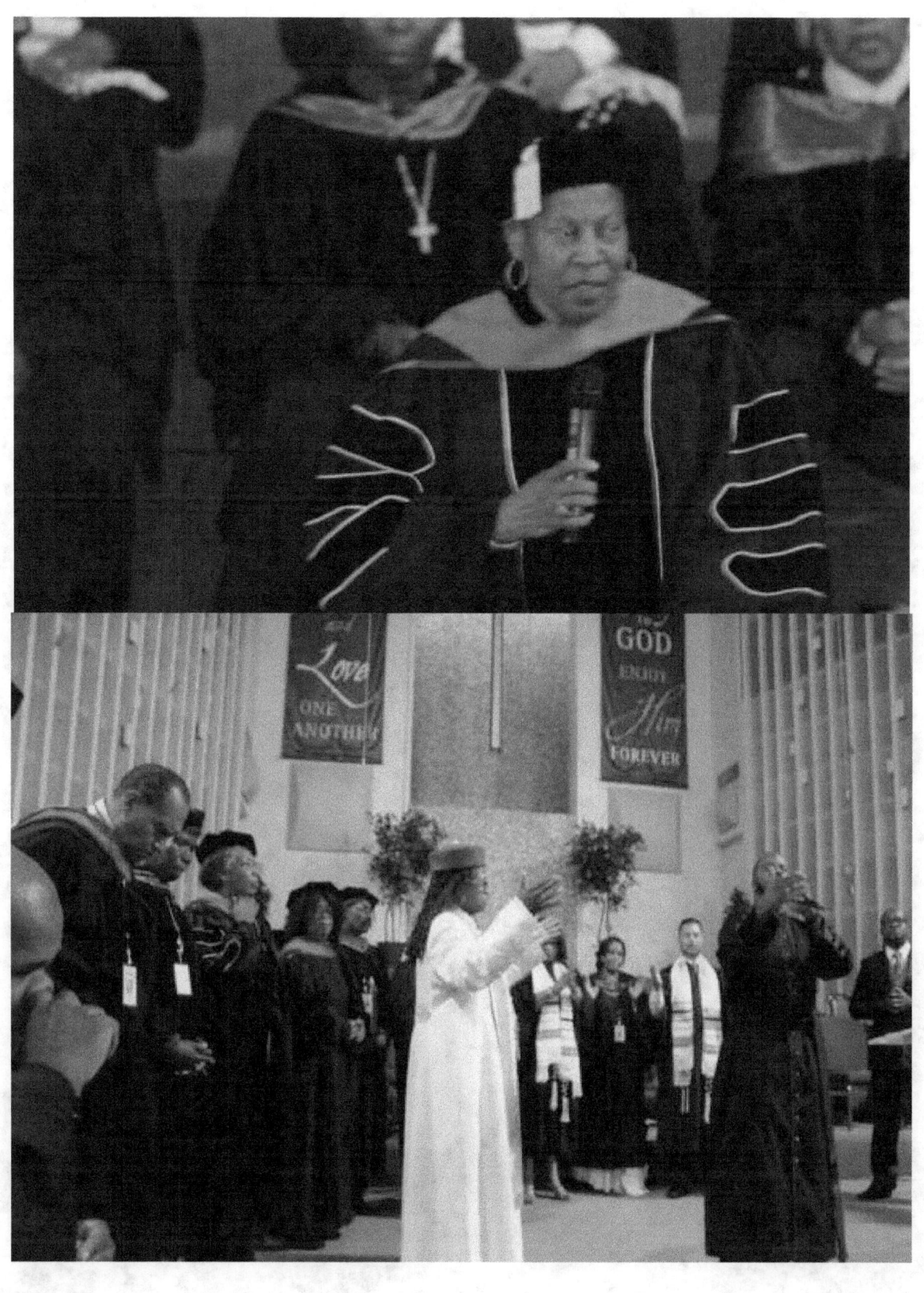

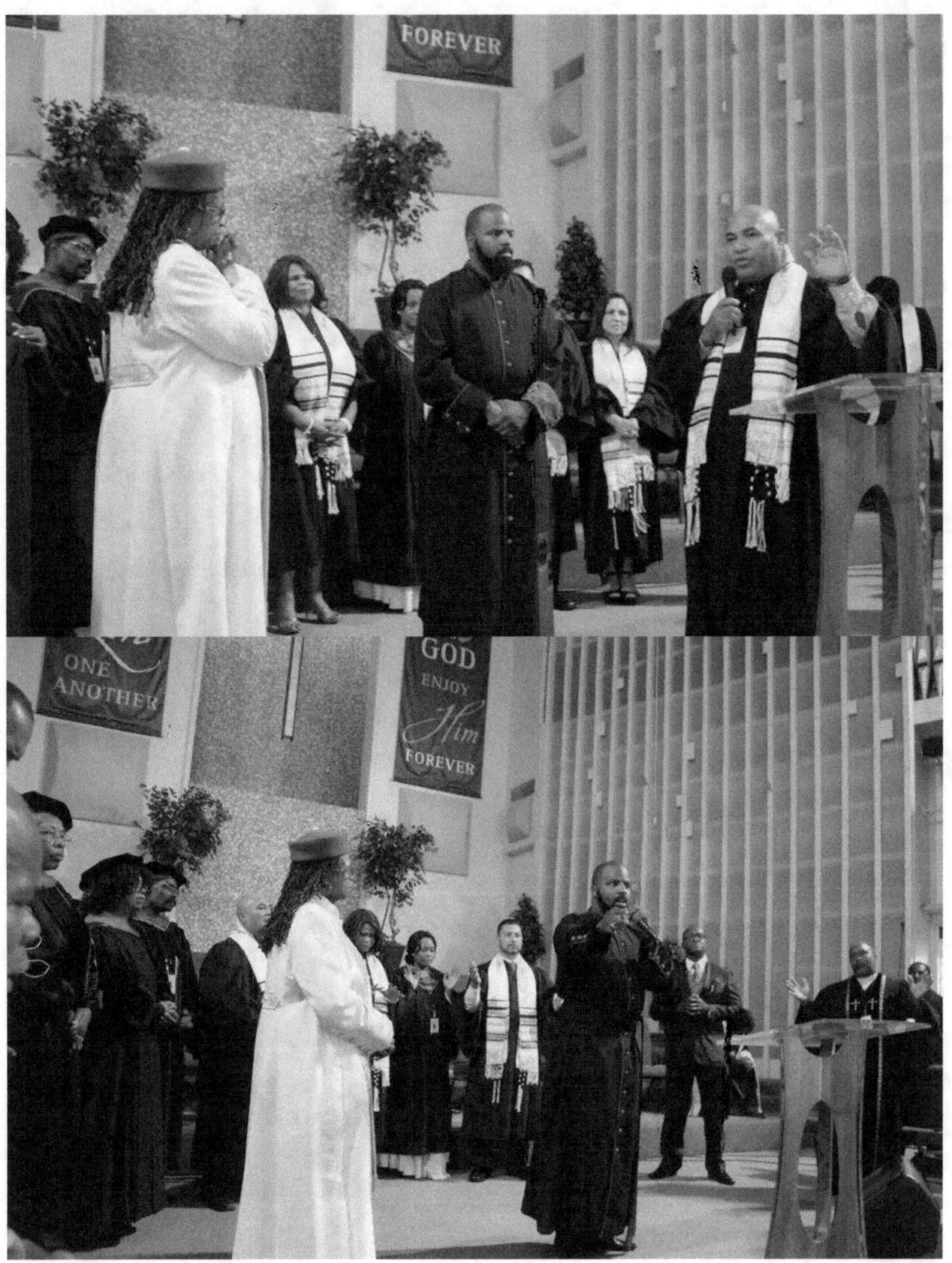

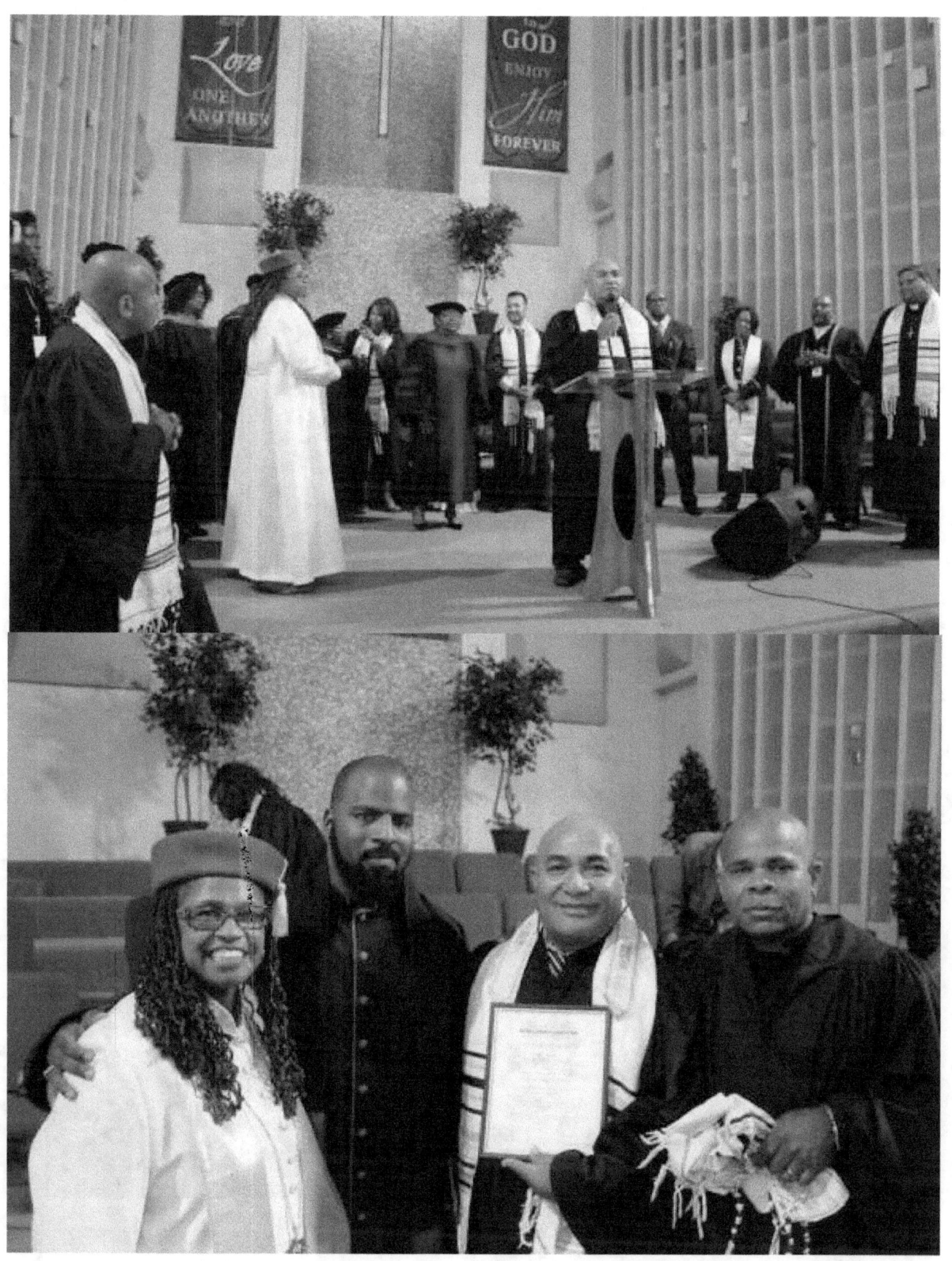

133

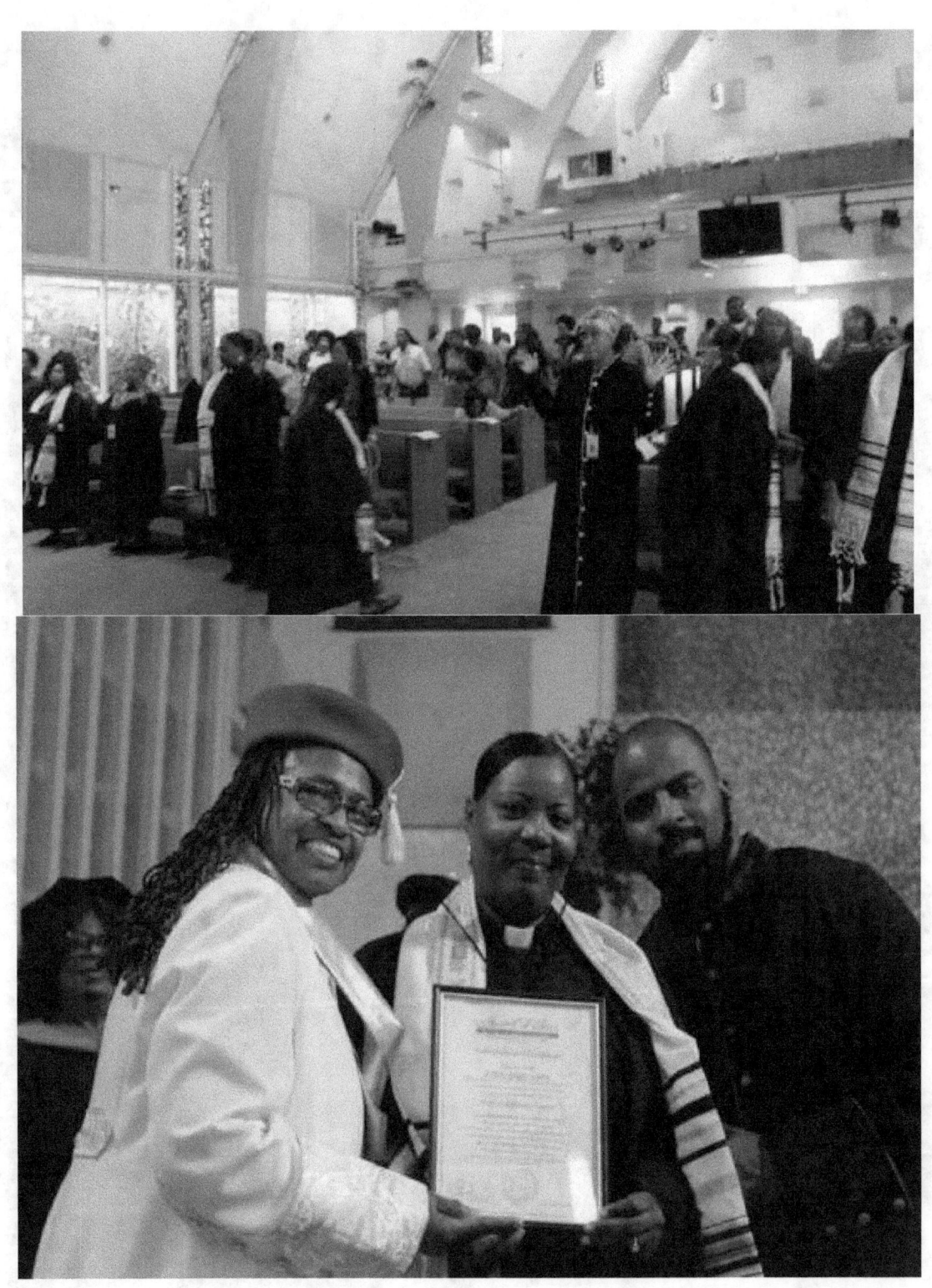

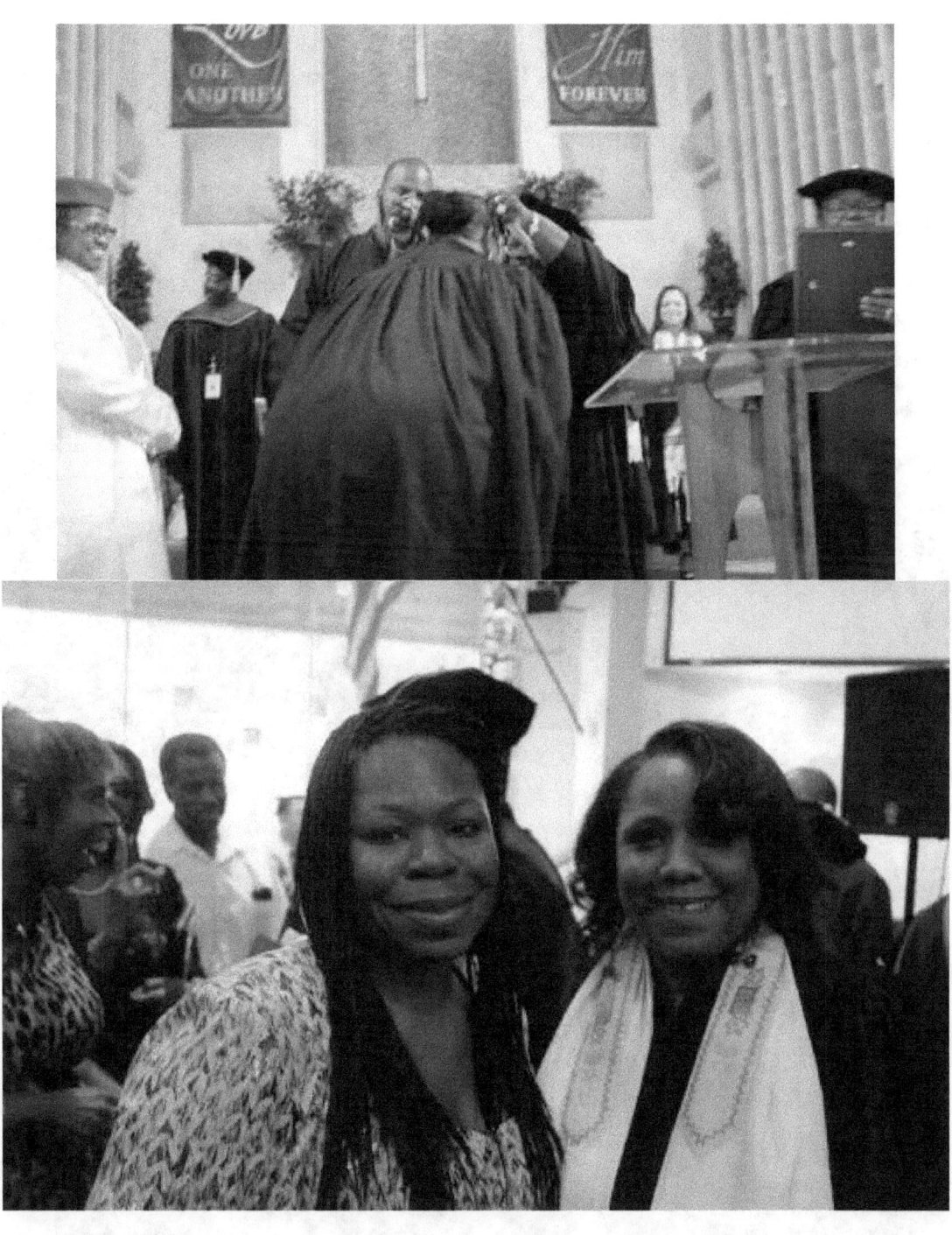

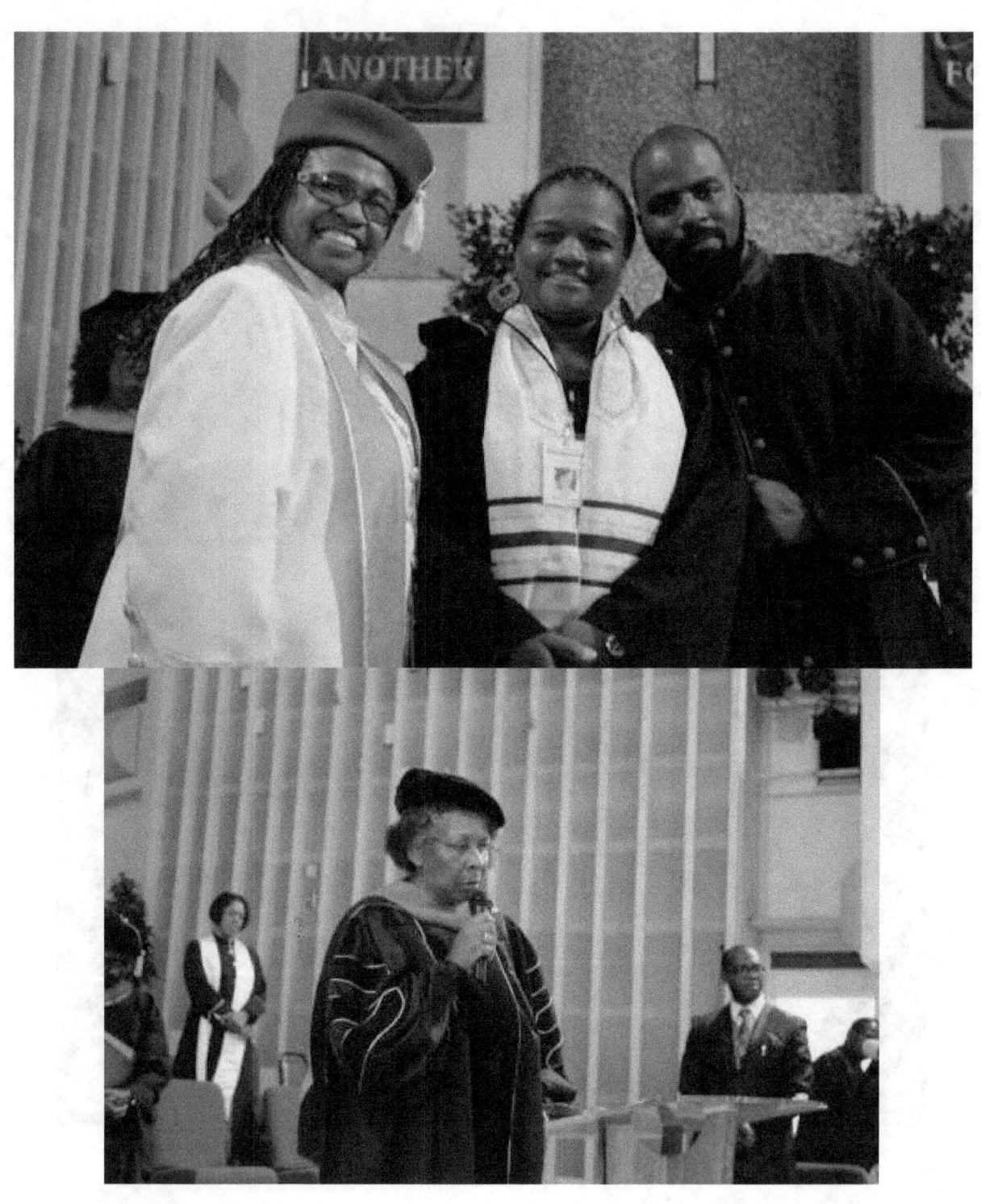

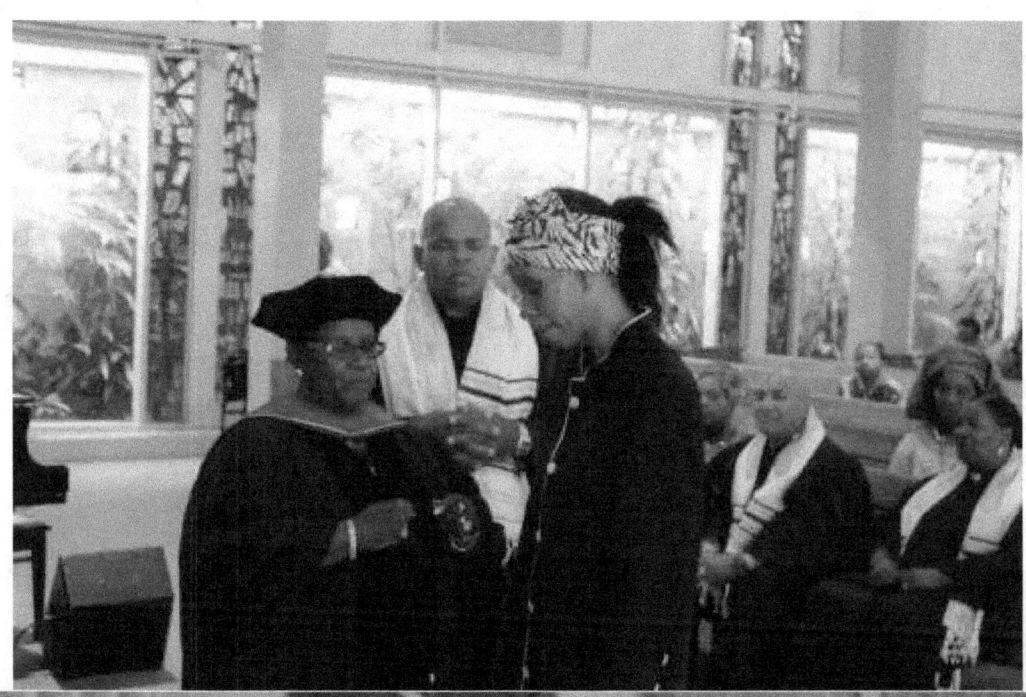

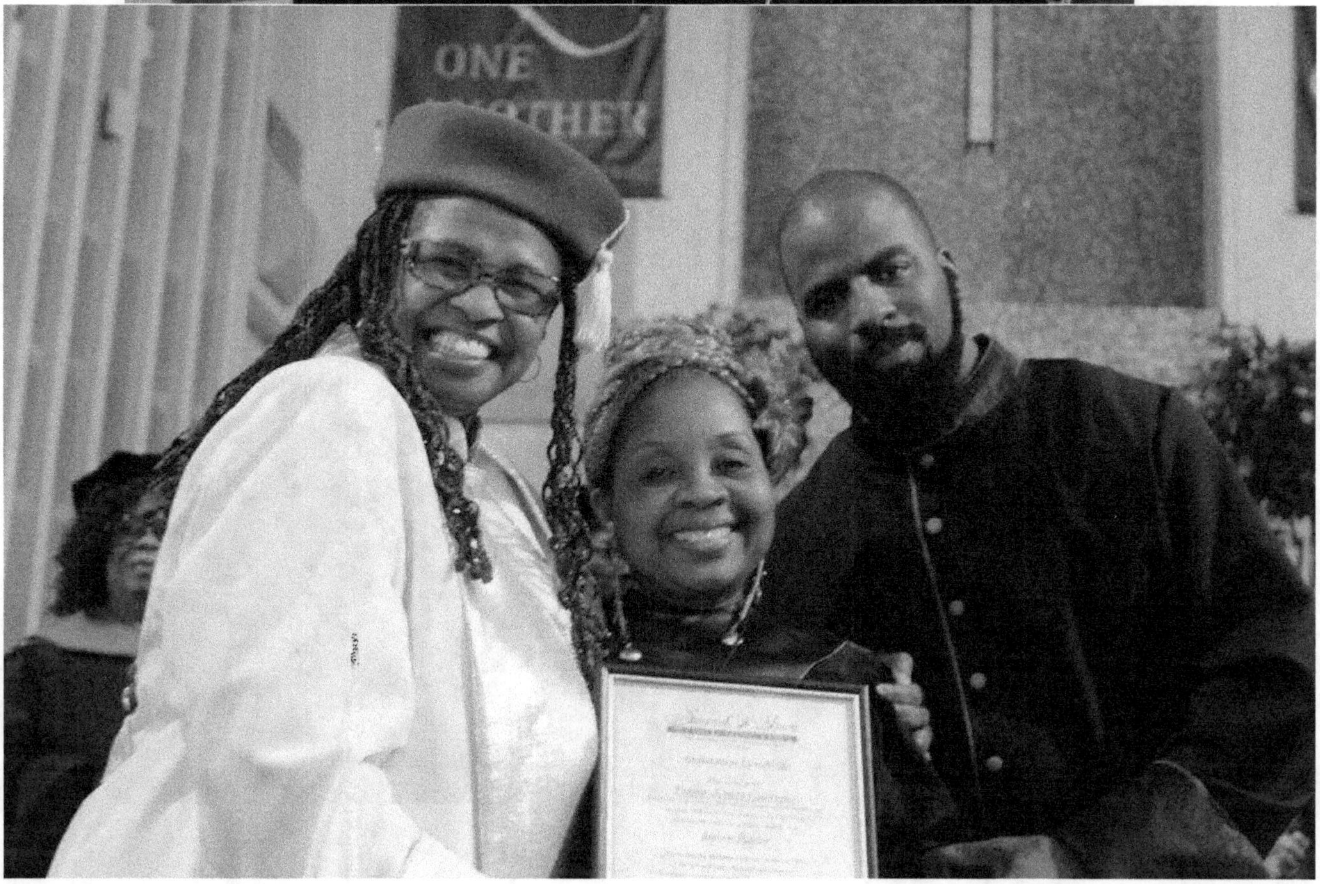

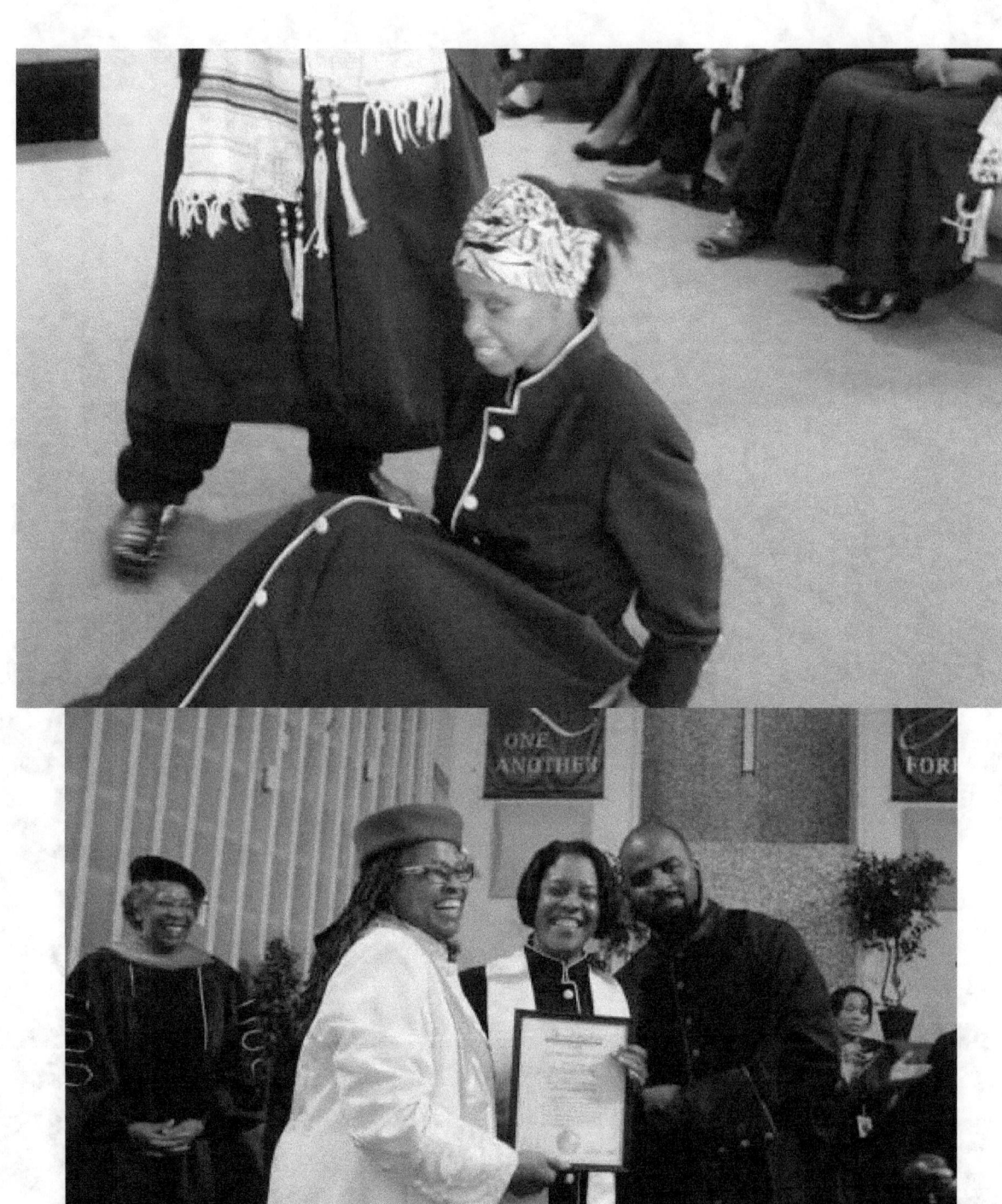

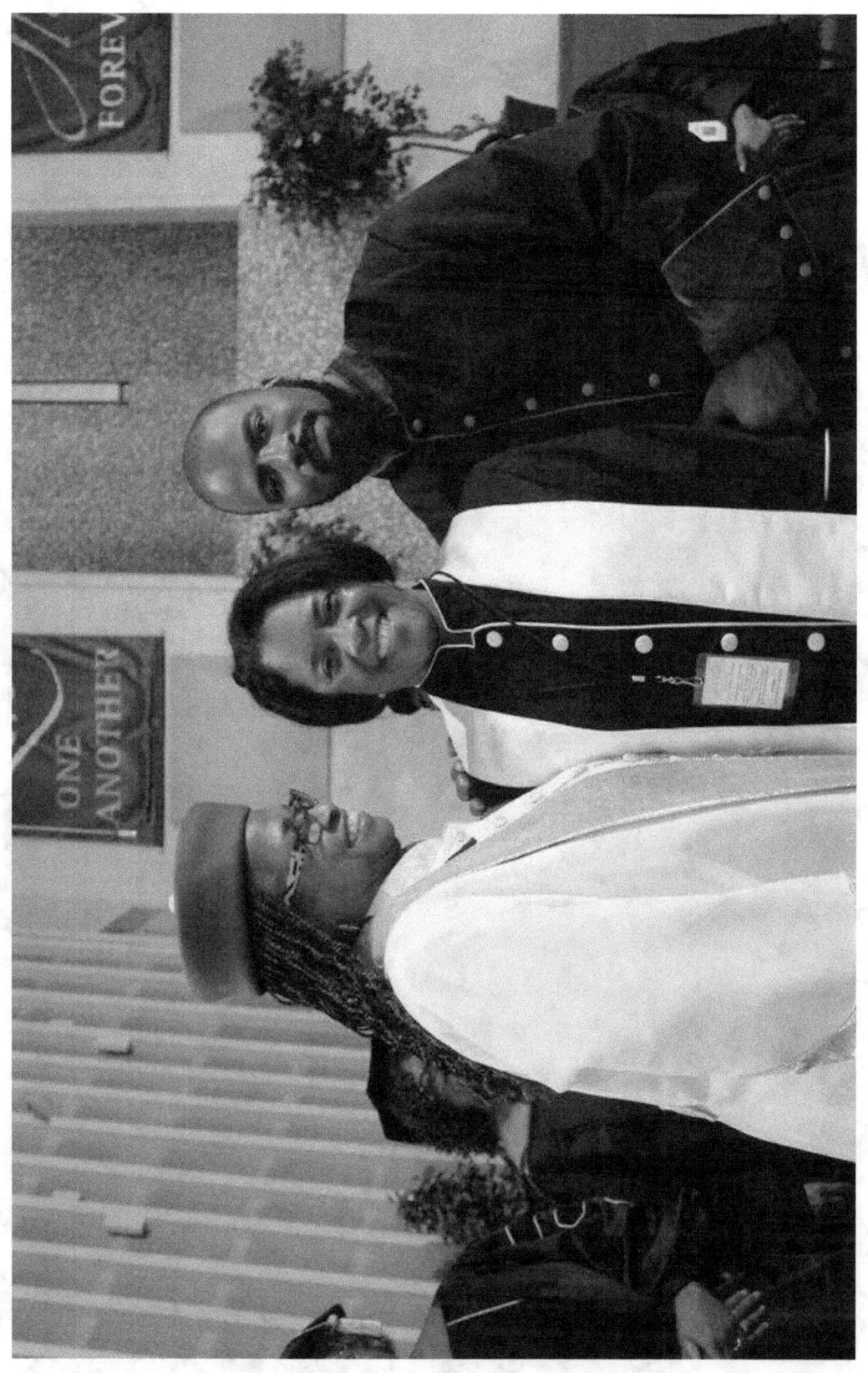

139

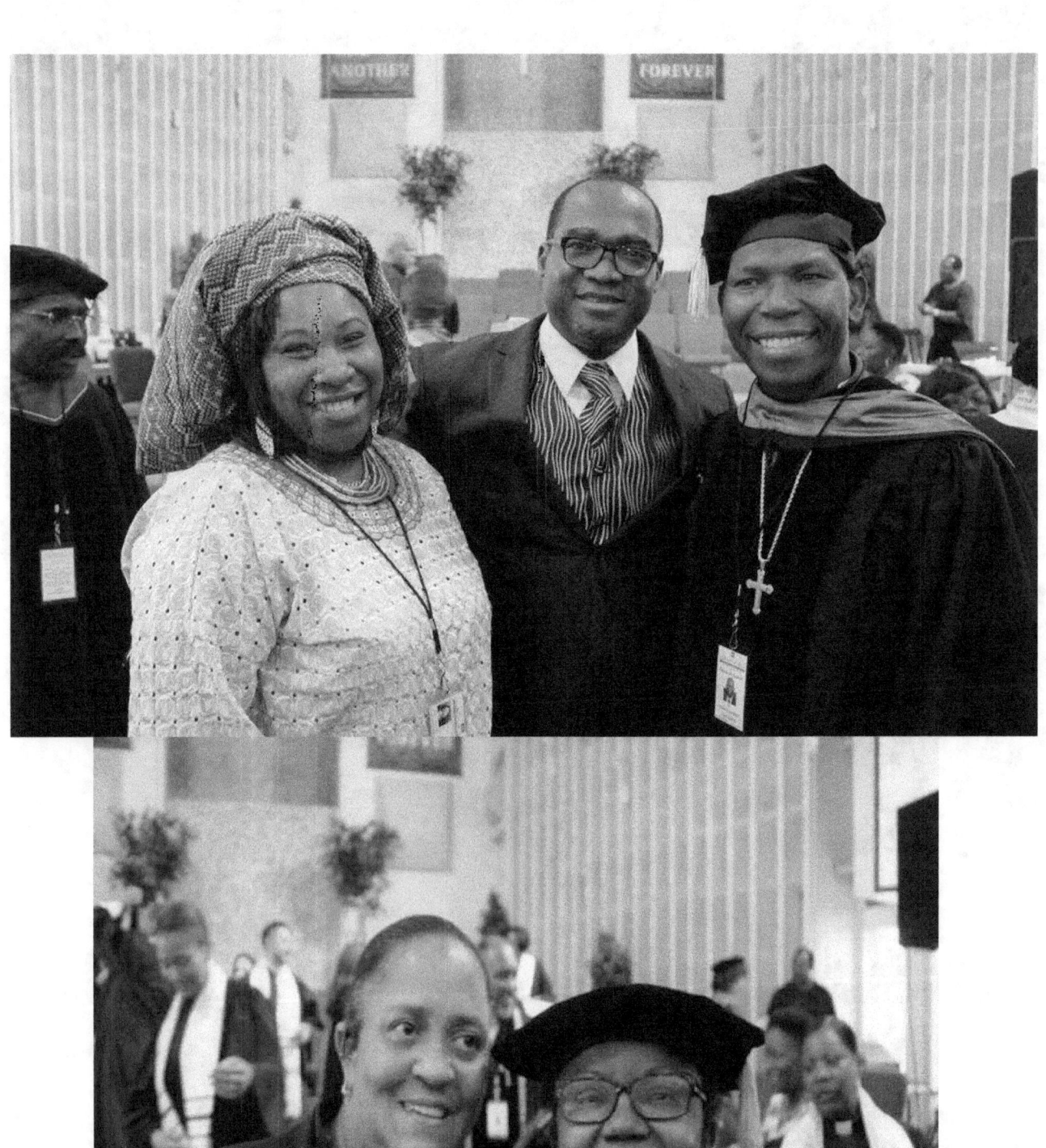

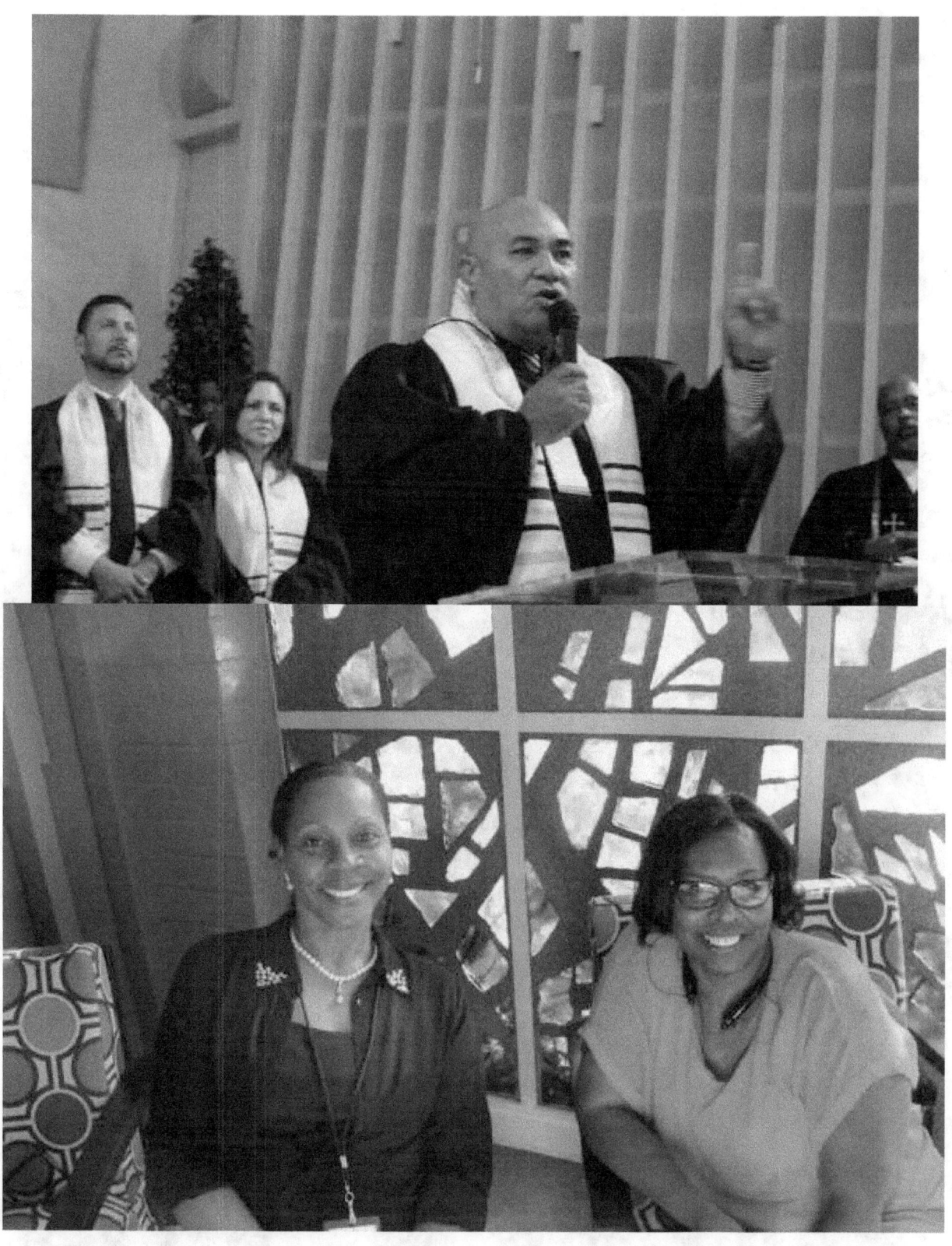

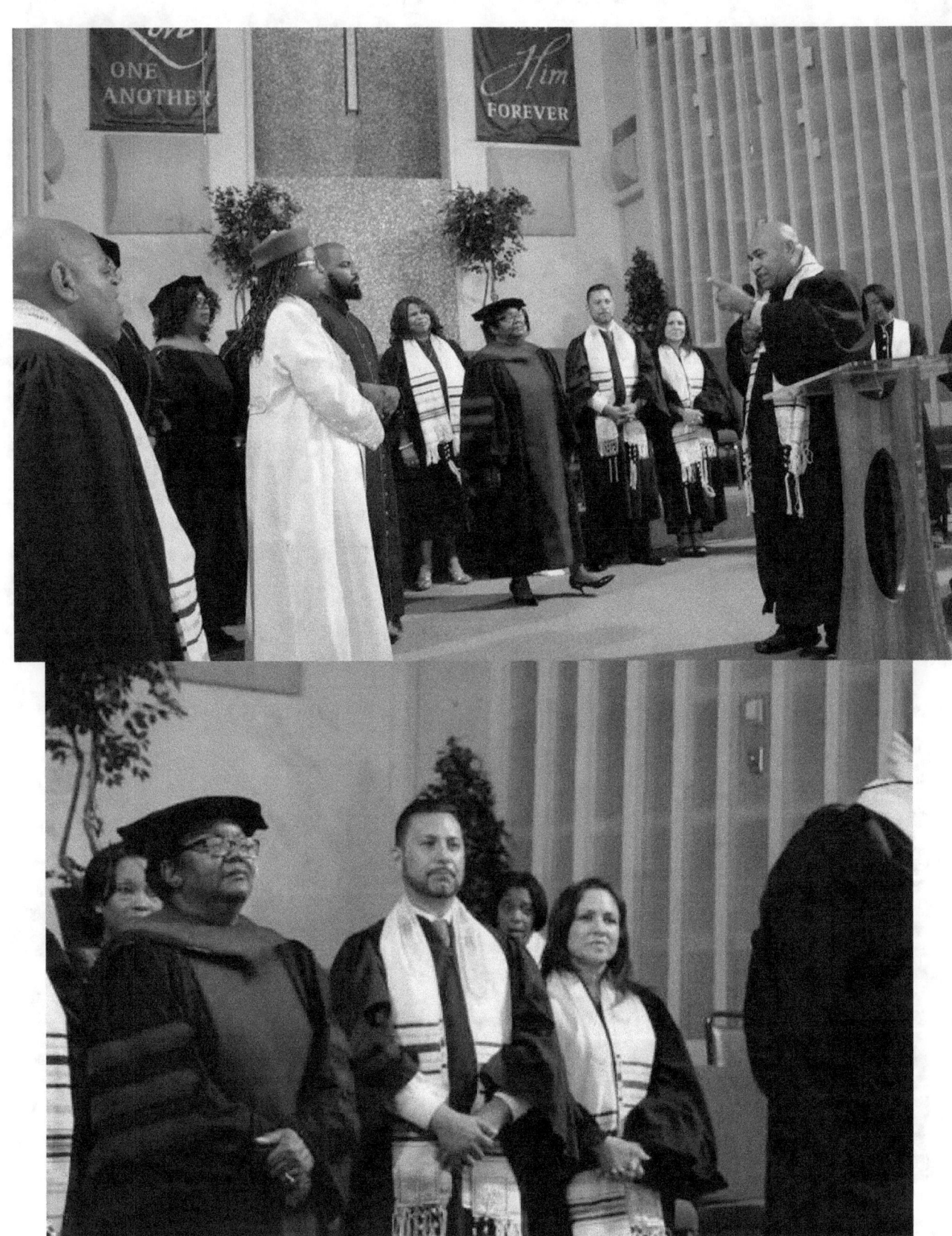

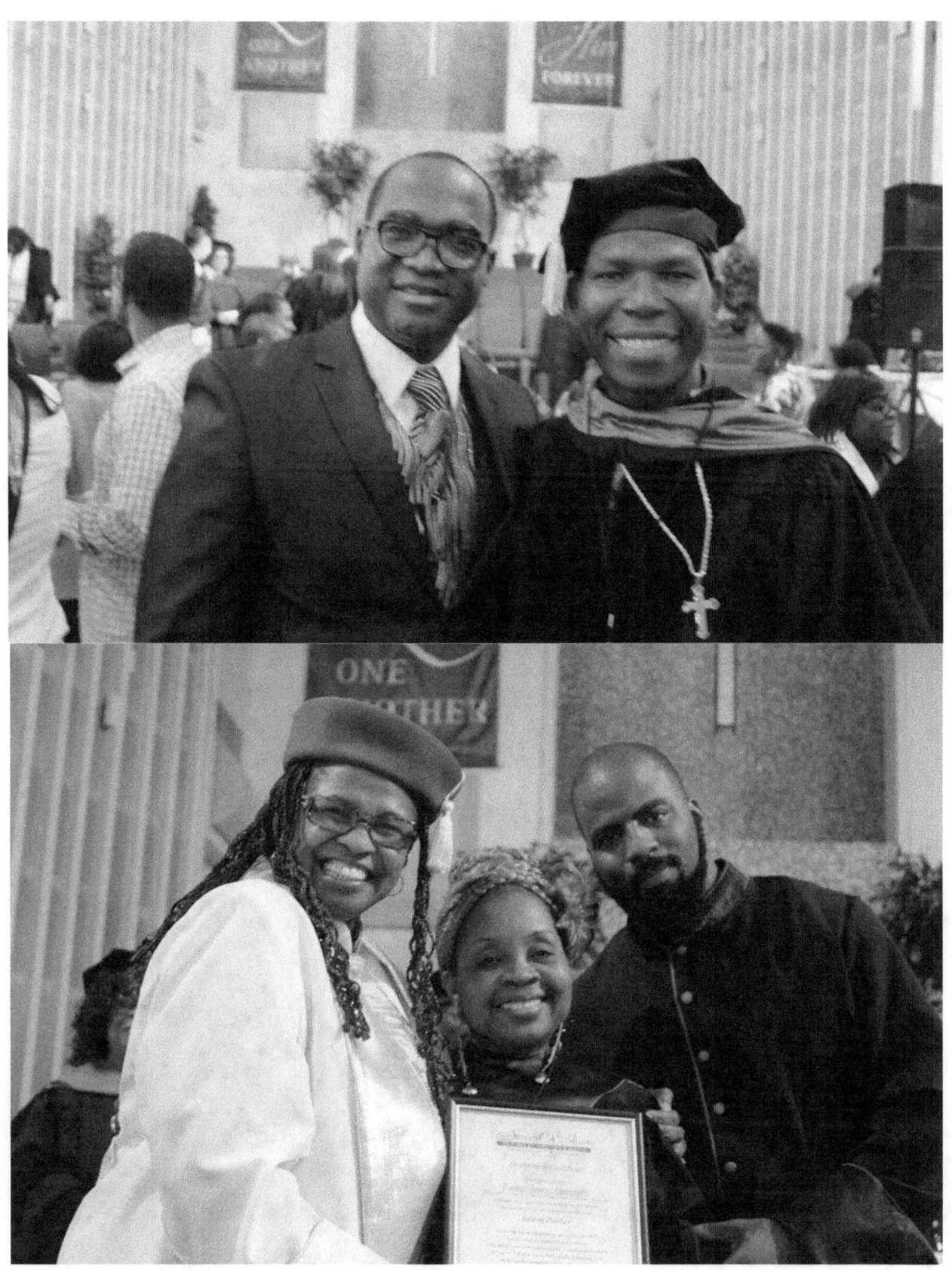

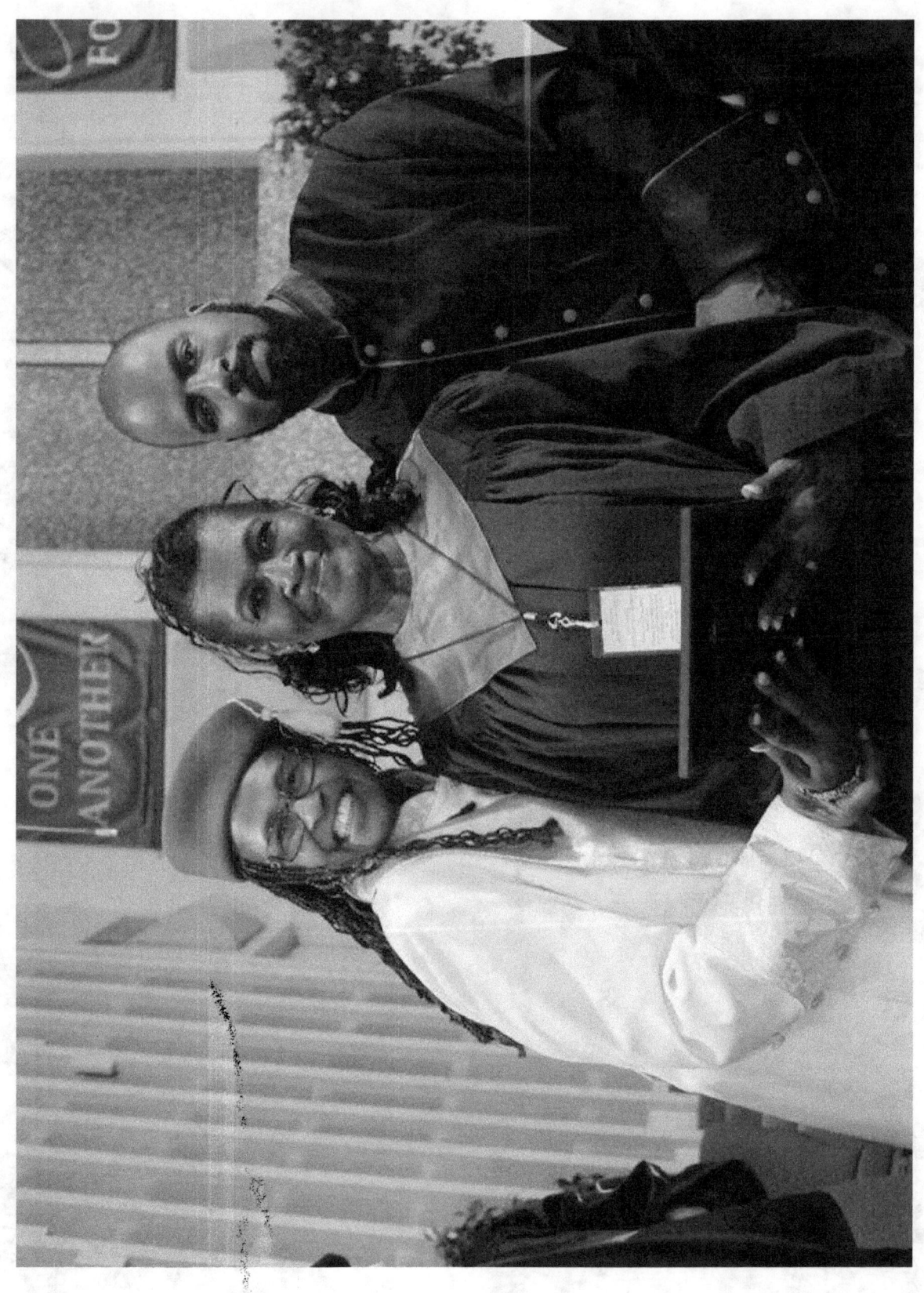

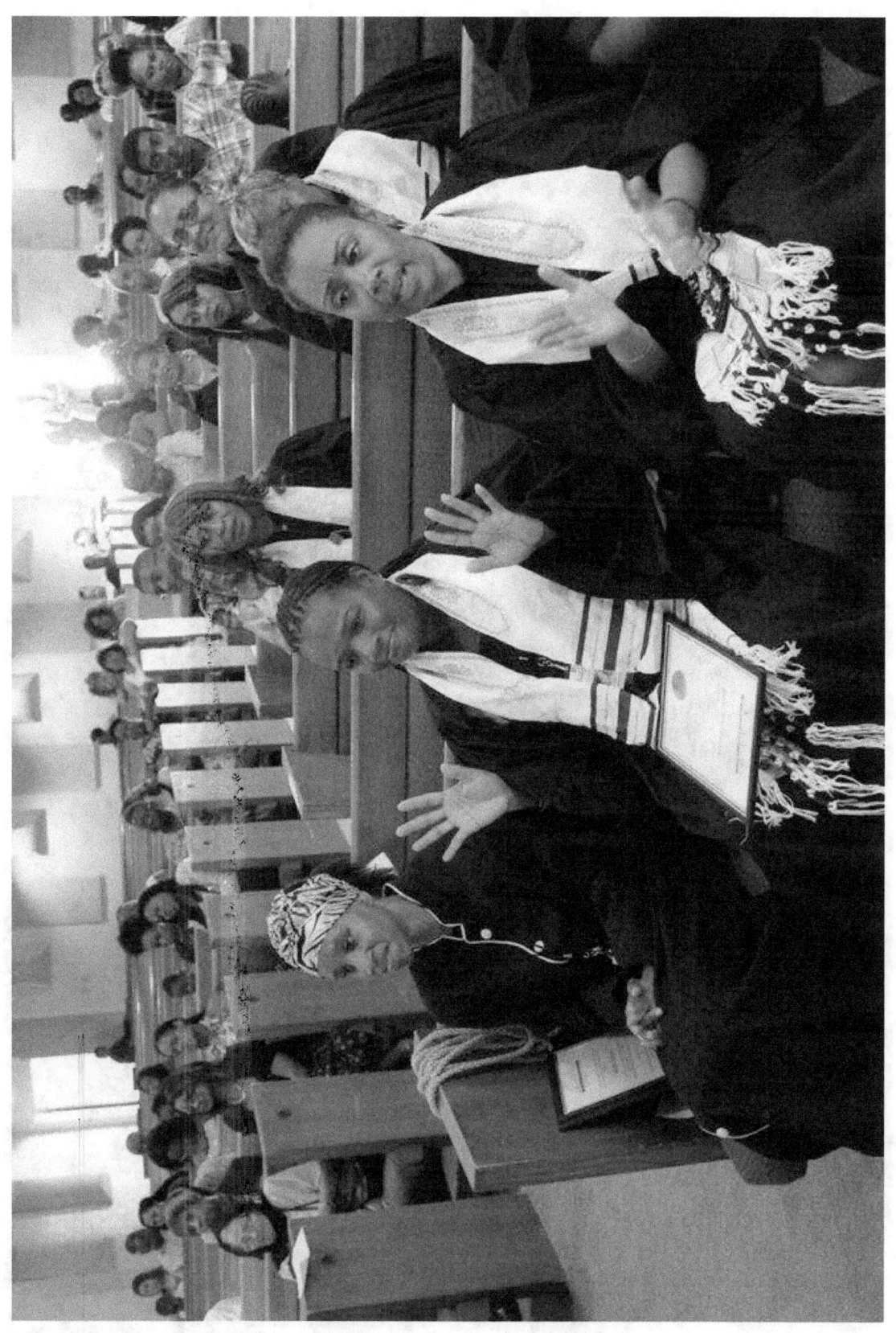

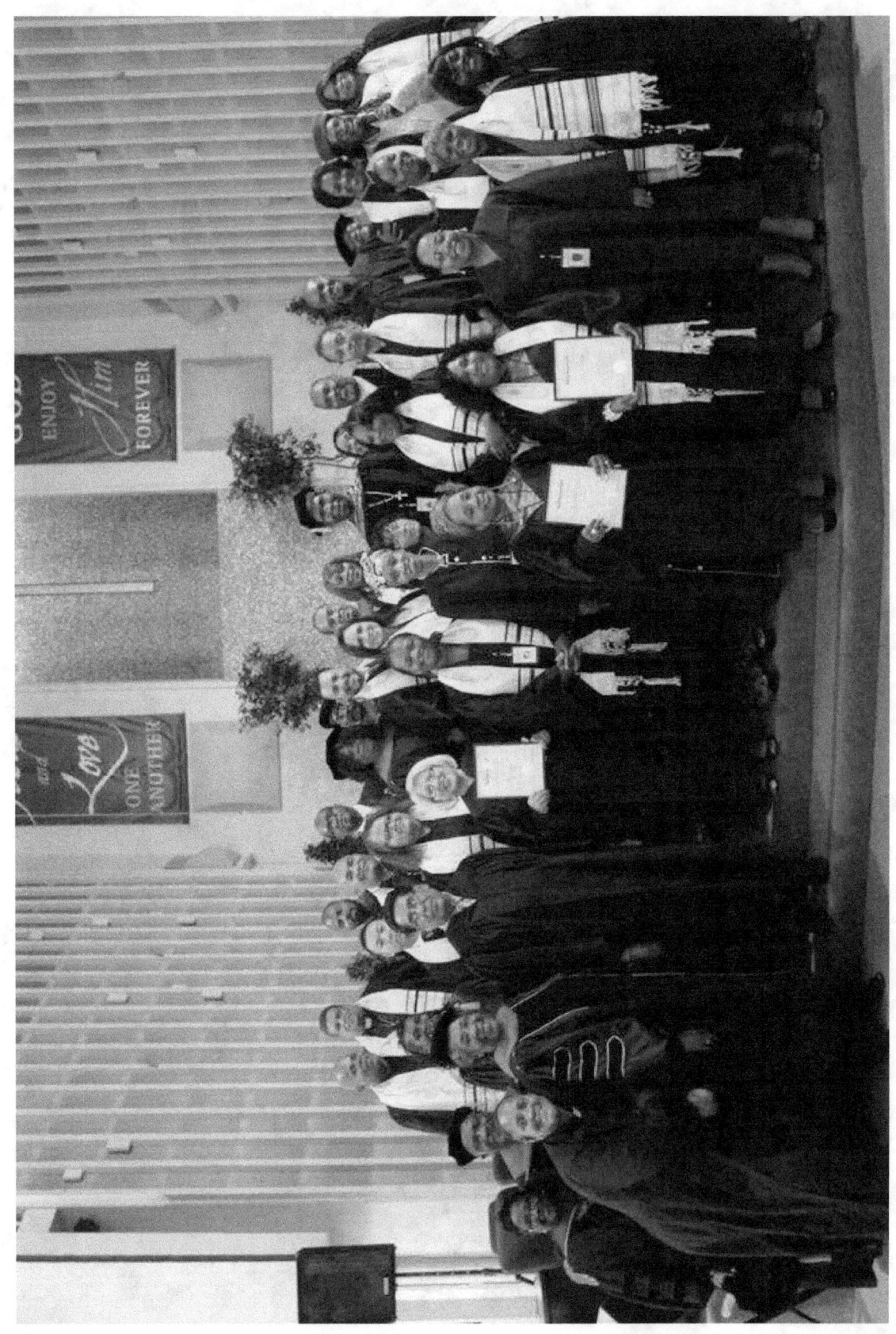

146

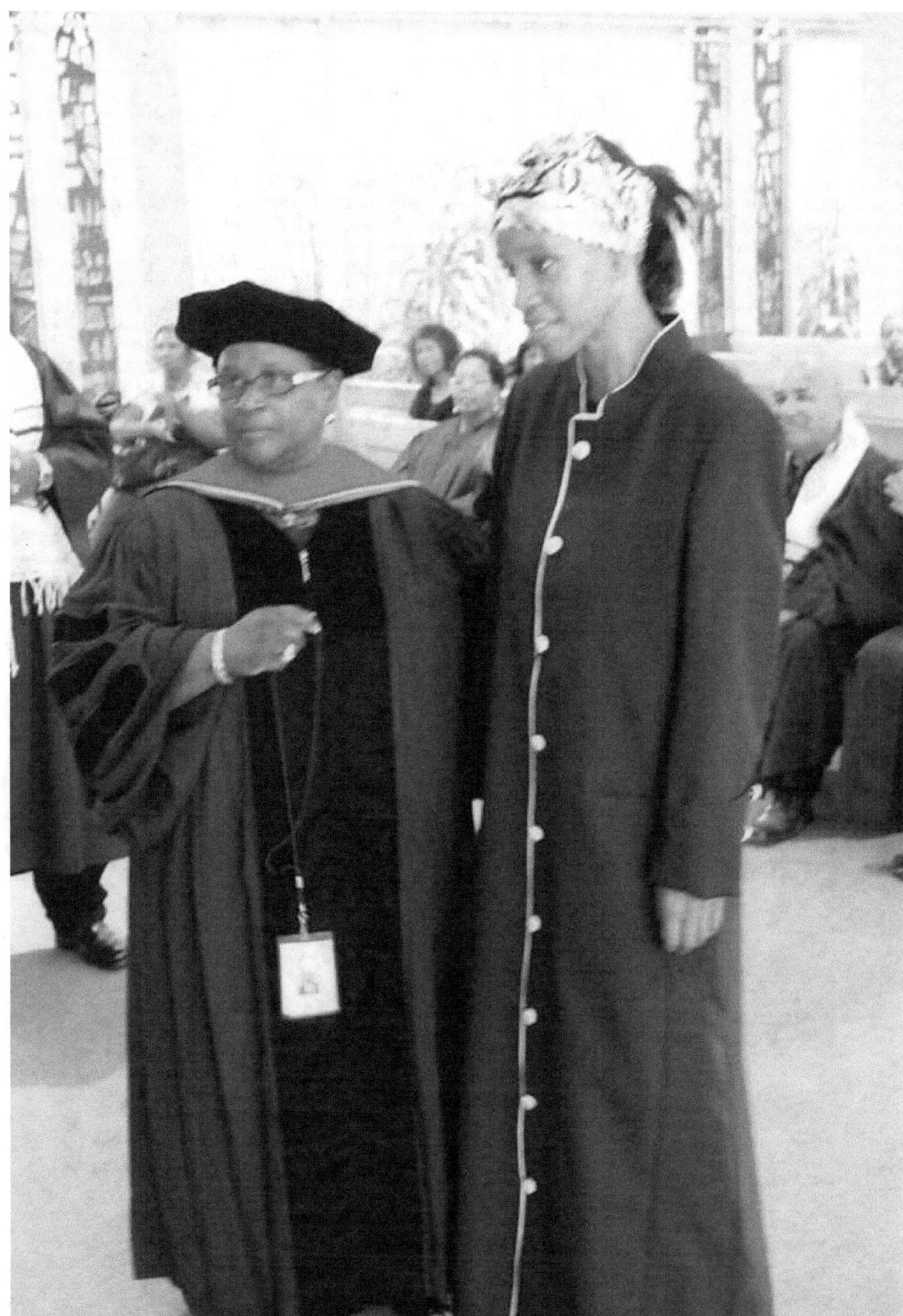

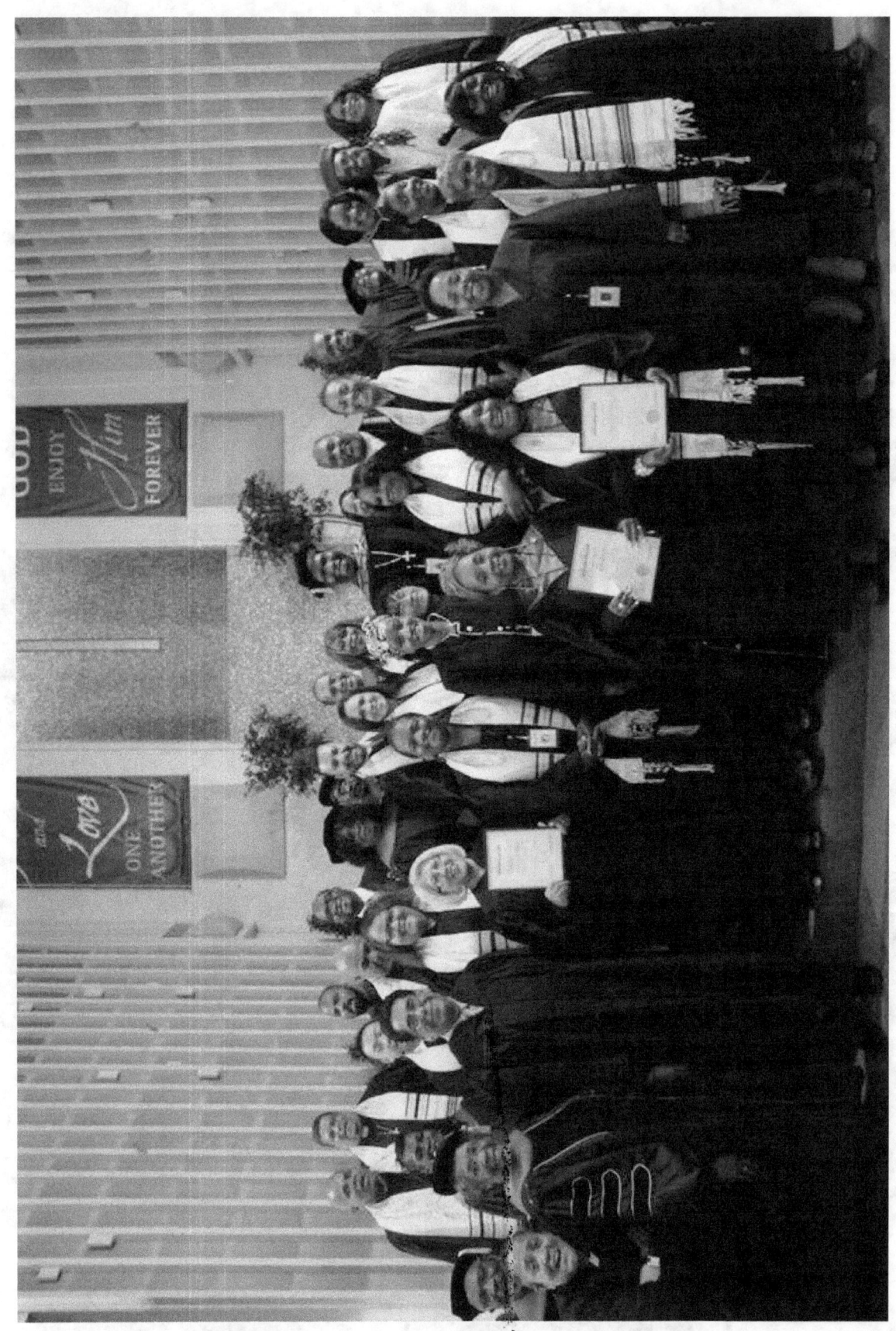

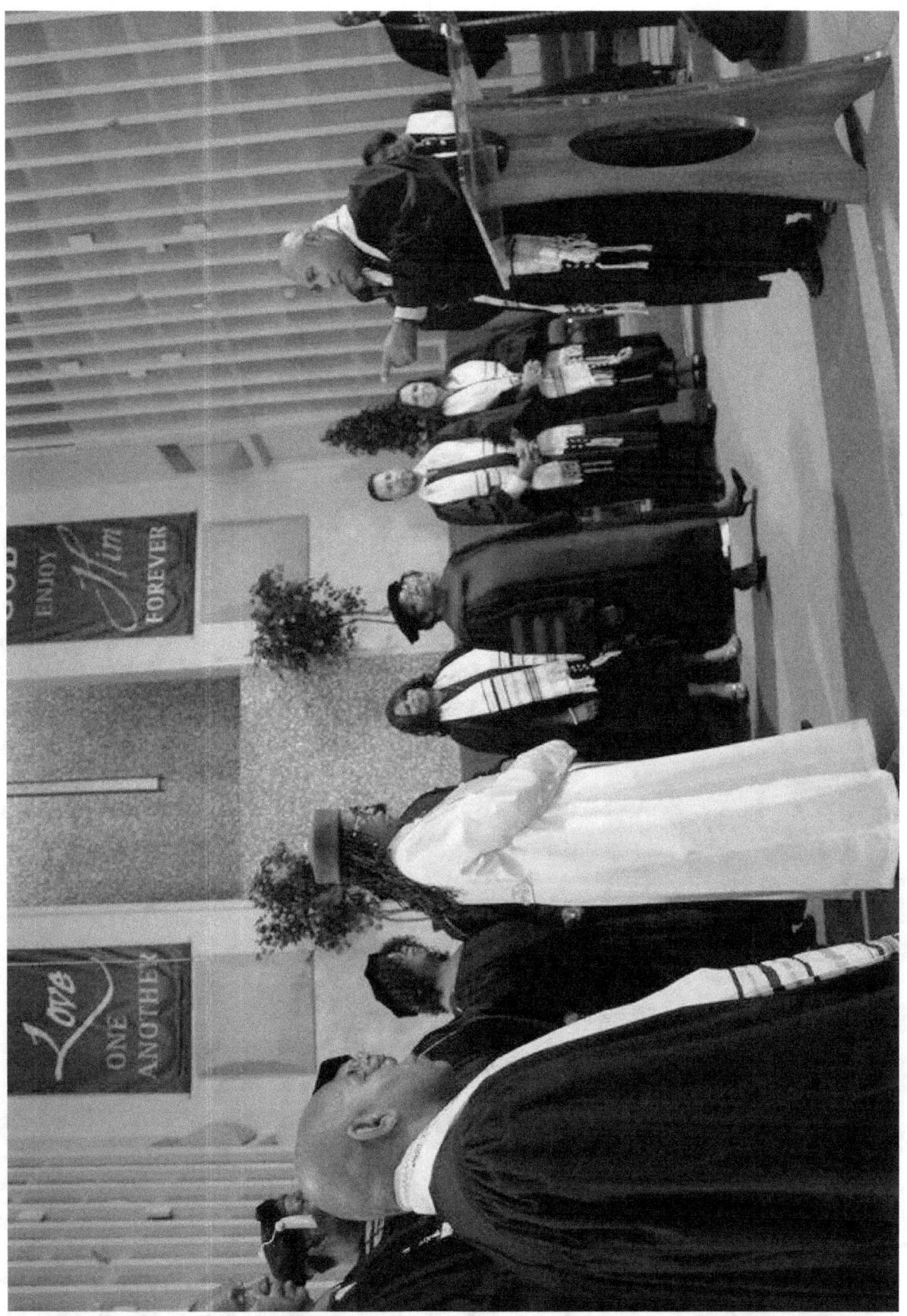

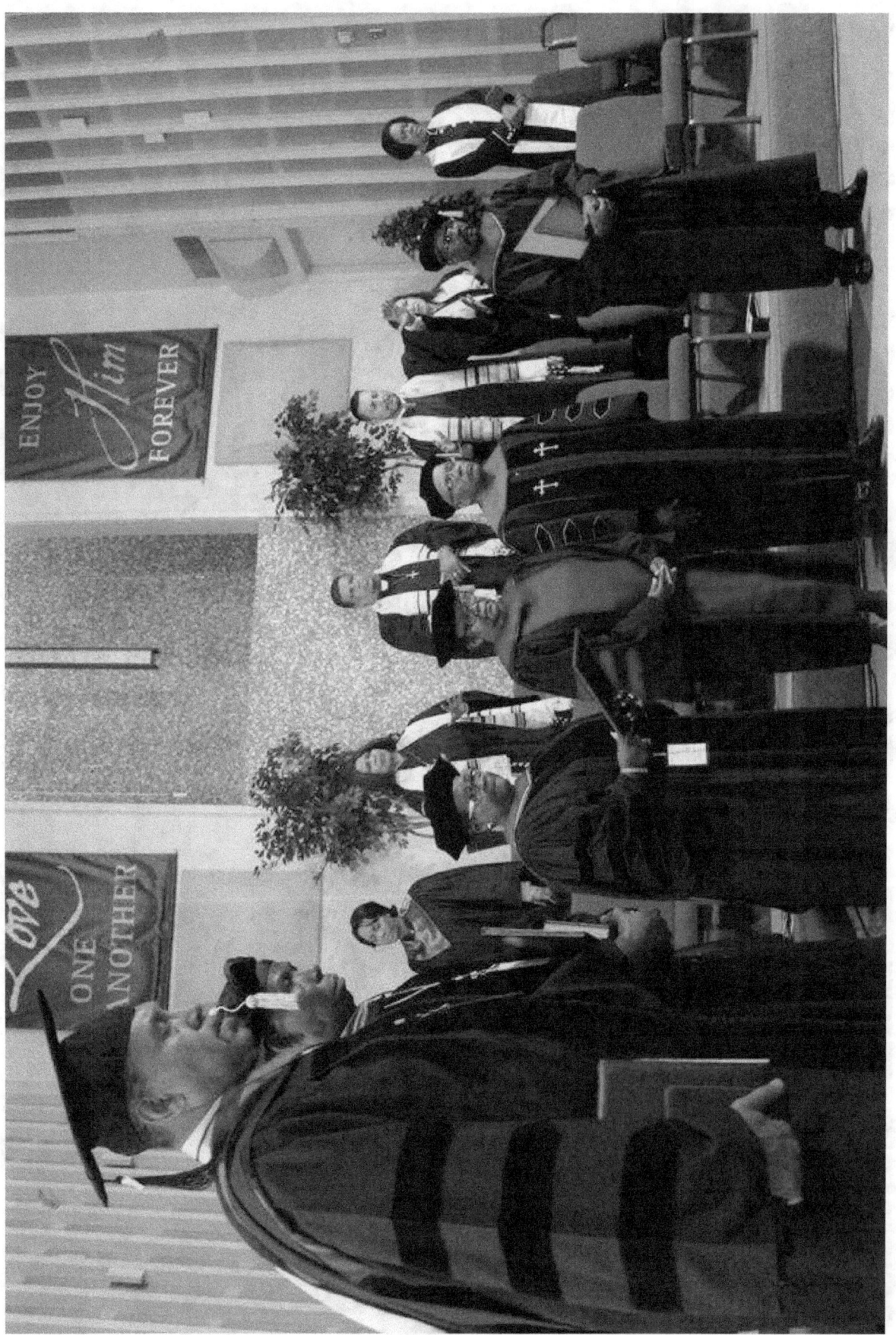

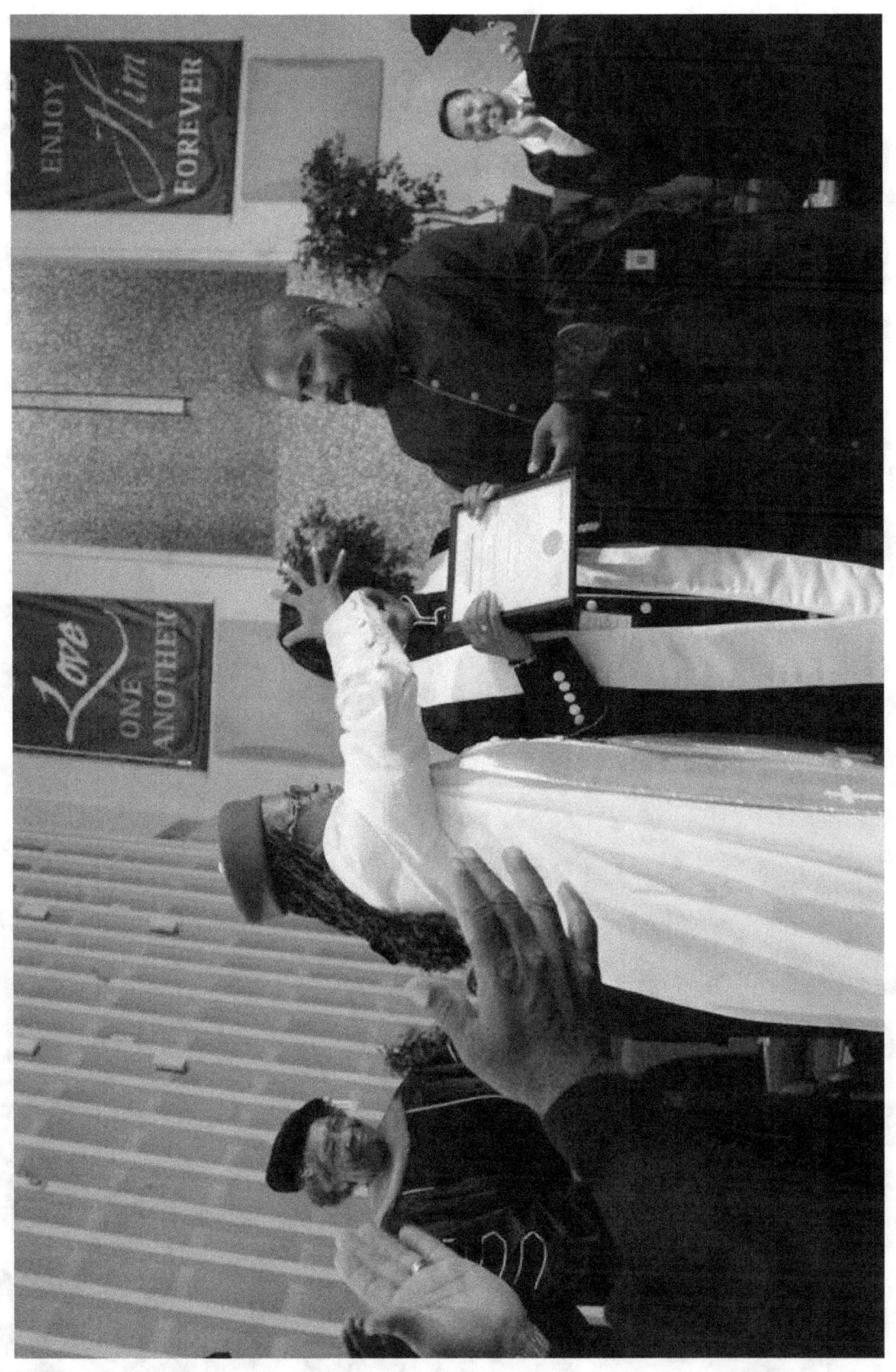

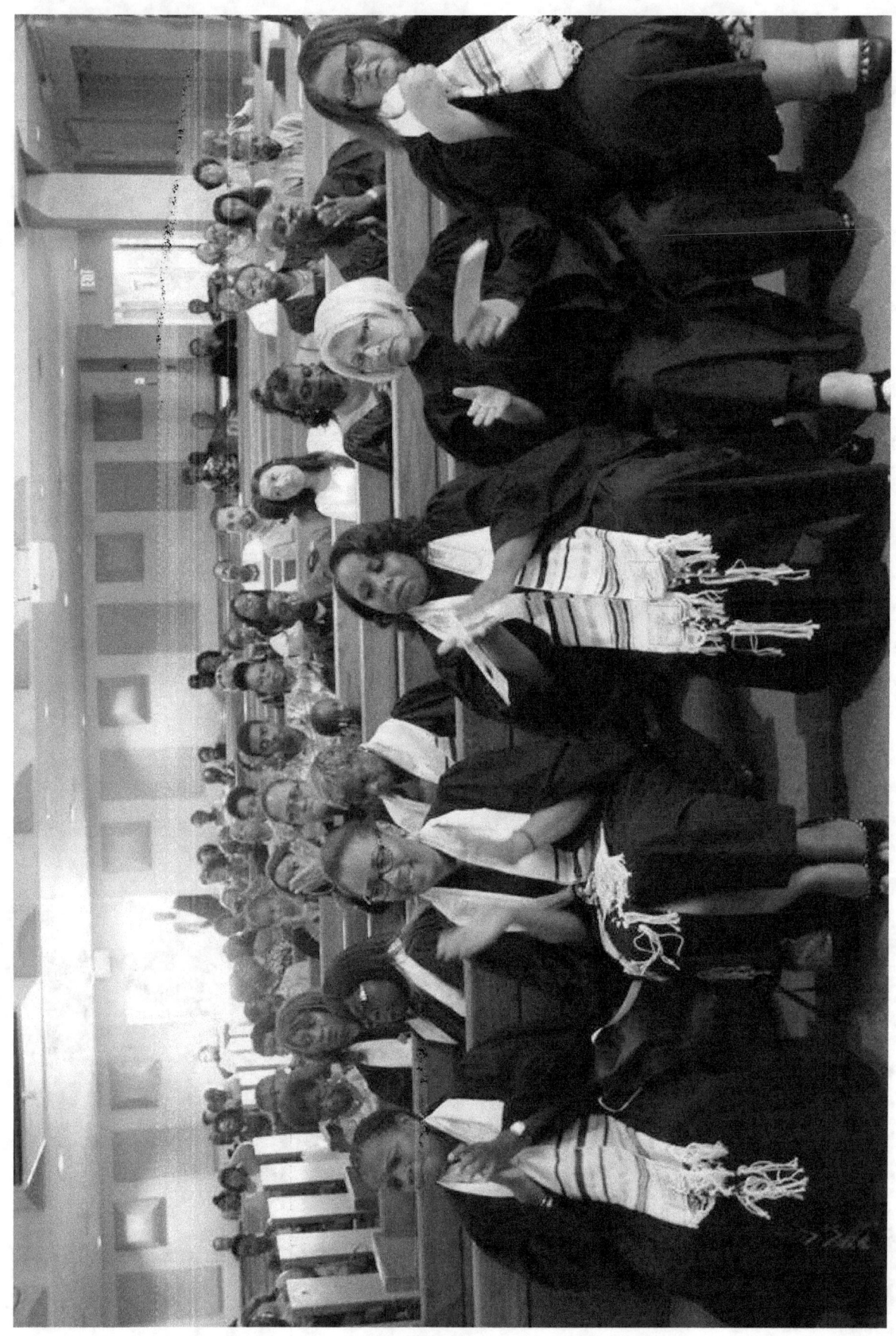

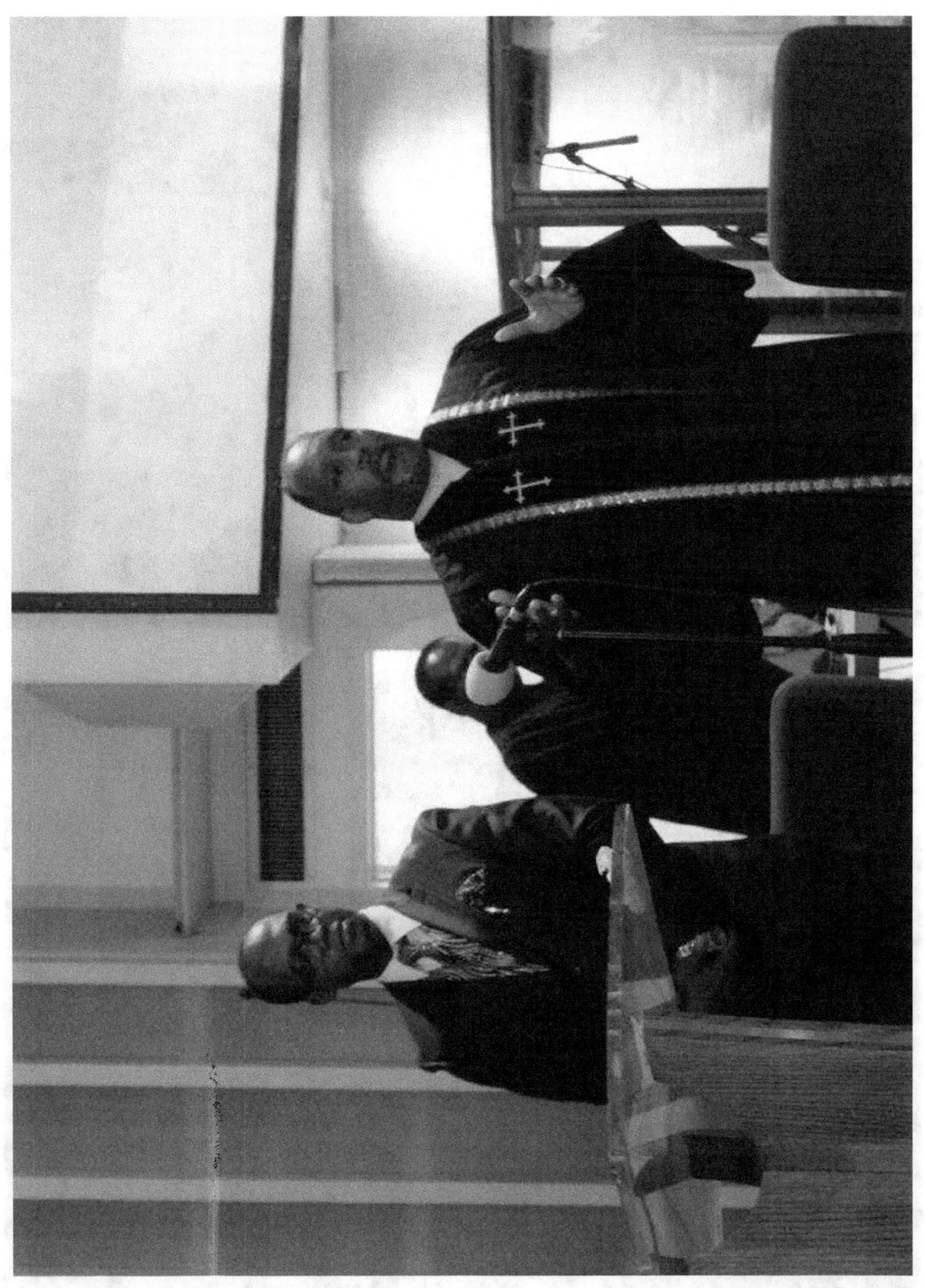

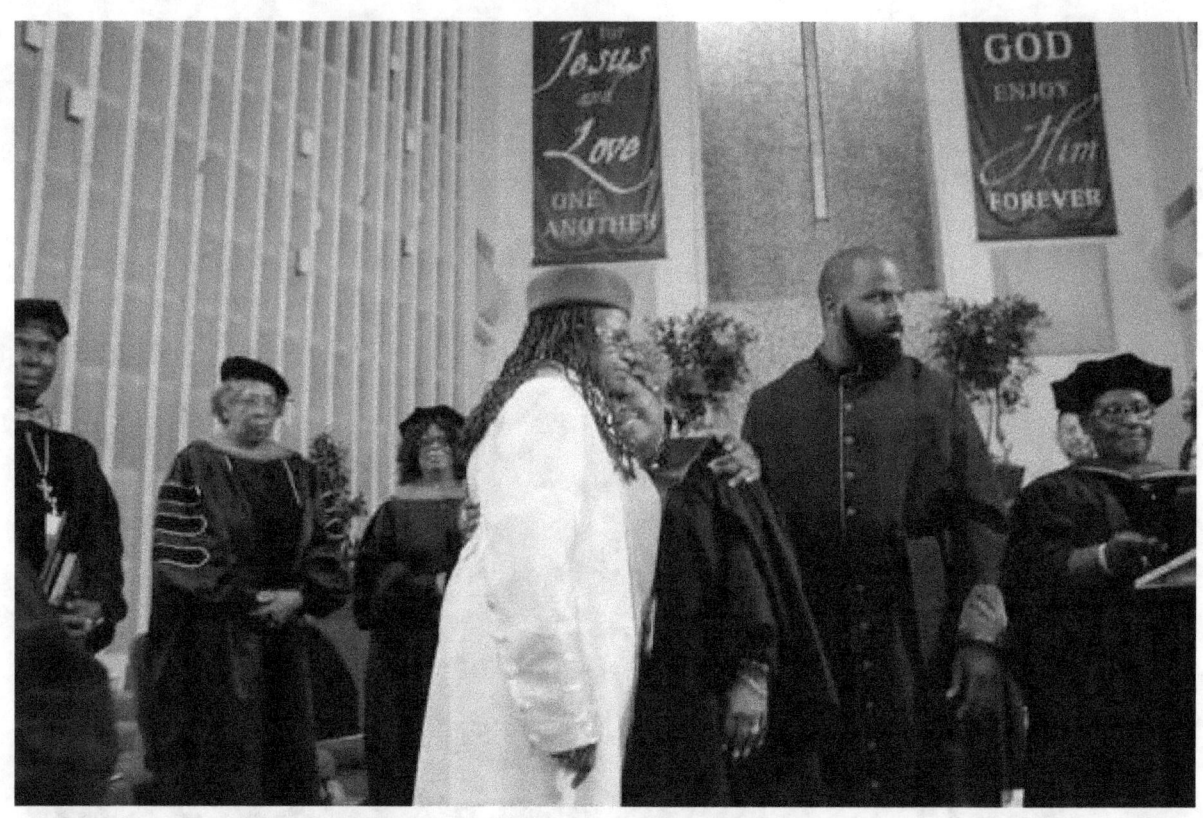

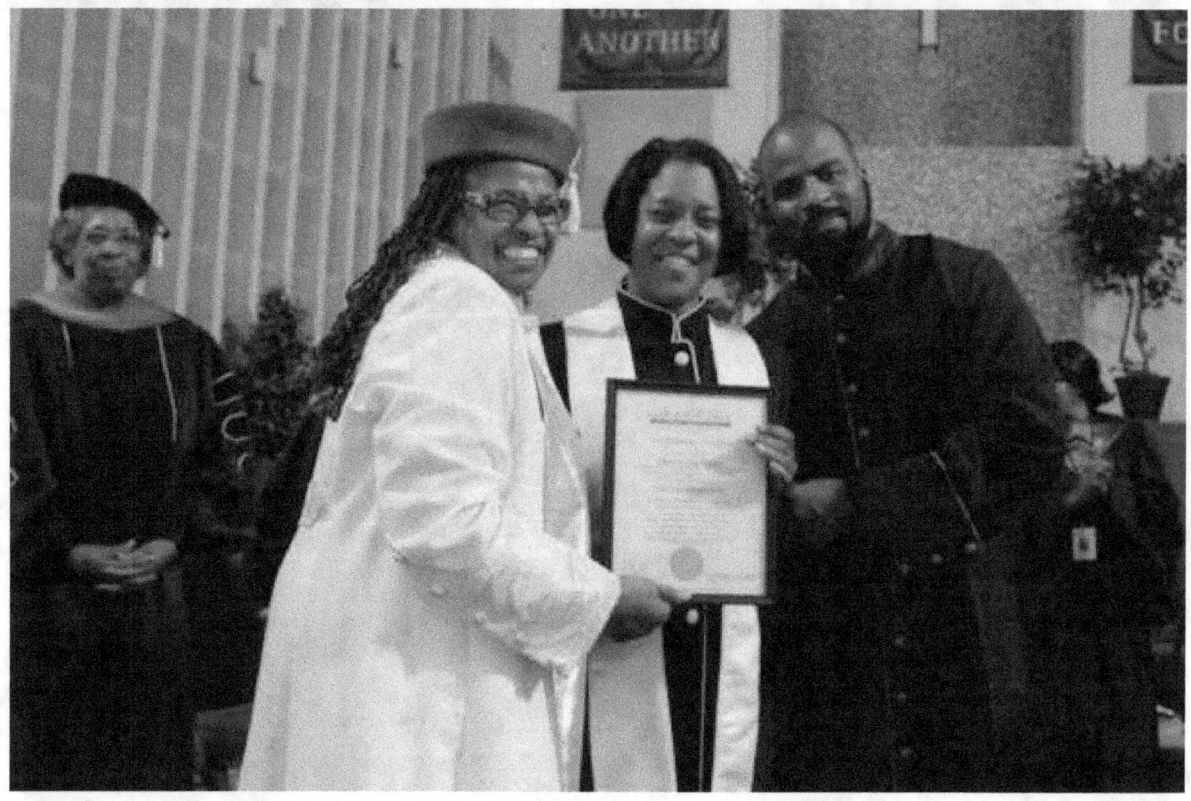

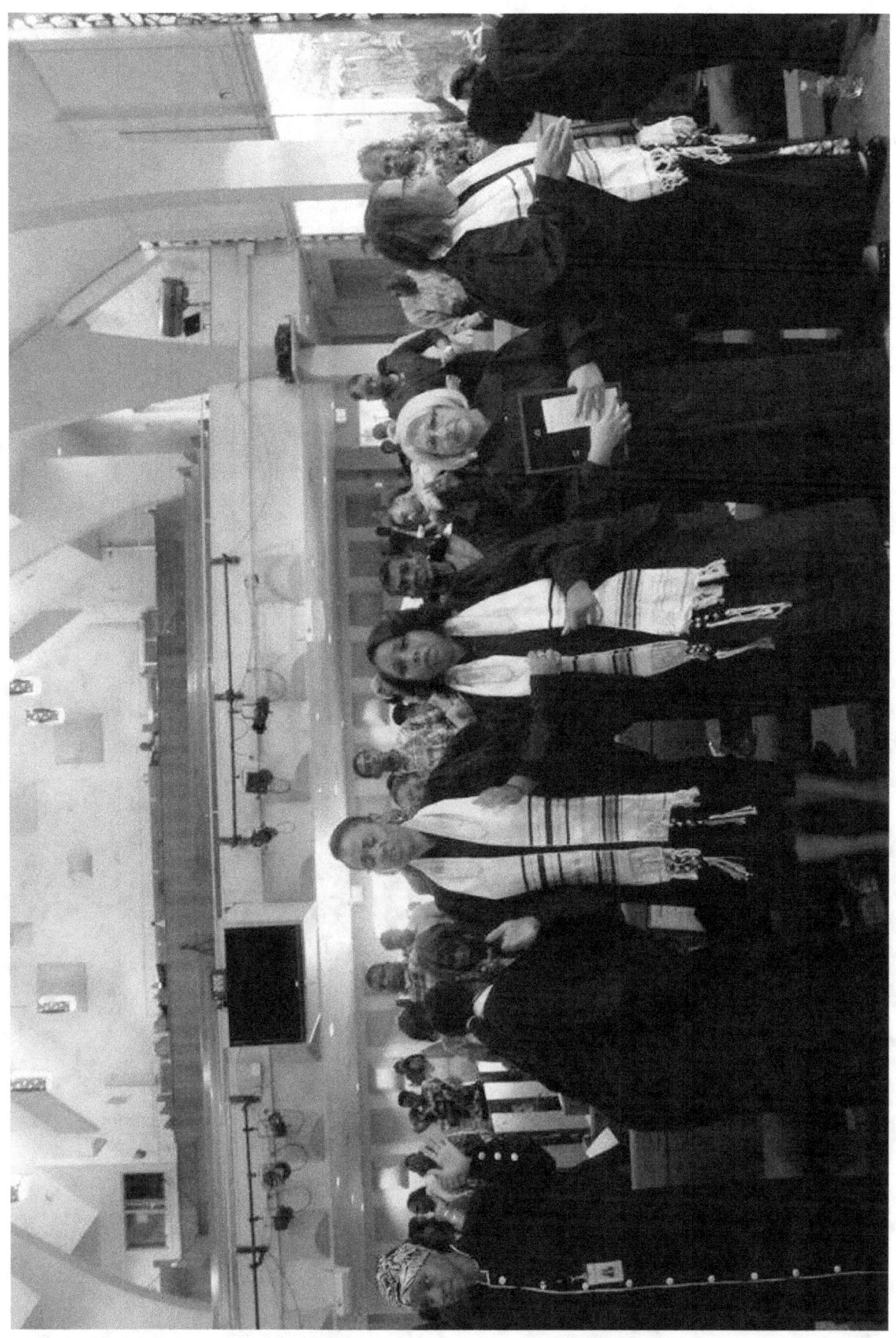

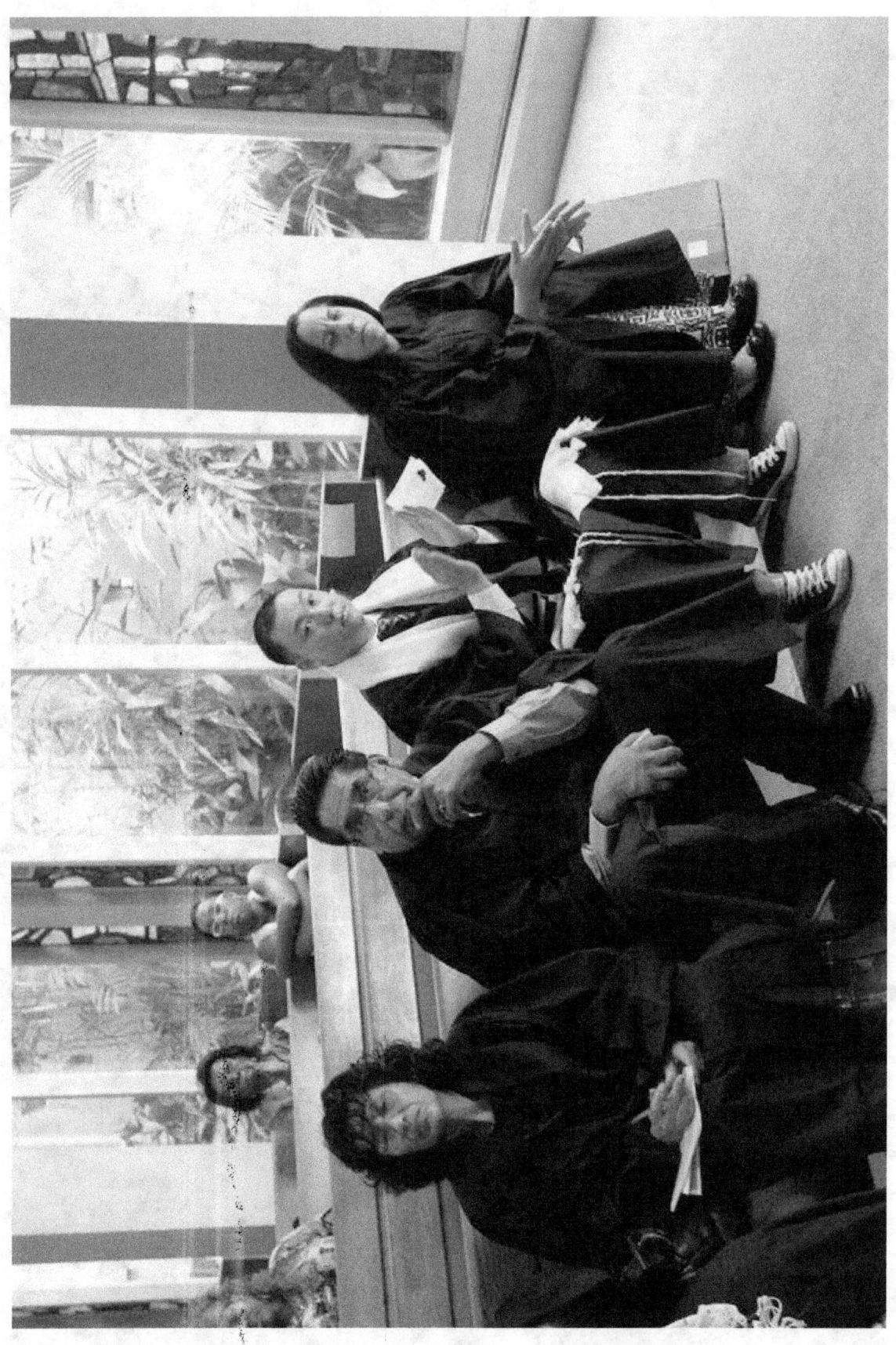

156

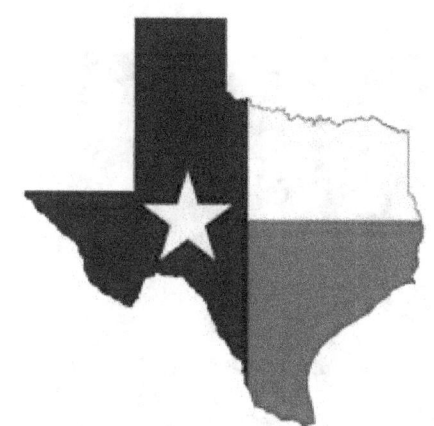

S.O.V.
Ministerial Training Center

Houston, Texas

Now Open Every Wednesday 7p-9p

NOW YOU can* earn your Ordination Certificate *Credentials Minister's License, *Get Ministry Diploma *Certificate of Leadership * Minister of Music *Psalmist *Missionary Certificate *Ministry of Helps Certificate Also Experience "Hands On" Ministry Training on Skid Row, Retirement Home, In House Ministry, Gospel Media and so much MORE! Everyone welcome to sit in workshops FREE!

Location: Sweet Home MBC

2503 16th St
Galena Park, TX 77547

Want more information? CALL Texas Campus:

Dean of Students

Dr. Kenneth Lee Thomas

1.909.529.1650 www.SaintsOfValue.org

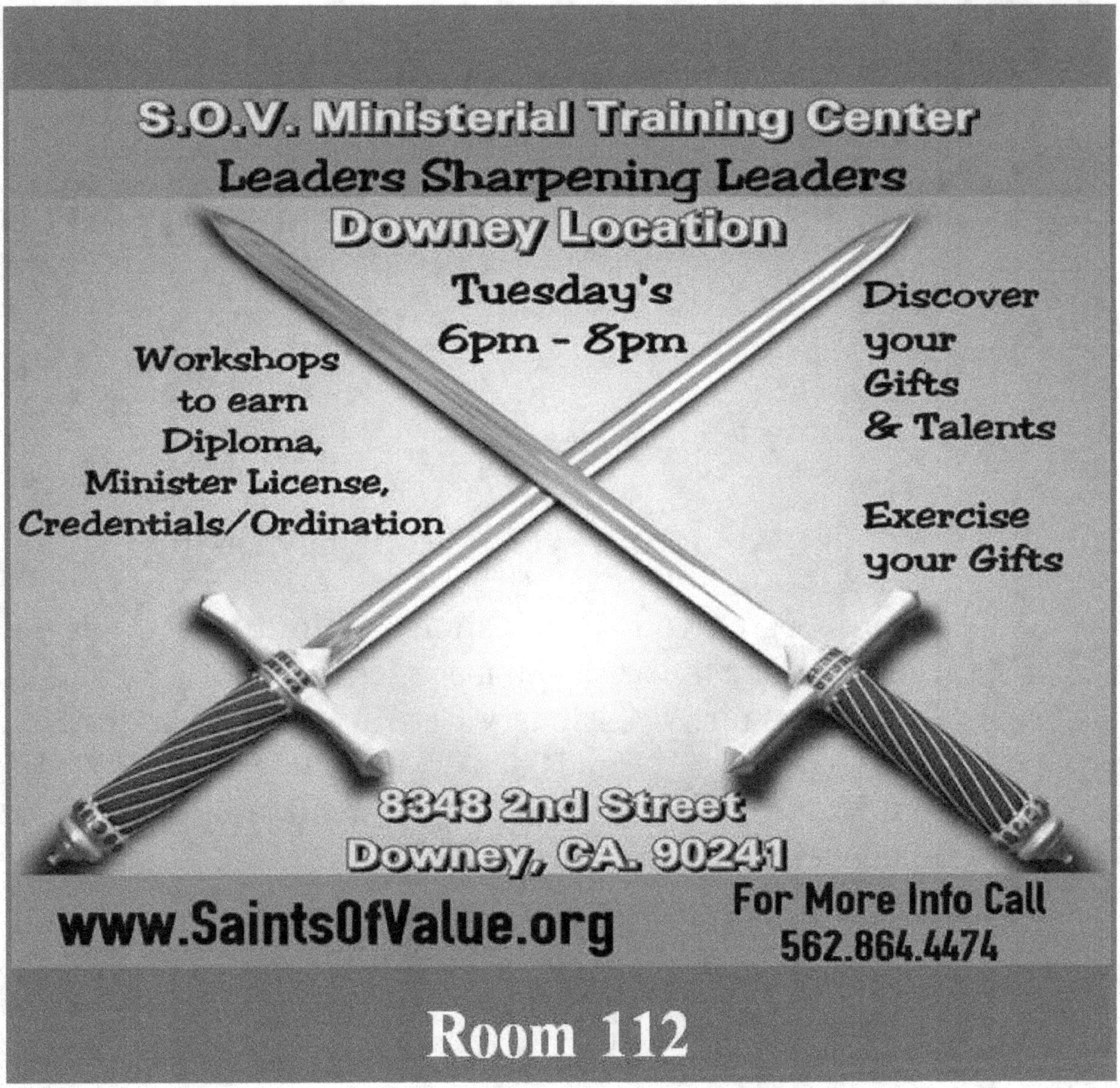

S.O.V. Ministerial Training Center
Leaders Sharpening Leaders
Downey Location

Tuesday's
6pm - 8pm

Discover
your
Gifts
& Talents

Workshops
to earn
Diploma,
Minister License,
Credentials/Ordination

Exercise
your Gifts

8348 2nd Street
Downey, CA. 90241

www.SaintsOfValue.org

For More Info Call
562.864.4474

Room 112

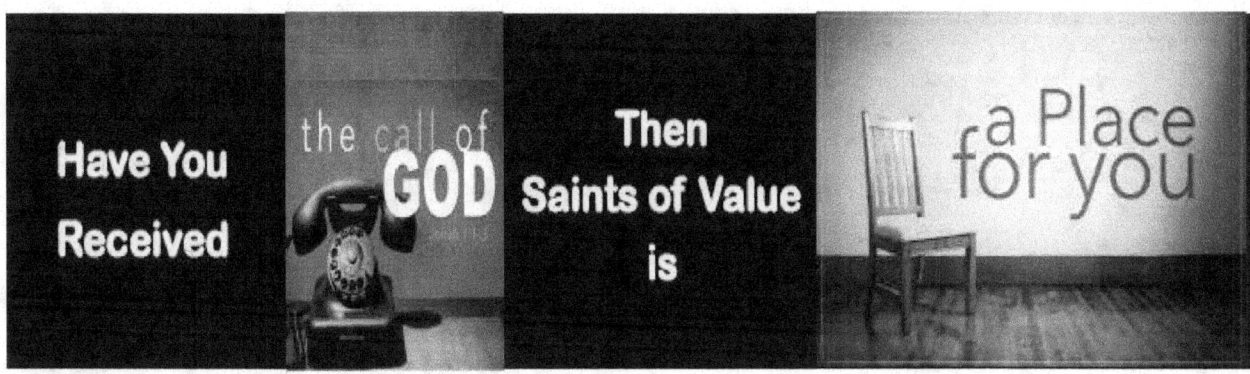
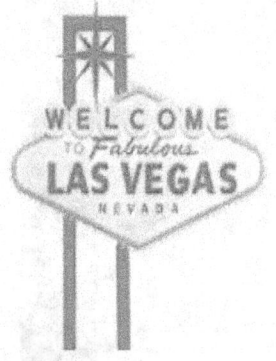
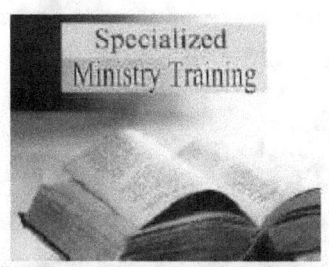
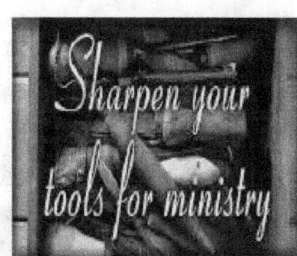
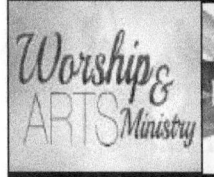

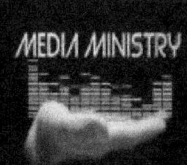
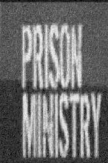
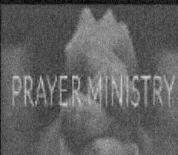
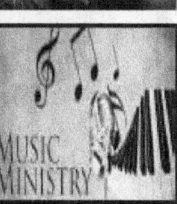

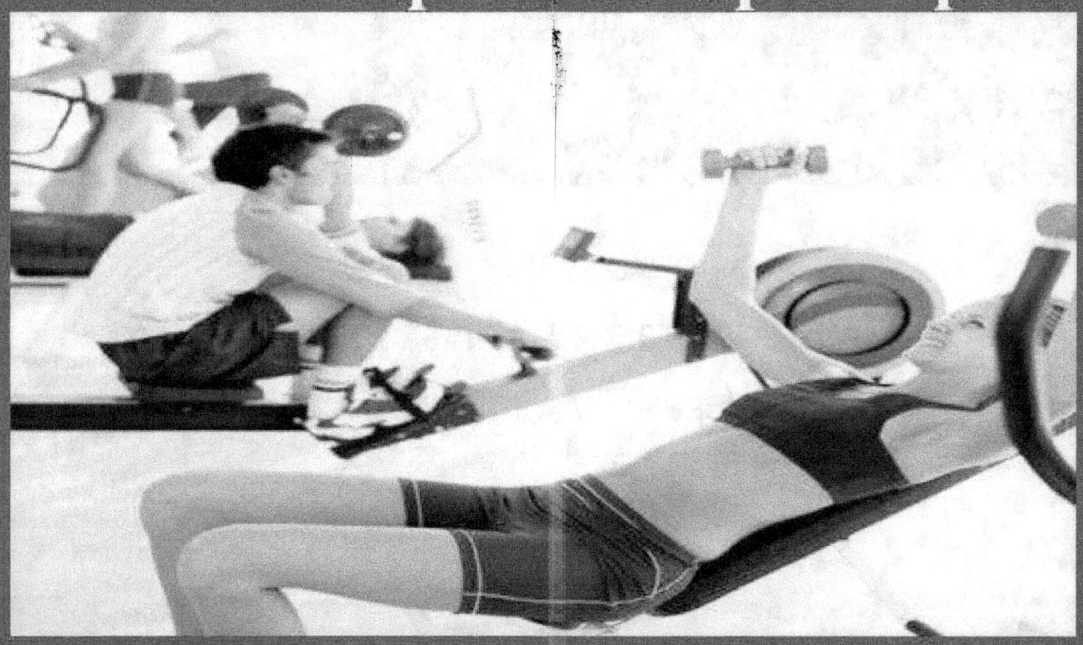
And Always Remember…

160

This Is The Place Where You! Discover YOU are
A Saint Of Value!

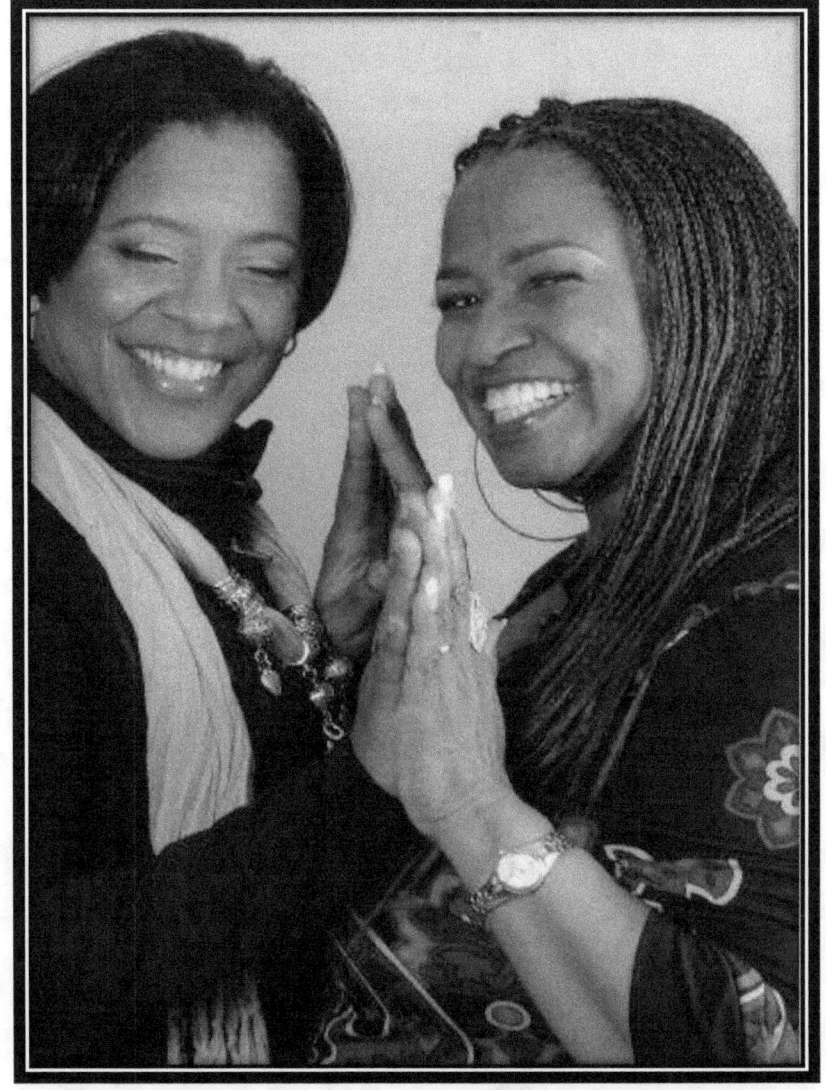

Apostle / Pastor Dr. Vicki Lee, S.O.V. Founder/CEO-Director
& Daughter: Youth Pastor Venus Lachelle Burton

Giving All The GLORY To GOD!
The Word of God Works!
And Know "Prayer" Changes Things